TRADE AND DEVELOPMENT

The China–Hong Kong Connection
The Key to China's Open-Door Policy

TRADE AND DEVELOPMENT

A series of books on international economic relations and
economic issues in development

Edited from the National Centre for Development Studies,
Australian National University, by Helen Hughes

Advisory editors

Juergen Donges, *Kiel Institute of World Economics*
Peter Lloyd, *Department of Economics, University of Melbourne*
Gustav Ranis, *Department of Economics, Yale University*
David Wall, *Department of Economics, University of Sussex*

Titles in the series

Helen Hughes (ed.), *Achieving industrialization in East Asia*

Yun-Wing Sung, *The China–Hong Kong connection: The key to
China's open-door policy*

Kym Anderson (ed.), *New silk roads: East Asia and world textile
markets*

Rod Tyers and Kym Anderson, *Disarray in world food markets:
A quantitative assessment*

THE CHINA–HONG KONG CONNECTION

The Key to China's Open-Door Policy

YUN-WING SUNG

Department of Economics
Chinese University
of Hong Kong

CAMBRIDGE UNIVERSITY PRESS

CAMBRIDGE

NEW YORK   PORT CHESTER   MELBOURNE   SYDNEY

CAMBRIDGE UNIVERSITY PRESS
Cambridge, New York, Melbourne, Madrid, Cape Town, Singapore, São Paulo, Delhi

Cambridge University Press
The Edinburgh Building, Cambridge CB2 8RU, UK

Published in the United States of America by Cambridge University Press, New York

www.cambridge.org
Information on this title: www.cambridge.org/9780521108980

First published 1991
This digitally printed version 2009

A catalogue record for this publication is available from the British Library

National Library of Australia cataloguing in publication data
Sung, Yun-Wing.
The China–Hong Kong connection: the key to China's
open-door policy.
Bibliography.
Includes index.
ISBN 0 521 38245 9.
1. China — Foreign economic relations — Hong Kong.
2. Hong Kong — Foreign economic relations — China.
3. China — Politics and government — 20th century.
I. Title. (Series : Trade and development)

382.095105125

Library of Congress Cataloguing in Publication data
Sun, Yun-Wing.
The China–Hong Kong connection: the key to China's open door
policy/Yun-Wing Sung.
Includes bibliographical references and index.
ISBN 0 521 38245 9.
1. China — Commercial policy. 2. Hong Kong — Commerce.
3. Intermediation (Finance). I. Title.
HF1604.S87 1991
337.5105125 — dc20
91-14780
CIP

ISBN 978-0-521-38245-8 hardback
ISBN 978-0-521-10898-0 paperback

To my wife, Pauline
and my son, Samuel

Contents

Tables

Preface

The open-door policy that has evolved in China since 1979 has far-reaching implications for the Asian-Pacific region and the world. It has long been recognized that Hong Kong is the key to China's door to the outside world, and the focus of this book is on the multi-faceted roles of Hong Kong in China's open-door policy. The Chinese giant reaches out to the world on the back of the Hong Kong midget, and the Chinese leadership value Hong Kong so much that they have promised, in a formal agreement with Britain, that they will preserve the capitalist system in Hong Kong for fifty years after 1997.

Since 1979, China has built numerous direct links with the outside world. Paradoxically, the shares of China's merchandise trade, tourist trade, shipping, foreign loans and foreign investments handled by Hong Kong have been rising. In this book, in order to explain this paradox, a theory of intermediation is constructed and the theory is applied to analyse the roles of Hong Kong in China's merchandise trade, tourist trade, shipping, foreign loans and foreign investments. Besides the China–Hong Kong connections in trade and investment, the reform of China's trade regime is also described and analysed in detail.

The discussion takes account of developments up to June 1990. The open-door policy suffered a severe setback as a result of the violent suppressions of the pro-democracy movement in June 1989. The isolation of China after the Tiananmen incident implies that China will become even more dependent on Hong Kong in its economic relations with the outside world.

The idea for this book first grew out of a research project entitled 'China's entry to world markets' sponsored by the National Centre for Development Studies (NCDS) of the Australian National University in August 1985. I was then on sabbatical at the NCDS. Professor Helen Hughes, Director of the NCDS, has taken a deep interest in this book and has given me invaluable advice and encouragement. I have also benefited greatly from the assistance provided by the Centre.

David Wall read the first draft of the manuscript and offered many constructive suggestions. A significant part of the information in this book was obtained through interviews with experts in China and businessmen in Hong Kong, and I would like to thank them for their patience and support. Needless to say the views and any errors in this book are solely my responsibility.

Last, but not least, I would like to thank my wife for her affectionate encouragement and support.

Abbreviations

cif   cost, insurance and freight
CITIC   China International Trust and Investment Corporation
COEFE   cost of earning foreign exchange
EC   European Community
EER   effective exchange rate
ETDD   Economic and Technology Development Districts
FIAC   Foreign Investment Administrative Commission
fob   free on board
FTC   Foreign Trade Corporation
GDP   gross domestic product
GSP   General Scheme of Preferences
IEAC   Import–Export Administration Commission
LFTC   Local Foreign Trade Corporation
MFA   Multi-Fibre Arrangement
MFTC   Municipal Foreign Trade Corporation
MOFERT   Ministry of Foreign Economic Relations and Trade
NFTC   National Foreign Trade Corporation
OECD   Organization for Economic Cooperation and Development
SAFEC   State Administration of Foreign Exchange Control
SEZ   Special Economic Zone
SITC   Standard International Trade Classification

Symbols

HK$ Hong Kong dollar
US$ United States dollar
Y   renminbi = yuan (Chinese currency)
—   not available
..   not applicable
m   million
n.e.s.   not elsewhere stated

Introduction

The open-door policy that has evolved in China since the death of Mao Zedong and the Purge of the Gang of Four in 1976 has had far-reaching repercussions for the Chinese economy as well as for the world economy. The open-door policy is a vital part of China's new development strategy of intensive growth — growth through adaptation and diffusion of technology, especially foreign technology. Although China imported foreign technology, including capitalist technology, in Mao's era, the novelty of the 'open door' is the willingness to acquire technology through foreign investment. Moreover, foreign technology is broadly interpreted to include not only technology embodied in plant and equipment, but also knowledge, including management skills and even the practices and ideas of a modern society. The traditional mechanism of 'arm's-length' trade cannot adequately promote the transfer of this knowledge, and consequently closer interaction with foreigners through direct foreign investment has become a central element of the new development strategy. This recognition of the importance of direct foreign investment has accounted for the willingness of the Chinese to utilize special trade and various forms of industrial cooperation agreements.

Another vital aspect of China's modernization drive is the reform and partial marketization of China's Stalinist economic system. The open-door policy and the reform drive are mutually reinforcing. The commitment to the open-door policy forces China to modify a rigid economic system to facilitate economic interaction with world markets. Successful foreign enterprises in China, and ideas and examples from the outside world, have had significant demonstrative effects; the external sector has been a leader in China's reform drive. However, as East European experiences indicate, reform of a Stalinist economy is a long and tortuous process. The effectiveness of the open-door policy is limited by the lack of such reforms; China's door to the outside world will not be genuinely open until there has been a successful reform of its economic system.

1

Many of China's economic problems in the domestic as well as external sectors can be attributed to the inconsistencies in China's reform measures (Lin 1989: 1–24). Though China has decentralized economic power to local authorities and enterprises, the interest rate, exchange rate and the prices of many essential raw materials are still fixed at beneath equilibrium levels by planners. This implies chronic shortages, and a rationing of credit, foreign exchange, and essential raw materials. In the pre-reform era of the Stalinist system, planners favoured capital-intensive and heavy industrial projects in the rationing of resources. If interest rates, exchange rates and prices of essential materials are deregulated, many heavy industrial projects will show losses because they use large amounts of capital, imported equipment, energy, and materials. Such rationing benefits not only the heavy industrial sector but also the planners themselves who, in their enforcement of rationing, have acquired more power. In the thirty years of the pre-reform era, the interests of heavy industries and economic planners have been so firmly entrenched that the deregulation of interest rates, exchange rates and prices of essential materials has failed, despite the decentralization of economic power. In a decentralized regime, controlled interest rates imply inflation because loans are artificially cheap, while controlled exchange rates imply trade deficits because the value of imports (exports) is kept artificially low (high). Furthermore, controlled energy and raw material prices imply chronic shortages and inefficiency in resource allocation. Though the focus of this book is the open-door policy, it is clearly important to bear in mind the close link between the open-door policy and economic reforms.

Economic liberalization and the open-door policy have also introduced ideas of democracy and political reforms. One manifestation of this was the growth of a fully-fledged pro-democracy movement in Beijing, a movement which was suppressed on 4 June 1989. At the Fourth Plenum of the 13th Central Committee of the Chinese Communist Party held on 24 June 1989, Zhao Ziyang, the liberal general secretary of the Party, was ousted and replaced by former Shanghai mayor Jiang Zemin. The Party pledged to continue the policy of economic reforms and opening to the outside world, but communist principles and the leadership of the Communist Party would be strictly upheld. In other words, the policy of China's government would be one of political repression and economic liberalization. The choice of the new Party secretary, Jiang Zemin, reflects this policy. Jiang is a moderate technocrat who speaks English and French and has extensive experience in economic management and economic reforms. He has also proved to be strong in ideological control and stern in countering the student movement in Shanghai.

Events since June have demonstrated China's commitment to

political repression and economic liberalization. By July 1989, up to 7000 supporters of the pro-democracy movement had been arrested (*South China Morning Post* 21 July 1989) and Western newspapers and magazines were banned, even in hotels for foreigners. The Tiananmen incident has brought world condemnation and economic sanctions against China. The United States, the European Communities and Japan have suspended military sales and official loans to China, and Australia, New Zealand, Canada, Austria, Switzerland, Finland and the Scandinavian countries have suspended official contacts with China. In such an environment, it is perhaps not surprising that the Chinese Government has been eager to make gestures of further economic liberalization to assure investors. The Party chief Jiang Zemin and Prime Minister Li Peng have given their full support to the controversial plan to develop the Yangpu freeport in the Hainan SEZ (*South China Morning Post* 17 July 1989). According to a preliminary plan arrived at in mid-1988, the Hainan Government would lease 30 square kilometres of Yangpu, the island's best deep sea port, to a consortium headed by the Japanese construction giant Kumagai Gumi. The consortium would run the 'super-special zone' along Western lines, though sovereignty of the area would still be vested with China. The plan had been held up by conservative opposition in the autumn of 1988, but after the suppression of the pro-democracy movement, was approved in order to convince the world of China's commitment to the open-door policy. Whether the plan will come to fruition is still unknown because Kumagai Gumi was reported to be having second thoughts about the plan after the Tiananmen incident. However, Yangpu port officials have since told Kumagai executives that Beijing might grant them more favourable terms (*South China Morning Post* 17 July 1989). After the Tiananmen incident, Chinese officials have also been more flexible in their negotiations with foreign investors, even proposing terms favourable to them (*Hong Kong Economic Journal* 12 July 1989). Beijing has also ordered Shenzhen to accelerate its development (*Ming Pao* 2 July 1989).

After the suppression of the pro-democracy movement, Beijing was quick to re-emphasize the strategic role of Hong Kong in China's open-door policy. The heads of China's trading companies in Hong Kong met Zheng Tuobin, the Chinese Minister for Foreign Trade in mid-June 1989. He stressed that the role of Hong Kong in relation to China had become more significant, as China's foreign economic relations were under severe stress after the Tiananmen incident. He emphasized that tourism, foreign loans and commodity exports were the three major sources of China's foreign exchange earnings, and that the first two sources had dwindled after the Tiananmen incident. (China relies mainly on commodity exports and Hong Kong is one of the major channels of China's commodity exports.) He also stressed that China would not punish the employees of China's companies in Hong Kong, even though many of them had openly supported the pro-democracy movement (*Wen Hui Pao* 30 June 1989).

The Chinese clearly view Hong Kong as a 'window' or a 'bridge' to the outside world. They value this 'window' so much that they have promised (in the Sino-British joint declaration) to preserve the capitalist system in Hong Kong for fifty years after 1997. Capitalist and free-wheeling Hong Kong has become the key in the opening of the socialist and rigidly regimented Chinese economy.

In terms of the provision of foreign capital to China from 1979 to 1989, Hong Kong has contributed over 59 per cent of all foreign investment (including direct foreign investment and commercial credit) and over 48 per cent of foreign commercial loans. Hong Kong is also China's foremost trading partner. In 1989, China's exports to and imports from Hong Kong were 48 and 32 per cent of total Chinese exports and imports respectively. Of these exports to Hong Kong, 17 per cent were consumed in Hong Kong, and 83 per cent were re-exported; of the imports into China, 29 per cent had been produced in Hong Kong and 71 per cent were re-exports. Hong Kong also played an important role in trans-shipment. The estimated shares of China's exports and imports trans-shipped through Hong Kong in 1989 were both 10 per cent. Thus, China–Hong Kong trade and trans-shipment accounted for 58 per cent of Chinese exports and 42 per cent of Chinese imports.

Besides trade and investment, Hong Kong facilitates China's open-door policy in many indirect ways. Hong Kong serves as a contact point, a channel for information and technology transfer, and a market and production training ground. Given the efficiency and versatility of the Hong Kong economy, the effect of Chinese policies on trade and investment will be manifested quickly, and Chinese planners can avail themselves of the rapid feedback mechanism of the Hong Kong economy to gauge the effectiveness of their policy.

Chapter 1 of this book traces the development of China's open-door policy. Chapter 2 outlines the multi-faceted roles of Hong Kong in China's open-door policy and develops an economic theory of middleman which is important in explaining the significance of Hong Kong in China's open-door policy. Chapter 3 outlines the new institutional setting that has evolved to handle China's international trade and investment. Chapter 4 evaluates the achievements of the open-door policy and its prospects. Chapters 5 to 7 focus on the roles of Hong Kong as financier, trading partner and middleman respectively. Chapter 8 contains concluding comments and an evaluation of future prospects.

1

The open-door policy

Antecedents of the open-door policy

Many elements of the open-door policy, including technology imports, foreign aid, loans and investment had been accepted in Mao's era. In the 1950s, China relied heavily on Soviet loans, technicians, turnkey projects and blueprints, and at least 150,000 Chinese technicians and workers were trained in the USSR. Joint stock companies with the USSR also existed.

The importance of maintaining an economic relationship with the capitalist world was not ignored in Mao's era. For example, China recognized the importance of maintaining ties with the capitalist world through Hong Kong, and left the colony in British hands in 1949 at a time when China could easily have taken it by force. When the Korean War broke out in 1950, China imported most of her strategic supplies from Hong Kong. Although the American-led United Nations trade embargo against China (after China's entry into the Korean War) prevented a rapid development of ties with the capitalist world, China continued to export to the capitalist world through Hong Kong. Chinese imports arriving via Hong Kong dwindled because of the United Nations trade embargo; nevertheless, significant quantities of strategic supplies were smuggled into China through Hong Kong.

After the Sino-Soviet rift of the early sixties, China became isolated. The much-publicized policy of self-reliance made a virtue out of necessity and was more in line with Mao's ideology. At a pragmatic level, China re-oriented her trade from the Soviet bloc to the Organization for Economic Cooperation and Development (OECD) countries, and began to import complete industrial plants from Japan and Western Europe during the period 1962–65. This process was halted in 1966 with the outbreak of the Cultural Revolution.

As the Cultural Revolution receded in 1970, Mao Zedong and Zhou Enlai initiated the *rapprochement* with the United States, and imports of industrial plants from OECD countries resumed on a large scale. In 1973, the State Council approved a plan to spend US$4.3 billion (the 'Four Three Program') on plant imports over a four-year period. However, this policy of massive plant imports, financed by oil exports, was resisted by the 'Gang of Four', and the campaign against Deng Xiaoping in 1975 cast doubt on the Four Three Program. It was not carried out thoroughly, but in 1978, Hua implemented an even larger import program, in the main based on the earlier program.

After the downfall of the Gang of Four in 1976, Hua Guofeng started his over-ambitious modernization plan which involved an unbalanced growth strategy, massive imports of industrial plants and an explicit commitment to an open-door policy. In 1978 alone, foreign contracts worth US$6.4 billion were signed. A program of massive plant imports was grafted onto the Stalinist strategy of extensive (and unbalanced) growth characterized by forced savings, high investment (especially in heavy industry), and neglect of efficiency and consumption. Hua's plan soon led to structural imbalances in the form of bottlenecks and a balance of payments deficit. The neglect of efficiency led to hasty and inappropriate plant imports. Very often, contracts on plant imports were concluded without feasibility studies and without estimations of the demand for complementary domestic inputs, as in the case of the giant Bao Shan General Iron and Steel Works near Shanghai.

Characteristics of the open-door policy

The failure of Hua's over-ambitious plan led to a fundamental re-orientation of China's developmental strategy. At the Party's historic Third Plenum in December 1978, Hua's Stalinist strategy was abandoned and a program of readjustment and reform was introduced to achieve balanced and intensive growth. Economic reforms and marketization were initiated to improve economic efficiency. Readjustment was introduced to rectify the imbalances engendered by the strategy for unbalanced growth, involving a shift of emphasis from heavy industry to agriculture and light industry, and also a lowering of the savings rate. The willingness to accept foreign investment, the most often noted feature of the open-door policy, can be explained by the change in development strategy. The rise in consumption following readjustment reduces the resources available for investment and exports, and the Chinese thus accept foreign investment to relieve savings and balance of payments constraints. As debt financing can lead to repayment problems in hard times, equity financing is also accepted.

Equity financing is also more effective in technology transfer. Under the new strategy of intensive growth, attention is being paid to the form and effectiveness of technology transfer. The importing of complete plants, as in Hua's era, eased, with priority being given to technology imports intended to modernize China's existing plants. The fact that much of this technology was 'disembodied' and undocumented illustrates China's willingness to cope with the frictions and tensions typical of joint ventures.

The open-door policy should not be confused with free trade. Strict foreign exchange controls exist and China is trying to avoid importing goods which could be produced domestically. However, the novelty of the open-door is that China has to expand her exports rapidly to finance technology imports. International trade has thus become an active instrument in China's development strategy. The positive effects of exports on efficiency have also been important for the strategy of intensive growth. Zhao Ziyang emphasized that 'Putting China's products to the test of competition in the world market will spur us to improve management, increase variety, raise quality, lower production costs and achieve better economic results' (*Beijing Review* 21 Dec. 1981:24). Chinese exports as a proportion of national product rose to the record level of 13.5 per cent in 1987, compared with 5.3 per cent in 1977 and a low of 2.9 per cent in 1970.

Evolution of the open-door policy

The open-door policy has gone through three cycles of liberalization and retrenchment. Decentralization of the trading and investment systems was undertaken simultaneously with domestic economic reforms in 1979–80, 1983–84 and 1988. In each reform drive, selected regions of the country were opened up, i.e. given substantial autonomy in international trade and investment. All three reform drives led to inflation and balance of payment difficulties, and each was followed by a period of retrenchment. The Tiananmen incident dealt a severe blow to the open-door policy; this is analysed in detail at the end of the chapter.

(i) The first reform drive of 1979–80

Hua Guofeng's modernization plan led to a trade deficit in 1978 (Table 1.1). Hua's plan was replaced by a program of readjustment and reform at the Third Plenum in December 1978. In 1979 the reform drive gained momentum: the Ministry of Foreign Trade was reorganized and industrial ministries were given more power in foreign trade. Moreover, special autonomy in trade and investment was given to the provinces of Fujian and Guangdong and the three central municipalities, Beijing, Tianjin and Shanghai. Guangdong and Fujian were given the authority to operate Special Economic Zones (SEZs). Guangdong operates three SEZs: the Shenzhen and Zhuhai SEZs which are adjacent to Hong Kong and Macau respectively, and the Shantou SEZ which has close links to overseas Chinese populations, including a community in Hong Kong that originated in Shantou. Fujian operates the Xiamen SEZ which is opposite Taiwan and only a few miles from two coastal islands controlled by Taiwan. However, the reforms in the domestic and external sectors led to a loss of central control and internal and external balances continued to deteriorate during 1978–80 (Table 1.1). China's leaders concluded that the 1979 policy of readjustment had failed and severe retrenchment was needed (Sung and Chan 1987:8). In December 1980, a

Table 1.1 *Value and growth rates of Chinese trade*

Year	Exports		Imports		Trade balance US$m
	US$m	Growth rate (%)	US$m	Growth rate (%)	
1970	2,260	2.5	2,326	27.5	−66
1971	2,636	16.6	2,205	−5.2	431
1972	3,443	30.6	2,858	29.6	585
1973	5,819	69.0	5,157	80.4	662
1974	6,949	19.4	7,619	47.7	−670
1975	7,264	4.5	7,486	−1.7	−222
1976	6,855	−5.6	6,578	−12.1	277
1977	7,590	10.7	7,214	9.7	376
1978	9,745	28.4	10,893	51.0	−1,148
1979	13,658	40.2	15,675	43.9	−2,017
1980	18,272	33.8	19,550	24.7	−1,278
1980	18,120	—	20,020	—	−1,990
1981	22,007	21.5	22,015	10.0	−8
1982	22,321	1.5	19,285	−12.4	3,036
1983	22,226	−0.5	21,390	10.9	836
1984	26,139	17.6	27,410	28.1	−1,271
1985	27,350	4.7	42,252	54.1	−14,902
1986	30,942	13.1	42,904	1.6	−11,962
1987	39,437	27.7	43,216	0.7	−3,739
1988	47,540	20.4	55,251	27.8	−7,710
1989	52,486	10.4	59,142	7.0	−6,656
1990	62,070	18.3	53,360	−9.8	8,710

Sources: Data since 1980 were obtained from *Chinese Customs Statistics*; 1970–80 data were obtained from the Ministry of Foreign Economic Relations and Trade in Beijing.

second readjustment was announced, involving recentralization with emphasis on slow and balanced growth. Despite the second readjustment, export decentralization remained basically intact, although foreign exchange controls were strengthened and the Ministry of Foreign Trade regained control over a few commodities (Kueh & Howe 1984:832).

(ii) The second reform drive of 1983–84

Balance of trade was restored in 1981 and China accumulated a sizeable surplus in 1982–83. Internal balance was restored in 1982 and China embarked on another reform drive in 1983–84 (Sung & Chan 1987:11). In 1983, Hainan island, an island only slightly smaller than Taiwan, was granted a degree of autonomy exceeding that of the Special Economic Zones. In April 1984, fourteen coastal cities along the entire Pacific coast were declared open.[1] These cities provide virtually all of the port facilities in China, and accounted for 97 per cent of turnover in Chinese ports in 1983. They are also relatively industrialized, providing nearly one-quarter of China's gross value of industrial output, although their population share was only 8 per cent (Kueh 1986:15). In January 1985, China announced its intention of opening the entire Chinese Pacific basin. The first step was the opening of the Changjiang delta, the Zhujiang delta and the south Fujian triangle comprising the historic ports of Xiamen, Zhangzhou and Quanzhou in February 1985. The opening of the Liaoning and Shandong peninsulas was originally on the agenda for March 1985 (Kueh 1986:11), but the speed of events led to confusion, and the opening of the two peninsulas was shelved. In September 1984, the State Council approved a radical proposal to reform the foreign trade system, decentralizing autonomy in foreign trade to foreign trade corporations which were to become responsible for their own profits and losses. In view of the sizeable foreign exchange reserves built up since 1982, foreign exchange controls were relaxed in 1984 (Qi 1985a:47).

The radical reform proposals had barely been implemented when a massive trade deficit and runaway inflation forced planners to recentralize domestic reforms leading to a loss of control over investment and monetary expansion. The trade deficit was caused primarily by the relaxation of foreign exchange and import controls, especially in the open areas, leading to a surge of imports (Qi 1985a:47). To rectify the imbalance, planners imposed severe administrative controls on bank loans, foreign exchange and investment in early 1985.

---

[1] They include Dalian, Qinhuangdao, Tianjin, Yantai, Qingdao, Lianyungang, Nantong, Shanghai, Ningbo, Wenzhou, Fuzhou, Quangzhou, Zhanjiang and Beihai.

Although the 1984 proposed foreign trade reforms remained largely unimplemented, there was active discussion on economic and political reforms in 1984–85, and the reformers appeared to be preparing for another reform drive. The renminbi was devalued twice in 1985–86, and another devaluation was reportedly scheduled for 1987. However, the radical economic and political reform proposals and student unrests in December 1986 provoked a strong conservative backlash, culminating in the forced resignation of the Liberal leader Hu Yaobang. Following student demonstrations, price reforms and the planned devaluation of the renminbi were shelved to pacify social discontent over inflation (Sung & Chan 1987:19).

(iii) The third reform drive of 1988

The campaign against 'bourgeois liberalization' only held up reforms temporarily. At the Thirteenth Party Congress in November 1987 reforms gained the upper hand, and a third reform drive was launched in 1988. Hainan island became a separate province in mid-1988 with a higher degree of autonomy than before. The opening of the entire Chinese Pacific Basin continued with the opening of the Liaoning and Shandong peninsulas, the entire provinces of Guangdong (previously limited to the Zhujiang delta) and Fujian (previously limited to the south Fujian triangle), parts of Guangxi province and Hebei province, and eighteen additional coastal cities (*Hong Kong Economic Times* 14 June 1988). The areas opened in 1988 were as large as all the areas opened in the years from 1979 to 1987. By 1988, the population in the opened areas totalled 160 million. The open areas form a three-tier structure in terms of increasing degrees of autonomy: coastal open areas, coastal open cities and SEZs. The huge trade deficit of 1984–86 declined rapidly in 1987 and China's trade was close to balance in the first half of 1988. The radical 1984 trade reforms that were stalled in 1985 were resumed in 1987–88.

The most noticeable event of 1988 was price reforms. However, the price reforms were carried out in an overheated economy plagued by excessive investment and monetary growth. The price reforms precipitated panic buying and runs on the banks. In September, price reforms were shelved and the State Council imposed severe controls on investment and credit. A trade deficit again emerged in the second half of 1988 and trade controls were stiffened. As the macroeconomic imbalance was very severe, further reforms will have to wait until the economy is successfully stabilized. The official policy was that stabilization would last two years.

The regional orientation of the open-door policy

As the map suggests, Hong Kong plays an important role in the regional orientation of the open-door policy. Most overseas Chinese have their ancestral roots in the provinces of Guangdong and Fujian which were given special autonomy in trade and investment in 1979. Guangdong is adjacent to Hong Kong and over 80 per cent of the Hong Kong population speak Guangdong dialects. Fujian is adjacent to Guangdong and also quite close to Hong Kong. Besides its link to Hong Kong, Fujian has other overseas connections. Chinese communities in Taiwan, Singapore and Southeast Asia have their ancestral roots in Fujian and speak the Fujian dialect. Economic interaction between Hong Kong and Guangdong has developed rapidly, and Hong Kong investors employed over a million workers in industrial processing in Guangdong in 1986. Fujian has also developed barter trade with Taiwan fishermen. Such trade is illegal in Taiwan but is promoted by China as a means of developing links with Taiwan. The indirect trade between China and Taiwan via Hong Kong has also grown rapidly since 1979.

Besides their economic functions, the SEZs also serve the political purpose of luring Hong Kong, Macau and Taiwan back to Chinese sovereignty. It is no accident that the Shenzhen and Zhuhai SEZs are adjacent to Hong Kong and Macau respectively, and that the Xiamen SEZ is just a few miles from the two coastal islands controlled by Taiwan. China will resume sovereignty over Hong Kong and Macau in 1997 and 1999 respectively under the special arrangement of 'one country, two systems'. That is, the capitalism of Hong Kong and Macau will be preserved for fifty years under Chinese rule. A similar special arrangement has been promised for Taiwan. The scheme will appear more credible if China can demonstrate its tolerance of the development of capitalism in the SEZs.

The development of Shenzhen, the most developed SEZ, vividly illustrates the crucial role of Hong Kong in the open-door policy. In January 1979, the State Council created an industrial export zone at Shekou which is close to Hong Kong. The zone was to be developed and managed by the China Merchants Steam Navigation Co. (CMSNC), a Hong Kong based company controlled by the Chinese Ministry of Communications. According to Ho and Huenemann (1984:49), 'Hong Kong business interests suggested that the zone be expanded to encompass property development and tourism and suggested the name "Special Economic Zone" to reflect the broader

The China–Hong Kong Connection

scope'. Shekou thus became part of the Shenzhen SEZ, but continues to be managed by CMSNC. The 15 per cent corporate tax rate of SEZs was designed to match the profit tax rate of Hong Kong, which was 15 per cent from 1966 until 1975, but was raised to 16.5 per cent in 1987 and to 18.5 per cent in 1984.

Hong Kong also played an important role in the opening of Hainan island. Xu Jiatun, the highest ranking Chinese official in Hong Kong, is an adviser there, and Hong Kong capitalists were consulted by a number of Chinese officials, including Deng Xiaoping, on the opening of Hainan. In June 1988, Deng Xiaoping remarked that China would build 'a few Hong Kongs' on its soil, and that the situation in Hong Kong would remain unchanged even beyond the fifty years promised in the Sino-British joint declaration.

Deng re-iterated his policy of 'building a few Hong Kongs' in China after the suppression of the pro-democracy movement (*Miang Pao* 29 June 1989), and Deng's support for the plan of the Yangpu free port in Hainan was cited as an example of such a policy. In the same spirit, the plan to establish a stock market in Shenzhen would continue (*Hong Kong Economic Journal* 17 July 1989).

The open-door policy in historical perspective

Despite the severe setback for economic reform and the open-door policy after the Tiananmen incident, support for these strategies still appears to be very strong. The Fourth Plenum of the 13th Party Central Committee, convened in June 1989, pledged to continue the implementation of the principles and policies laid down since the historic Third Plenum of the 11th Party Central Committee in December 1978, which marked the inauguration of Deng's era of economic reform and open-door policy. The basic line laid down in 1978 was one which focused on economic construction, political orthodoxy, economic reform, and opening to the outside world.

The problem with Deng's policy is that he wants both communist orthodoxy and economic liberalization; but economic liberalization undermines communist orthodoxy in the long run. Despite the tension between political repression and economic liberalization, there are examples of successful economic development under repressive political regimes, namely, Taiwan, South Korea and Brazil. The tension between political orthodoxy and economic liberalization is much stronger within communism than within capitalism for the simple reason that in capitalist countries, private property rights and the market system can function quite well under political repression. In communist countries, the emphasis on orthodoxy hampers marketization and economic reforms.

Among communist countries, East Germany can be cited as an example where communist orthodoxy and an open-door policy have co-existed for a long time. East Germany had some success with a strategy of intensive growth through technocratic improvements of central planning rather than genuine economic decentralization. However, it is unlikely that China will succeed by following the East German strategy because the Chinese economy is much less amenable to central planning. In comparison with the East German economy, the Chinese economy is much larger and much more heterogeneous and regionalized. China's planning apparatus is very crude and centralized planning has largely failed. China's economic success since 1978 was achieved through economic decentralization and liberalization, which slowly undermined the communist orthodoxy.

The tension between communist orthodoxy and economic liberalization accounts for many of the twists and turns of Chinese politics since 1978. In the economic imbalances following the first and second reform drives, conservatives unleashed attacks on the reformers and their policies in 1980–82 and in 1985–87 (Sung & Chan 1987). Student unrest in December 1986 triggered a strong conservative backlash, leading to the forced resignation of the liberal leader Hu Yaobang and a campaign against 'bourgeois liberalization'. The Tiananmen incident and the ousting of Zhao Ziyang in June 1989 can be regarded as the culmination of the tension between communist orthodoxy and economic liberalization.

These twists and turns since 1978 have surprised most observers, but the open-door policy appears to be supported by all factions of the party with the exception of the far-Left. China has remained committed to the open-door policy despite setbacks in 1979–80, 1984–86, 1988 and in 1989. With the exception of the far-Left, most Chinese leaders realize that access to foreign technology is essential to China's modernization. However, the Party old guard also clings tenaciously to communist orthodoxy, which serves its vested interest. The tension between communist orthodoxy and economic reforms may continue for a long time until the passing away of the old guards. In its relationship with other countries, China has explored a one-sided interaction with the socialist bloc and has also tried self-reliance. Both policies failed and China has had little choice but to open its door to the world. Barring major wars and disasters, it seems that economic rationality is likely to triumph over ideology in the long run.

2

The pivotal role of Hong Kong

In examining the role of Hong Kong in China's trade, it is important at the outset to distinguish between trans-shipment, entrepôt trade, and direct trade.

Trans-shipment means that goods are consigned directly from the exporting country to a buyer in the importing country, although the goods are transported via an entrepôt and may be temporarily stored at the entrepôt for onward shipment. Trans-shipped goods may change their mode of transportation at the entrepôt: Chinese goods, for example, are carried by train or coastal vessels to Hong Kong where they are consolidated into containers. Trans-shipped goods are not usually regarded as part of the trade of the entrepôt and they do not clear customs because they represent goods in transit and are not imported into the entrepôt.

Unlike trans-shipment, entrepôt trade is indirect trade, as imports for re-export are consigned to a buyer in the entrepôt and the buyer takes legal possession of the goods after clearing customs. These imports may then be processed before being re-exported; processing may include packaging, sorting, grading, bottling, drying, assembling, decorating, diluting, or even minor manufacturing (such as the pre-shrinking of grey cloth). According to the official definition in Hong Kong, any manufacturing process that permanently changes the shape, nature, form, or utility of the basic materials used in manufacture would turn the product into a domestic export, that is, an export manufactured in Hong Kong. This would qualify the item to be classified as being of Hong Kong origin, a qualification in some cases for inclusion in quotas (in the case of clothing and textiles) and for generalized and other preferences. The Hong Kong government requires detailed production records from those manufacturers who claim Hong Kong origin for their manufactures. Heavy fines are imposed if false records are produced. However, the forging of production records by small manufacturers to claim Hong Kong origin for Chinese merchandise is not unknown.

15

Direct trade includes domestic exports and retained imports. According to the Hong Kong government, retained imports are defined as the difference between total imports and re-exports, and the re-exports margin is ignored. Conceptually, retained imports should be the difference between total imports and imports for re-export. However, it is difficult to obtain information on the value of imports for re-export as the importer may not be able to ascertain at the time of importation whether a certain import will be re-exported. The Hong Kong definition therefore understates the value of retained imports by the re-export margin.

In 1988, the Hong Kong Trade Development Council conducted a large-scale survey of Hong Kong exporters/importers, and the re-export margins for Chinese goods and third countries' products were estimated at 16 per cent and 14 per cent respectively (Hong Kong Trade Development Council 1988). For convenience, the re-export margin is taken to be 15 per cent in this study. Imports for re-export are thus estimated to be 85 per cent of the value of re-exports, and retained imports are correctly defined as the difference between total imports and imports for re-export.

The role of Hong Kong in China's open-door policy can be summarized under four main functions: financier, trading partner, middleman, and facilitator (Table 2.1). The first three of these are considered in much greater detail in Chapters 5–7.

Hong Kong as financier

Hong Kong's share of foreign investment in China (including direct foreign investment and commercial credits) was 65 per cent (Table 2.2) in 1988, and dropped slightly to 58 per cent in 1989.

By contrast, Hong Kong's share in China's foreign loans is quite small, though the share rose from 0.6 per cent in 1983 to 9.4 per cent in 1989 (Table 2.2). This is partly due to the fact that Hong Kong does not extend official loans to China. However, China-backed companies began to raise funds in Hong Kong's stock market through share placements in 1987 (*South China Morning Post* 18 June 1987), and there are signs that China may make more use of Hong Kong's stock market in the long run.

Hong Kong plays a leading role in syndicating loans to China. The share of China's foreign loans syndicated in Hong Kong rose from 6 per cent in 1979–82 to 31 per cent in 1987 (Table 2.2). However, the share dropped to 10 per cent in 1989. This fall was related to the recentralization of the power to borrow foreign funds in 1988–89. (The relationship between centralization and loan syndication is explained in a later chapter.)

Table 2.1 *A summary of the role of Hong Kong in China's open-door policy*

Financier	Direct investment Indirect investment Loan syndication	
Trading partner	Commodity trade Services trade	
Middleman	Commodity trade	entrepôt trade trans-shipment brokerage in direct trade
	Services trade	tourism loan syndication business consultancy
Facilitator	Contact point Conduit of information and technology Training ground	marketing production

Hong Kong as trading partner

This refers to direct trade only, entrepôt trade being covered under the middleman function. Chinese trade statistics do not distiguish between direct and indirect trade. Moreover, the Chinese figures for total imports from Hong Kong (including both imports via Hong Kong and imports of Hong Kong goods) are appreciably lower (26 per cent lower in 1986) than Hong Kong's corresponding figures for exports to China (including both re-exports and domestic exports). It appears that, in Chinese statistics, a considerable portion (around 35 per cent in 1986) of China's imports via Hong Kong is attributed to the country of origin while the rest is attributed to Hong Kong. To distinguish between direct trade and entrepôt trade, and to remedy the deficiency of China's statistics, this study uses Hong Kong statistics to calculate China's trade with Hong Kong. Time lags and differences between fob and cif prices are ignored. China's exports via Hong Kong are taken to be Hong Kong's imports of Chinese goods for re-export. China's exports retained for internal use in Hong Kong are taken to be Hong Kong's retained imports from China. China's imports via Hong Kong are taken to be Hong Kong's re-exports to China. China's imports of Hong Kong goods are taken to be Hong Kong's domestic exports to China.

Tables 2.3 and 2.4 summarize the shares of Hong Kong in China's exports and imports respectively. Hong Kong's imports are disaggregated into retained imports and re-exports from 1966 and Hong Kong's exports are disaggregated into domestic exports and re-exports from 1960.

Table 2.2 *Hong Kong's contribution to utilization of foreign capital (contracted) in China* (US$m)

Year	Foreign investment		China's utilization of foreign capital (contracted) Foreign loans[a]					Total	From Hong Kong
	Total	From Hong Kong[b]	Total	Hong Kong as				
				lender	centre of syndication	sub-total		
		(i)		(ii)	(ii)	(ii)		(iii)
1979–82 (average)	1,384	919 (66)	1,240	19 (1.5)	7.5 (6.0)	9.4 (7.6)	2,624	1,013 (38.6)
1983	1,917	642 (34)	1,513	9 (0.6)	104 (6.9)	11.3 (7.5)	3,430	755 (22.0)
1984	2,875	2,175 (76)	1,916	51 (2.7)	250 (13.0)	301 (15.7)	4,791	2,476 (51.7)
1985	6,333	4,134 (65)	3,534	73 (2.1)	513 (14.5)	586 (16.6)	9,867	4,720 (47.8)
1986	3,330	1,773 (53)	8,401	244 (2.9)	1,538 (18.3)	1,782 (21.2)	11,737	3,555 (30.3)
1987	4,319	2,331 (54)	7,817	401 (5.1)	2,400 (30.7)	2,801 (35.8)	12,136	5,132 (42.3)
1988	6,189	4,033 (65)	9,814	580 (5.9)	1,945 (19.8)	2,525 (25.7)	16,002	6,558 (41.0)
1989	6,294	3,645 (58)	5,185	488 (9.4)	718 (13.8)	1,206 (23.2)	11,479	4,851 (42.3)

Figures in brackets represent:
  (i) Percentage share of total foreign investment in China.
  (ii) Percentage share of total foreign loans to China.
  (iii) Percentage share of China's total utilization of foreign capital.

[a] Foreign loans exclude foreign currency loans from the Bank of China.
[b] Including Macau (most are from Hong Kong).
Sources: Syndicated loans: *Asian Finance* and *Asian Banking*.
Other data: *Almanac of China's Foreign Relations and Trade*, various issues.

Table 2.3 Hong Kong's imports from China

Year	Total imports			Retained imports			Imports for re-export		
	US$m	(i)	(ii)	US$m	(i)	(iii)	US$m	(i)	(iv)
1931–38 (average)	87	31.5	37.3	28	7.2	8.0	60	21.4	2.0
1948	108	86.6	20.7	—	—	—	—	—	—
1950	137	24.8	20.7	—	—	—	—	—	—
1951	151	20.0	17.7	—	—	—	—	—	—
1952	145	17.6	22.0	—	—	—	—	—	—
1955	157	11.1	24.2	—	—	—	—	—	—
1960	207	11.2	20.2	—	—	—	—	—	—
1966	487	20.5	27.4	394	16.6	26.3	94	3.9	29.1
1970	470	20.8	16.1	373	16.6	14.9	97	4.3	20.2
1975	1,383	19.0	20.3	1,083	14.9	19.4	300	4.2	21.3
1977	1,741	22.9	16.6	1,286	17.0	14.9	455	6.0	21.6
1979	3,038	22.2	17.7	2,076	15.2	15.1	962	7.1	24.1
1981	5,276	24.0	21.5	3,325	15.1	18.1	1,951	8.8	26.2
1983	5,888	26.5	24.4	3,588	16.1	20.5	2,300	10.4	29.8
1984	7,131	27.5	24.9	4,075	15.7	20.9	3,056	11.7	28.6
1985	7,568	27.7	25.5	3,790	13.8	20.8	3,778	13.8	28.0
1986	10,462	33.8	29.5	4,842	15.6	22.0	5,620	18.2	35.8
1987	14,776	37.4	30.5	5,591	14.2	19.6	9,185	23.3	39.2
1988	19,406	40.8	30.4	5,084	10.7	15.0	14,322	30.1	40.6
1989	25,215	48.0	34.9	4,698	9.0	13.7	20,517	39.1	54.3

(i)   Percentage share of China's exports.
(ii) Percentage share of Hong Kong's total imports.
(iii) Percentage share of Hong Kong's retained imports.
(iv) Percentage share of Hong Kong's re-exports.

Sources: Hong Kong data: 1931–38, Tom (1957); 1948–89, Hong Kong Trade Statistics; 1966–89, Review of Overseas Trade. Chinese data: 1931–48, Yearbook of International Trade Statistics; 1950–79, Chinese Statistical Yearbook; 1981 and after, Chinese Customs Statistics.

Table 2.4 Hong Kong's exports to China

Year	Total exports			Domestic exports			Re-exports		
	US$m	(i)	(ii)	US$m	(i)	(iii)	US$m	(i)	(iv)
1931–38 (average)	87	21.3	39.5	9	2.1	7.6	79	19.2	7.6
1948	71	42.0	17.7	—	—	—	—	—	—
1950	221	37.8	33.9	—	—	—	—	—	—
1951	281	23.4	36.1	—	—	—	—	—	—
1952	91	8.1	17.9	—	—	—	—	—	—
1955	32	1.8	7.2	—	—	—	—	—	—
1960	21	1.1	3.1	2	0.1	0.5	19	1.0	10.0
1965	13	0.6	1.1	3	0.2	0.4	10	0.5	3.6
1970	11	0.5	0.4	5	0.21	0.2	6	0.2	1.2
1975	33	0.5	0.6	6	0.08	0.1	28	0.4	2.0
1977	44	0.6	0.5	7	0.09	0.09	38	0.5	1.8
1979	383	2.5	2.5	121	0.8	1.1	263	1.7	6.6
1981	1,961	8.9	9.0	523	2.4	3.6	1,438	6.5	19.3
1983	2,531	11.8	11.5	856	4.0	6.0	1,675	7.8	21.6
1984	5,033	18.4	17.8	1,443	5.3	8.2	3,590	13.1	33.6
1985	7,857	18.6	26.0	1,950	4.6	11.7	5,907	14.0	43.7
1986	7,550	17.6	21.3	2,310	5.4	11.7	5,241	12.2	33.4
1987	11,290	26.1	23.3	3,574	8.3	14.3	7,716	17.8	32.9
1988	17,030	30.8	27.0	4,874	8.8	17.5	12,157	22.0	34.5
1989	18,816	31.8	25.7	5,548	9.4	19.3	13,268	22.4	29.9

(i)   Percentage share of China's imports.
(ii) Percentage share of Hong Kong's total exports.
(iii) Percentage share of Hong Kong's domestic exports.
(iv) Percentage share of Hong Kong's re-exports.

Sources: Hong Kong data: 1931–38, Tom (1957); 1948–89, *Hong Kong Trade Statistics*; 1966–89, *Review of Overseas Trade*.
Chinese data: 1931–48, *Yearbook of International Trade Statistics*; 1950–79, *Chinese Statistical Yearbook*; 1981 and after, *Chinese Customs Statistics*.

Some useful pre-war data are also available. From 1931 to 1938, 37 per cent of Hong Kong's imports came from China. Twenty per cent of these imports were consumed locally, 10 per cent were re-exported to China, and 70 per cent were re-exported to non-Chinese countries. In the same period, the Chinese market accounted for 40 per cent of Hong Kong's exports. Of the exports to China, 10 per cent were produced locally, 11 per cent originated in other parts of China, and 79 per cent consisted of re-exports of non-Chinese origin (Tom 1957:11). Hence, 80 per cent of the imports from China and 90 per cent of the exports to China represented entrepôt trade. Hong Kong's entrepôt trade accounted for 25 per cent of China's exports and 19 per cent of China's imports.

After the Second World War, China conducted most of its trade through Hong Kong and the Hong Kong–China trade recovered to pre-war levels. China's feverish buying prior to, and during, the Korean War, and the closure of major Chinese ports after the 1949 revolution, led to Hong Kong's exports to China trebling during the period 1948–50, representing 38 per cent of total Chinese imports. Hong Kong's imports from China also rose to 25 per cent of total Chinese exports in 1950. However, the United Nations embargo on the export of strategic commodities to China on 18 May 1951, following China's entry into the Korean War, led to a sharp fall in Hong Kong's exports to China. The United States ban on all imports from China also led to a stagnation in Hong Kong imports from China in the early 1950s, and Hong Kong's share of exports fell from 25 per cent in 1950 to 11 per cent in 1955.

In addition to the United States embargo, the communist takeover resulted in a drastic cut in the import of consumer goods and also a re-orientation of China's trade to communist countries. Trade between Eastern bloc countries tended to be state-to-state direct trade, and China arranged most of its purchases of capital goods through East Berlin. Hong Kong's exports to China continued to fall throughout the 1950s. After the Sino-Soviet rift in the early 1960s, China re-oriented its trade to capitalist countries. However, most of China's imports were wheat and capital goods which were handled directly by China's state trading companies, and Hong Kong's exports to China continued to fall in the 1960s. In 1970, Hong Kong's exports to China were less than 0.5 per cent of China's imports.

The picture of Hong Kong's imports from China was rather different. China's need to earn hard currency meant that it had to continue to export to Hong Kong. Hong Kong's imports from China grew in the late 1950s, representing some 11 per cent of China's exports. In the 1960s, following the Sino–Soviet rift, China's exports to Hong Kong grew absolutely as well as relatively. In 1966, just before the Cultural Revolution, Hong Kong's imports from China represented 21 per cent of China's exports and 27 per cent of Hong

Kong's imports. In 1966, the first year that disaggregated data became available, only 19 per cent of Hong Kong's imports from China were re-exported, a much lower percentage than the pre-war level. It appears that Hong Kong's re-export of Chinese goods had stagnated while Hong Kong's retained imports of Chinese goods had increased rapidly. This increase can be attributed to the rapid growth of Hong Kong and to China's need to earn hard currency.

China's total exports and its exports to Hong Kong stagnated in the period 1966–70 due to the Cultural Revolution, and China's share of Hong Kong imports fell to 16 per cent in 1970. The *rapprochement* with the United States in the early 1970s brought about another expansion of China's total exports and its exports to Hong Kong during 1970–75.

Dramatic changes in the trade pattern occurred in the late 1970s. In the period 1966–75, the share of China's exports re-exported through Hong Kong stayed at roughly 4 per cent. After 1976, it rose rapidly, and re-exports exceeded retained imports in 1986. In 1988, 74 per cent of Hong Kong imports from China were re-exported, accounting for 30 per cent of China's exports. For Chinese imports from Hong Kong, the changes were even more dramatic: from 1977 to 1987, total exports, domestic exports and re-exports of Hong Kong to China grew 257 times, 511 times, and 203 times respectively. Hong Kong re-emerged as a major entrepôt for China, and China also became a major market for Hong Kong products.

Hong Kong was the largest final market (i.e. excluding Chinese exports via Hong Kong) for Chinese exports in the late 1960s and early 1970s, but the Hong Kong market was overtaken by the Japanese market and the US market in 1973 and 1987 respectively. However, the Hong Kong market still accounted for 9 per cent of China's exports in 1989. China continues to regard Hong Kong as its largest market, as Chinese trade statistics disregard the substantial re-exports of Chinese products via Hong Kong. Hong Kong's domestic exports to China have grown from negligible amounts to US$5548 million in 1989. In 1984, Hong Kong became the third largest supplier of goods to China after Japan and the United States. The rapid growth of Hong Kong's domestic exports is, in part, due to Hong Kong investment in processing/assembling operations in China. Hong Kong firms supply such operations with the required raw materials and components, part of which are made in Hong Kong. It should be noted that China regards Hong Kong as its largest supplier from 1987 onwards, as Chinese trade statistics regard a substantial part of the re-exports of Hong Kong to China as imports from Hong Kong.

China's exports retained in Hong Kong have declined absolutely in 1988 and their share of China's total exports has declined sharply.

Their share of Hong Kong's retained imports also stagnated from 1984 to 1986 and declined sharply in 1987. China has been unable to capture the higher end of Hong Kong's market, which was dominated by Japan. Given the increasing affluence of Hong Kong and the Japanese dominance in vehicles, capital goods, and quality consumer durables and consumer goods, the future for Chinese products in Hong Kong is not very bright.

Trade in services, mostly tourism, is also important. The number of Hong Kong tourists visiting China is not known exactly because the Chinese statistics on tourist arrivals combine Chinese visitors from Hong Kong, Macau, and Taiwan in the same category. Hong Kong statistics on the number of Hong Kong residents departing for China understate the number of Hong Kong tourists visiting China because a substantial number of Hong Kong residents visit China via Macau. In 1978, the number of compatriots from Hong Kong, Macau and Taiwan visiting China totalled 1.6 million, and from Hong Kong statistics, the number of Hong Kong residents visiting China and Macau was 1.3 million and 2.1 million respectively. If 10 per cent of the Hong Kong residents visiting Macau travelled to China, the estimate for the number of Hong Kong residents visiting China would be 1.5 million (Table 2.5). This estimate appears to be reasonable as Hong Kong's population was ten times that of Macau at the time, and Hong Kong should account for the lion's share of the traffic. In 1978, the number of tourists visiting China from Taiwan was negligible.

By 1989, the number of 'compatriots' visiting China had increased to 23 million, and from Hong Kong statistics, the numbers of Hong Kong residents visiting China and Macau were 15.2 million and 4.9 million respectively. Even if as many as one-third of Hong Kong residents visiting Macau travelled to China, the estimate of Hong Kong residents visiting China would only be 16.8 million (Table 2.5), leaving 6.1 million visitors to be accounted for by 'compatriots' from Taiwan and Macau. The number of Taiwanese visitors was relatively insignificant because Taiwan only relaxed its restrictions on visits to China in late 1987. It is well known that the majority of Taiwanese visiting China enter China through Hong Kong, and the number of Taiwanese visiting Hong Kong in 1989 was only 1.1 million. Thus, Macau appears to account for over 5 million person-trips in 1989. As the population of Macau was only half a million, this implies an average of 10 trips per person in 1989.

Strange as such figures may seem, the estimates in Table 2.5 are reasonable. The 1989 estimate for Hong Kong implies an average of 2.9 trips per person. As Hong Kong is small in area, a lot of Hong Kong people make one-day trips to China at weekends for leisure. About 700 Hong Kong housewives in Sheung Shui (a Hong Kong town near Shenzhen) earn a living by travelling to Shenzhen everyday,

Table 2.5 *Hong Kong's contribution to China's tourism* (thousands)

Year	Total tourists visiting China	Compatriots from Hong Kong, Macau and Taiwan	Hong Kong residents			Foreigners		
			Total	(i)	(ii)	Total	(iii)	(iv)
1978	1,809	1,562	1,501	(83)	(74)	248	—	—
1979	4,204	3,821	3,526	(84)	(80)	383	—	—
1980	5,703	5,139	4,324	(76)	(74)	564	(46)	(40)
1981	7,767	7,053	5,065	(65)	(68)	714	(40)	(34)
1982	7,924	7,117	5,287	(67)	(68)	807	(40)	(34)
1983	9,477	8,564	6,476	(68)	(69)	913	(40)	(36)
1984	12,852	11,670	8,916	(69)	(70)	1,182	(40)	(39)
1985	17,833	16,378	11,983	(67)	(70)	1,455	(45)	(43)
1986	22,819	21,269	12,990	(57)	(64)	1,550	(50)	(44)
1987	26,902	25,087	15,559	(58)	(65)	1,815	(55)	(61)
1988	31,695	29,773	18,092	(61)	(65)	1,922	(71)	(61)
1989	24,501	22,972	16,843	(69)	(73)	1,530	(75)	(67)

Figures in brackets represent:

(i)   Percentage share of Hong Kong visitors in China's total tourist arrivals.
(ii) Percentage share of Hong Kong visitor's expenditure in total tourist expenditure in China.
(iii) Percentage share of foreign visitors who leave China via Hong Kong.
(iv) Percentage share of foreign visitors who enter China via Hong Kong.

Sources: Number of Hong Kong tourists: *Hong Kong Monthly Digest of Statistics*, various issues. Foreigners leaving and entering China via Hong Kong: Census and Statistics Department, Hong Kong.
Other data: *Chinese Statistical Yearbook*, various issues.

selling duty-free cigarettes, jeans, T-shirts and buying cheap meat, fruits and vegetables on the way back (*South China Morning Post* 11 Oct. 1988). Macau is much smaller than Hong Kong and leisure trips to China are even more frequent. Hong Kong people going to China have to purchase train or long-distance bus tickets, whereas Macau people can walk to China. An appreciable number of people in Macau earn their living through border trade with China. The opening up of China to tourists thus explains the very rapid increase in the number of Macau compatriots visiting China.

Table 2.5 assumes that, of the Hong Kong residents visiting Macau, 10 per cent travelled to China in 1978. This fraction rose to one-third by 1987 due to the development of tourist facilities in Zhuhai (which is adjacent to Macau). As the number of Hong Kong residents visiting China directly were more than three times those visiting Macau in 1987, this estimate of Hong Kong residents visiting China (directly and through Macau) is not very sensitive to variations in this fraction. Hong Kong's share in China's tourist arrivals declined from 84 per cent in 1979 to 58 per cent in 1987. The decline is largely due to the rapid rise in the share of Macau in tourist arrivals. However, the number of Hong Kong visitors has grown faster than the number of foreign visitors. Hong Kong's share in China's tourist arrivals and expenditure rose in 1989 due to the sharp drop in foreign tourism after the bloody suppression of the pro-democracy movement in 1989. The number of Chinese tourists visiting Hong Kong has also grown rapidly. However such trips are usually paid for by Hong Kong relatives of the Chinese tourists.

The level of expenditure of Hong Kong tourists in China is available from the general household surveys of Hong Kong and it is thus possible to estimate the contribution of Hong Kong tourists to tourist expenditure in China. Hong Kong accounted for 79 per cent of tourist expenditure in China in 1979, but the share declined to 65 per cent in 1987.

Hong Kong as middleman

Hong Kong plays the role of middleman both in commodity and services trade, including tourism, financial services, and business consultancy. A middleman creates opportunities for trade and investment by lowering transaction costs. In commodity trade, China's indirect trade via Hong Kong exceeded its direct trade with Hong Kong in recent years and China is relying more and more on the Hong Kong entrepôt (Tables 2.3 and 2.4). Hong Kong is also an important centre for trans-shipment for China. The value of trans-shipped goods is not available as they do not go through customs, but their weight is known. From 1983 to 1988, trans-shipment of goods to (from) China via Hong Kong has increased 15 (2.5) times. In 1988, trans-shipment of goods to (from) China represented 31 (21) per cent of goods transported to (from) China by weight. This implies that a significant portion of China's trade is trans-shipped via Hong Kong.

Hong Kong trading firms also appear to perform an important brokerage role for China's direct trade. In 1988, the amount of China's direct trade conducted through Hong Kong brokers was estimated to be US$15 billion, representing 7 per cent of China's total trade (Hong Kong Trade Development Council 1988). As for tourist trade, Hong Kong is the foremost gateway into China for tourists. Many foreigners also join package tours of China organized in Hong Kong, and the percentage of foreign tourists visiting China via Hong Kong has been increasing since 1984–85 (Table 2.5). Loan syndication, which has been discussed under the financier function, can also be viewed as a middleman function performed by Hong Kong. Hong Kong was the centre for raising 80 per cent of China's syndicated loans (excluding soft loans and non-syndicated loans) in the period 1985–88. Hong Kong is also the foremost centre for consultancy services for China.

In commodity trade as well as tourist trade, the relative importance of direct trade with Hong Kong has declined whereas the relative importance of indirect trade via Hong Kong has increased. As for bank loans, Hong Kong is not a significant leader, but the relative importance of Hong Kong as a syndication centre is again increasing. (Table 2.2) The dominant role of Hong Kong in direct foreign investment also conceals a middleman function. The investments of Taiwan and South Korea in China are concealed through Hong Kong subsidiaries, and multinational companies also like to test the Chinese investment environment through their Hong Kong subsidiaries.

Hong Kong as facilitator

The Chinese value Hong Kong as a contact point with the world. Hong Kong is the major centre for China's trade and also the centre for consultancy services to China. Although multinationals can now set up offices in China, office space is so scarce that many companies operate from hotels. Hotels in China are crowded and travel and communication are still inconvenient. Many multinationals set up their offices in Hong Kong and travel to China for business. If the volume of business grows, they set up an office in China as well. The same pattern is observed in investment: multinationals often test the investment climate in China through their Hong Kong subsidiaries, and will invest directly only if the initial investment is profitable.

Many foreign firms still deal with China via a Hong Kong agent (Sung 1985:53).

Chinese trading corporations representing various ministries, provinces, cities and even countries and brigades have also converged on Hong Kong since 1979. According to one estimate, the number of Chinese cadres sent to Hong Kong on business in the last few years totalled 50,000 (*The Nineties* Feb. 1985:34).

Another indication of the role of Hong Kong as a contact point is the mushrooming number of exhibitions held by Chinese export agencies in Hong Kong. China's contact point in international trade used to be the Canton trade fair, the disadvantage of this being that foreign traders can only attend by invitation, whereas all interested parties can attend an exhibition in Hong Kong. It is no accident that the investment symposium for China's nineteen open cities and districts was held in Hong Kong in November 1984. More than 1100 businessmen from twenty-three countries attended the seminar (*South China Morning Post* 15 Nov. 1984:3). All open cities and districts are trying to establish offices in Hong Kong. In 1984, Chinese export agencies held eleven large-scale exhibitions in the Hong Kong Exhibition Centre, accounting for one-quarter of all exhibitions at the Centre, and many smaller exhibitions of Chinese exports were held elsewhere in Hong Kong (*Pai-Shing Magazine* Sept. 1984:10).

The growth of consultancy services for China's trade is a further indication of Hong Kong's close relationship with China. According to *Intertrade* (Oct. 1984:2) half of the foreign law firms in Hong Kong provide legal advice to the China trade. China has sent about a dozen of its lawyers to Hong Kong law firms for practical training. In 1983, China's foremost trading corporation in Hong Kong, China Resources Co. Ltd, set up a consultancy firm, China Resources Trade Consultancy Company Ltd (CRTC), which provides advice to both foreigners and Chinese export firms. CRTC has also established a subsidiary in Hong Kong to provide consultancy services. The support services for the China trade can be very specialized. For example, Sara Beattie Ltd offers temporary Hong Kong headquarters to traders, and is equipped with Telex facilities to receive messages and orders for transmission to corporate headquarters in Europe or the United States. The offices are staffed by European secretaries, trilingual interpreters and translators (Sung 1985:54).

Nationals of countries that do not have diplomatic relations with China often conduct business with China in Hong Kong. Since Taiwan allowed its citizens to meet their Chinese relatives in a 'third country' in July 1987, companies that specialize in arranging such meetings have been established in Hong Kong (*The Nineties* Sept. 1987).

The Chinese also value Hong Kong as a conduit of market information and technology transfer. Before the open-door era, Chinese shoe exporters posted designers at visitor disembarkation points to watch shoe designs (*Hong Kong and Macao Economic Digest* 6 1982 (14):35). Since 1979, the effort to obtain information from Hong Kong has been more systematic. China has sought the services of Hong Kong consulting companies in obtaining market and technical information, and also in upgrading China's management and technical expertise. Hong Kong academics are active on the China lecture circuits and China has established companies in Hong Kong that specialize in gathering market and technical information.

To utilize Hong Kong as a market and production training ground, China has invested heavily in banking, real estate, shipping, retailing, and recently also in manufacturing. Chinese investment in Hong Kong was estimated to be US$6 billion by 1985 (*The Economist* 11 May 1985), exceeding the amount of Hong Kong direct investment in China (US$4.2 billion between 1979 and 1985). In 1985, China became the third largest investor in Hong Kong manufacturing after the United States and Japan. China's investment in manufacturing concentrates on high-technology electronics in firms producing integrated circuits; in fact, China has taken over the largest electronic firm (Conic) in Hong Kong. China's investment in Hong Kong manufacturing totals US$570 million. The engineers in the high-technology electronics firms come mostly from China, and these firms have attracted public attention because of an initial United States ban, later lifted, on supplying training and equipment to them (Sung 1985:63). China also uses Hong Kong as a market testing ground to gauge consumer acceptance of its new products through its vast distribution network.

The theory of international trade in intermediary services

Since the inauguration of the open-door policy, China has established numerous direct links with the rest of the world, including diplomatic, commercial, and transportation links. Paradoxically, the middleman role of Hong Kong is becoming more prominent, and an increasing share of China's commodity trade, tourist trade and loan syndication is handled through Hong Kong (Tables 2.2 to 2.5). To try to explain this paradox, it is useful to construct a theory of intermediation. The theory has strong predictions for entrepôt trade and services trade. However, due to lack of data for the latter, the predictions for entrepôt trade will be discussed in greater detail. Data on the entrepôt trade of Singapore are also included to illustrate this theory of intermediation, partly because Singapore is trying to take advantage of China's open-door policy, and also partly because Singapore is a major entrepôt. The usual explanation of entrepôt trade in terms of transportation cost is inadequate because it ignores the importance of transaction costs. It is useful to classify re-exports into processed re-exports and pure re-exports. Processed re-exports refer to re-exports that have been physically treated (packaged, sorted and so on), whereas pure re-exports have not been changed in any physical way.

Pure re-exports are difficult to account for theoretically because re-exports involve higher costs than trans-shipment (other things being equal) owing to two factors: first, re-exports have to clear the customs of an entrepôt twice, whereas trans-shipped goods do not have to clear the customs of the entrepôt at all, resulting in fewer delays and lower storage costs; and second, trans-shipped goods are insured and financed just once, whereas re-exports have to be insured and financed twice — first when they are imported into the entrepôt, and second when they are re-exported. While transportation costs determine trans-shipment, pure re-exports are determined by both transportation costs and transaction costs, and processed re-exports involve processing costs as well.

It has been suggested that the rapid increase in Hong Kong investment in processing/assembling operations in China is the main reason for the rapid increase in China's indirect trade through Hong Kong. Many Hong Kong manufacturers have shifted their production across the border due to rising wages in Hong Kong. In 1988, about two million workers in Guangdong were employed in factories set up by Hong Kong investors (*Hong Kong Economic Times* 15 May 1989). Most of these processing/assembling operations import their materials and components from Hong Kong or through Hong Kong, and export their products through Hong Kong. According to a survey of the Hong Kong Census and Statistics Department during the third quarter of 1988, Hong Kong investment in processing/assembling operations in China accounted for 37 per cent of Hong Kong's re-exports to China, 55 per cent of Hong Kong's re-exports of Chinese origin, and 74 per cent of Hong Kong's domestic exports to China (*South China Morning Post* 3 Mar. 1989).

Though Hong Kong investment in China is undoubtedly a significant factor in the rapid growth of Hong Kong re-exports, such investment explains processed re-exports rather than pure re-exports. In the case of pure re-exports, the Hong Kong investor in China can always trans-ship the raw materials, components and finished products via Hong Kong instead of re-exporting them through Hong Kong. Moreover, Hong Kong investment in processing operations in

China cannot explain the increasingly important role of Hong Kong as a middleman in tourist trade, loan syndication, and other services. It is thus worthwhile to construct a theory of international trade in intermediary services to analyse the role of Hong Kong as a middleman. A theory of international trade in intermediary services should include the following elements: (i) an explanation of the need for intermediation; (ii) an analysis of the economy of scale and economy of agglomeration in supplying intermediary services, as these economies increase the efficiency of intermediation, and (iii) an analysis of the provision of intermediary services by a foreign firm (versus a domestic firm).

(i) The need for intermediation

Intermediation can be accounted for by the existence of transaction costs, as there is no need for intermediation in the frictionless Walrasian model, where every economic agent is linked costlessly to everyone else. A model in which intermediaries emerge endogenously was constructed by Townsend (1978). Although his model is highly abstract, his justification for intermediaries can be described simply. Townsend assumed that establishing a bilateral trade link between economic agents involves a fixed transaction cost. Thus, an exchange structure in which everyone is linked to everyone else (the Walrasian model) is generally inefficient; efficient structures minimize the number of bilateral trade links and necessarily involve intermediation. Increasing the number of households in a trading coalition decreases risks, but increases the number of links and transaction costs. A trade-off is involved, and Townsend used a core equilibrium concept to show how equilibrium is arrived at in such an economy.

(ii) Economies of scale and of agglomeration

Whenever there are fixed costs and non-increasing marginal costs (or increasing marginal costs that are small relative to fixed costs), economies of scale will arise. Regardless of the existence of economies of scale, the Townsend model has shown that fixed costs in establishing trade links are by themselves sufficient to account for intermediation, though the existence of economies of scale in the production of intermediary services would enhance the need for intermediation. Yamamura (1976:184–5) argues that significant economies of scale exist in the production of trading services, as the production of these services usually involves large fixed costs and small or declining marginal costs. In the production of market information, which is an integral part of intermediation, he argues that considerable costs are involved, and the same market information is useful in many transactions.

Traders and firms supplying financial and business services tend to agglomerate in a city, suggesting that there are significant external economies involved. This implies that once a city acquires a comparative advantage in providing intermediary services, the advantage feeds upon itself, and more traders and intermediaries will come to the city, making the city even more efficient in intermediation. There are in fact external economies on both the demand and supply sides in intermediation. External economies on the demand side operate through searching: an increase in the number of potential trading partners makes trade easier. Traditional economic theory, with its frictionless Walrasian model, has ignored the fact that it is costly to search for opportunities to trade. Stuart (1979) made externality through search the centrepiece of a trade model. He contrasted his model with traditional location theory, which predicts that traders will be evenly dispersed throughout the population because a seller's location is a form of product differentiation, and spatially separated sellers can thus be regarded as 'spatial monopolists'. However, Stuart argued that, besides the disagglomerative force stressed by traditional theory, agglomeration can result from desires of buyers to search in market places where there are relatively many sellers. Thus the addition of a new seller to a market place might increase the drawing power of the market place sufficiently to increase the demands faced by the sellers already there (Stuart 1979:17). Stuart's model suggests that agglomeration should be most prevalent in the trading of heterogeneous goods under conditions of low search and travel costs. A rise in heterogeneity increases the need to search in a market place with many sellers. A decline in travel costs will shrink cost differentials between market places and will lead some buyers to shift from small (local) market places to larger (more distant) ones.

External economies on the production side are also important in trade. Hicks (1969:47–9), in his discussion on ancient city states that thrived on trade, observed that there are genuine external economies in trade. An increase in the number of merchants in a trading centre permits specialization and the division of labour, not only by lowering costs, but also by lowering risks. Each trader only has fair knowledge of his immediate environment, and imperfect information implies risks. The larger the number of traders, the easier it is to acquire information, and the easier it is to arrange multilateral contracts or develop specialized contracts such as insurance and off-sets.

Hicks's analysis can be elucidated using the Townsend model: there is a trade-off between decreasing risks and increasing fixed costs of transactions as the number of trade links increases. In a city, the fixed cost of transactions is lowered by proximity and efficient communications, facilitating the formation of large trading networks that lower risk. In addition to lowering risk, other externalities are present in production. Lucas (1985) stressed the importance of agglomeration, especially in service industries, because people in the same trade can interact and learn from one another. He called this 'externality of human capital'.

(iii) The provision of intermediary services by foreign firms

Internal trade is most often handled by domestic traders, for they are most familiar with the domestic environment. In international trade, there are two main reasons for the choice of a foreign firm in providing intermediary services. First, cultural heterogeneity implies variations in transaction costs in trade. For instance, Hong Kong and Singapore are cosmopolitan and bilingual by virtue of their colonial origins, and their traders can lower the transaction costs of trade between their hinterlands and the outside world. Second, a less developed country may lack the skills to participate effectively in international trade. The skills required for international trade include a good knowledge of English, familiarity with modern business practice, the ability to work in different cultural and legal environments and proficiency with complex contractual agreements. The supporting industries of international trade (shipping, air transport, communications, finance, insurance, and business services) are also capital- or skill-intensive.

Sung (1984) quantified the factor requirements of the manufacturing exports and services of Hong Kong. Import–export trade is found to be much more capital- and skill-intensive than wholesale trade, retail trade and manufacturing exports. The supporting industries of international trade (shipping, air transport, communications, storage, finance, insurance, and business services) are also more capital- and skill-intensive than manufacturing exports (Table 2.6).

A foreign firm can set up a local base of operation through direct foreign investment instead of providing intermediary services from a foreign base through the channel of international trade. However, many less developed countries, including China, are less eager to attract foreign investment in services than in manufacturing.

Setting up a local base of operation may not be desirable due to factor prices. Intermediation is not a labour-intensive activity and the low wages in developing countries are not a decisive inducement. The shortage of local skills can be a handicap. Furthermore, economies of scale and economies of agglomeration in intermediation weaken the incentive of foreign trading firms to set up local bases as these are not as efficient as the large home base.

Table 2.6 *Capital- and skill-intensities of selected industries in Hong Kong (1980)*

	Depreciation-labour ratio[a] (HK$/man-year)	Skill ratio[b] (%)
Manufacturing exports	2,683	2.49
Import/export trade	5,328	7.03
Wholesale trade	2,945	2.90
Retail trade	2,851	2.03
Shipping	21,160	5.16
Air transport	9,465	12.23
Communication	16,146	12.40
Storage	12,992	2.85
Finance	5,706	5.52
Insurance	4,618	8.12
Business service	11,989	29.95

[a] Since data on capital stock are not available, depreciation is used as a proxy.
[b] Percentage share of professionals and technical workers (major group $\frac{0}{1}$ of the International Standard Classification of Occupations) in the total number of employees.
Source: Sung (1984).

The efficiency of large trading centres

The theory presented here predicts that a decline in travel and communication costs will lower the fixed cost of transaction, and thus the fraction of world trade handled through intermediation will decline. However, declining travel costs also raise the attractiveness of large trading centres relative to small ones, and the fraction of world trade handled through large trading centres may not decline. The secular decline of the fraction of world trade handled through intermediation is quite evident. For instance, before the modern era, goods usually changed hands many times in long distance trading. Chinese-European trade was usually handled by Indian and Arab middlemen, but these middlemen lost their livelihood with the advent of modern communications. However, large entrepôts, including Hong Kong, Singapore, Gibraltar, Bahrain, and Puerto Rico, continued to thrive. The large Japanese trading companies which handle a substantial portion of Japan's foreign trade also continued to thrive (Yamamura 1976).

Table 2.7 shows that the shares of the re-exports of Hong Kong and Singapore in world exports have risen since 1962 and 1975 respectively, confirming this theory on the efficiency of large trading centres.

The share of Hong Kong's re-exports in world exports has increased from 0.73 per cent in 1938 to 1.47 per cent in 1989 (the share was declining from 1951 to 1962 due to the United Nations' embargo and China's isolation). To remove the erratic 'China factor', we can look at Hong Kong's re-exports from market economies to other market economies (Table 2.8). The rapid recovery of Hong Kong's entrepôt trade after 1962 was partly due to the recovery of trade with China. However, this factor did not become important until Deng's open-door policy was adopted in 1978. During the period 1962–78, most of the expansion of Hong Kong's re-exports arose from the increased trade among market economies. From 1968 until 1977, Hong Kong re-exports of Chinese goods accounted for one-quarter of total re-exports; re-exports to China were very small, and re-exports from non-Chinese sources to non-Chinese countries (predominantly from market economies to market economies) accounted for over 70 per cent of re-exports. Since the re-exports from market economies to market economies are determined mostly by market forces, the efficiency of Hong Kong in entrepôt trade is evident.

From 1977 to 1989, the share of re-exports supplied by China increased from 25 per cent to 54 per cent (including re-exports from China to China); the share of re-exports from other countries to China jumped from 2 per cent to 26 per cent; and the share of re-exports from other countries to other countries decreased correspondingly from 73 per cent to 19 per cent. Although trade with China has dominated over non-China trade since 1978, the latter has continued to exhibit healthy growth. Relative to world trade, the share of non-Chinese entrepôt trade rose from 0.11 per cent in 1968 to 0.15 per cent in 1978, and rose again to 0.28 per cent in 1989, again confirming the comparative advantage of Hong Kong in entrepôt trade.

In the case of Singapore, the Korean War led to a boom in entrepôt trade and the re-exports of Singapore rose to 1.8 per cent of world exports in 1951. The end of the Korean War led to a collapse in rubber prices, which was unfavourable for Singapore's re-exports. Re-exports continued to stagnate in the period 1956–62. The main reasons for this were the transfer of a tin ore smelting works from Singapore to Butterworth (Malaysia) in 1958, the 1957 recession in the West, and the 1961 fall in the price of rubber due to releases from strategic stockpiles in the United Kingdom and the United States (Ng 1971:163).

The confrontations with Indonesia from September 1962 until August 1966 meant that Singapore lost her chief supply of rubber and petroleum and also a substantial market for manufactures, though

Table 2.7 *Re-exports of Singapore and Hong Kong*

Year	Singapore's re-exports[a]		Hong Kong's re-exports[b]	
	US$m	Per cent of world exports	US$m	Per cent of world exports
1938	—	—	167	0.73
1948	701	1.23	404	0.61
1950	—	—	577	0.95
1951	1,481	1.80	680	0.83
1956	1,048	1.01	367	0.35
1960	1,065	0.84	187	0.15
1962	1,037	0.73	187	0.13
1964	815	0.47	237	0.14
1967	777	0.36	362	0.17
1970	955	0.30	477	0.15
1973	1,850	0.32	1,267	0.22
1975	2,199	0.25	1,412	0.16
1977	3,461	0.31	2,108	0.19
1979	5,861	0.36	4,002	0.24
1981	7,024	0.36	7,463	0.38
1983	8,019	0.44	7,740	0.43
1984	8,574	0.45	10,681	0.56
1985	8,001	0.41	13,497	0.70
1986	7,772	0.37	15,705	0.74
1987	10,064	0.41	23,439	0.96
1988	14,699	0.52	35,281	1.26
1989	16,338	0.54	44,411	1.47

[a] Prior to 1956, re-exports were not distinguished from exports in the official series. Re-exports in 1948 and 1951 are estimated to be 94 per cent of exports. Ninety-four per cent is the ratio of re-exports to exports in 1956 and 1960. Indonesian trade is excluded from 1964.
[b] Prior to 1959, re-exports were not distinguished from exports in the official series. Figures for 1938 are estimates taken from Tom (1938), and figures for 1948–56 are estimates taken from Chung (1969). See sources below.
Sources: World exports data: *Yearbook of International Trade Statistics.* Singapore data: 1948–51, *Yearbook of International Trade Statistics*; 1956, Legislative Assembly, Sessional paper no. Cmd.3 of 1958; 1960–67, Department of Trade, *Annual Report*, various years; 1970 and after, Singapore, *Yearbook of Statistics*, various years. Hong Kong data: 1938, Tom (1957); 1948–56, Chung (1969); 1960 and after, *Hong Kong Trade Statistics*, various issues.

some smuggling continued during the confrontation. However, although Singapore's entrepôt trade recovered rapidly in the late 1960s, this was not reflected in official statistics, because trade with Indonesia was excluded from official figures after the confrontation. Official figures indicated that Singapore's re-exports dropped in the period 1962–70, but entrepôt trade expanded. The contribution of entrepôt trade to gross domestic product (GDP) is a more reliable

Table 2.8 *Distribution of the re-exports of Hong Kong*

Year	From China to:		From other countries to:			Total
	China (US$m)	Other countries (US$m)	China (US$m)	Other countries (US$m)	% of world exports	(US$m)
1931–38 (average)	10 (4.8)[a]	63 (31.6)	69 (34.7)	58 (28.9)	0.31	200 (100)
1968	—	91 (25.8)	96 (1.4)	257 (72.8)	0.11	353 (100)
1970	—	114 (23.9)	5 (1.0)	358 (75.1)	0.12	477 (100)
1973	—	309 (24.4)	43 (3.4)	915 (72.2)	0.16	0.1267 (100)
1975	—	353 (25.0)	28 (2.0)	1,031 (73.0)	0.12	1,414 (100)
1977	—	535 (25.4)	37 (1.8)	1,536 (72.9)	0.14	2,108 (100)
1978	—	781 (27.7)	46 (1.6)	1,990 (70.6)	0.15	2,817 (100)
1979	—	1,132 (28.3)	263 (6.6)	2,607 (65.1)	0.16	4,002 (100)
1980	—	1,687 (27.9)	932 (15.4)	3,424 (56.7)	0.17	6,043 (100)
1981	52 (0.7)	2,243 (30.1)	1,386 (18.6)	3,782 (50.7)	0.19	7,463 (100)

Table 2.8 *continued*

| Year | From China to: | | From other countries to: | | | Total |
	China (US$m)	Other countries (US$m)	China (US$m)	Other countries (US$m)	% of world exports	(US$m)
1982	91 (1.2)	2,329 (31.9)	1,226 (16.8)	3,659 (50.1)	0.20	7,305 (100)
1983	136 (1.8)	2,570 (33.2)	1,539 (19.9)	3,495 (45.2)	0.19	7,740 (100)
1984	270 (2.5)	3,325 (31.1)	3,320 (31.1)	3,766 (35.3)	0.20	10,681 (100)
1985	395 (2.9)	4,040 (30.0)	5,512 (40.6)	3,554 (26.3)	0.18	13,512 (100)
1986	541 (3.4)	6,072 (38.7)	4,700 (29.9)	4,392 (28.0)	0.21	15,705 (100)
1987	793 (3.4)	10,013 (42.7)	7,716 (32.9)	4,917 (21.0)	0.20	23,435 (100)
1988	1,144 (3.2)	15,706 (44.5)	11,013 (31.2)	7,418 (21.0)	0.26	35,281 (100)
1989	1,548 (3.5)	22,590 (50.9)	11,721 (26.4)	8,552 (19.3)	0.28	44,411 (100)

[a] Figures in brackets represent percentage share of Hong Kong's total re-exports.

Sources: Review of Overseas Trade, various issues; 1931–38 data, Tom (1957); *Yearbook of International Trade Statistics.*

indicator: it did not suffer from the exclusion of Indonesian trade statistics, recovered to the pre-confrontation level by 1967 and then grew at the rapid rate of 18.7 per cent per year in the period 1967–70. From 1970 until 1989, Singapore's re-exports grew at an average rate of 17 per cent per year, and its share of world exports rose from 0.3 per cent to 0.54 per cent, although the recessions of 1975 and 1985 have resulted in setbacks. Taking into account distortion due to the exclusion of Indonesian trade, it can be concluded that Singapore's re-exports stagnated from 1956 until 1967 (actually declining slightly in real terms), but have grown rapidly since 1967, recovering part of the lost ground (in terms of share of world exports) since 1956.

According to conventional wisdom, suppliers can easily cut out middlemen in order to trade directly, and the prospects of entrepôt trade are limited. The 1961–64 Singapore Development Plan concluded that entrepôt trade 'has very limited possibilities of expansion' (Singapore Ministry of Finance 1961:10), but Singapore's re-exports

Table 2.9 *Commodity composition of the re-exports of Hong Kong and Singapore* (per cent)

Year	Hong Kong[a]			Singapore[b]		
	Food-stuffs (0, 1)	Crude materials (2–4)	Manufactures (5–8)	Food-stuffs (0, 1)	Crude materials (2–4)	Manufactures (5–8)
1948[a]	15.7	28.6	55.7	—	—	—
1956[b]	—	—	—	16.1	56.1	21.7
1960[b]	18.0	18.1	63.7	15.3	57.5	21.1
1965	19.3	13.2	66.5	—	—	—
1969	11.5	7.6	80.4	16.2	55.6	24.2
1974	8.0	10.7	80.9	10.1	51.9	33.9
1975	8.8	9.3	81.5	12.5	39.4	43.9
1980	5.7	9.1	82.8	9.3	35.8	52.2
1985	6.0	6.1	87.4	10.5	22.3	67.2
1986	6.3	5.6	87.0	13.2	16.6	66.3
1987	5.3	5.7	88.6	10.4	15.5	70.4
1988	5.4	5.2	89.4	9.1	16.5	71.5
1989	4.7	4.8	40.2	8.1	11.5	77.4

[a] The commodity composition of exports is used instead of that of re-exports since the latter is not available. Re-exports were 90 per cent of exports in 1948.
[b] The commodity composition of exports is used for these years because that of re-exports is not available. Re-exports were 94 per cent of exports in both years.
Sources: Hong Kong data: *Hong Kong Trade Statistics*. Singapore data: 1948, 1960, *Yearbook of International Trade Statistics*; 1965–80, *Yearbook of Statistics*; 1985 and after, *Singapore Trade Statistics*.

have grown rapidly since 1967. The growth in Hong Kong's re-exports since 1962 has been even more dramatic. A critical evaluation of conventional wisdom is evidently required.

Product heterogeneity and intermediation

The present theory predicts that product heterogeneity increases search costs and the demand for intermediation. Manufactures are usually more heterogeneous than crude materials and this may explain the different fortunes of entrepôt trade in Hong Kong and Singapore. Hong Kong's re-exports were dominated by manufactures as early as 1948 (the first year that data were available) while Singapore's re-exports were dominated by crude materials (chiefly tin and rubber) until 1974 (Table 2.9). The share of Hong Kong's re-exports in world exports has risen continuously since the early 1960s. However, the share of Singapore's re-exports in world trade fell from 1.8 per cent in 1951 to 0.25 per cent in 1975 because Malaysia and Indonesia tried to cut out the Singaporean middleman. Suppliers of rubber and tin found it relatively easy to develop port and processing facilities and to export directly. From 1955–57 until 1967–68, the proportion of Malaysian rubber and tin re-exported through Singapore fell considerably (Ng 1971:174), and the entrepôt trade of Singapore stagnated. However, the end of confrontation with Indonesia in 1966 boosted entrepôt trade. The political turmoil in Indonesia hampered its ability to process and export crude materials directly, and the proportion of Indonesian exports going through Singapore rose from the pre-confrontation level of 30 per cent in 1960 to over 60 per cent in 1967 (Buchanan 1972:112–13). The escalation of the Vietnam War also boosted Singapore's entrepôt trade. By 1975, although Malaysia and Indonesia were no longer dependent on Singapore for the export of crude materials and the Vietnam War was drawing to a close, East Asian countries were prospering and were importing machinery and manufactures through Singapore. Since 1975, the share of manufactures in Singapore's re-exports continued to rise sharply. The structural transformation of Singapore's entrepôt trade from crude materials to machinery and manufactures implies good growth prospects due to the higher search costs associated with heterogeneous manufactures. During the period 1975–89, Singapore's re-exports grew at an average annual rate of 15 per cent, and its share of world trade also rose rapidly.

This theory predicts that the demand for intermediation will be higher in services trade than in commodity trade because the 'products' of services tend to be tailored to individual requirements and are thus more heterogeneous than commodities. This is consistent with this author's limited data on services trade which indicates that China's reliance on the Hong Kong middleman in loan syndication and in tourism is even more pronounced than in commodity trade.

The commodity composition of China's indirect trade via Hong Kong is analysed in detail in Chapter 7. The results again confirm the importance of product heterogeneity in intermediation, for the share of China's trade in manufactures handled via Hong Kong is much higher than the corresponding shares of China's trade in agricultural products or crude materials.

Intermediation and decentralization

Traditionally, China preferred direct trade partly because direct trade can be used as a political instrument. Now, with worldwide political recognition and a pragmatic foreign policy, there is less need to use direct trade in this way, and economic instead of political factors predominate in China's choice of Hong Kong as an entrepôt and centre of intermediation.

China lacks skills in intermediary services, including insurance, finance, communications, marketing and legal services. Such skills are abundant in Hong Kong. Furthermore, intermediation demands flexibility, fast responses to changing world demand and quick identification of profitable opportunities. The Hong Kong economy enjoys minimal government intervention and is renowned for its flexibility and resilience. It is not surprising that the rigidly controlled and regulated Chinese economy depends on Hong Kong for intermediation.

Since China's adoption of an open-door policy in 1979, it is easier to trade directly with China. The fixed cost of establishing a direct trade link has decreased and this should lead to a rise in direct trade relative to indirect trade. However, China started to decentralize its foreign trade system in 1979, replacing vertical channels of command by horizontal links. The supervision and coordination costs of command are decreased, but transaction cost increases, creating a huge demand for intermediation. Before 1979, establishing trade links with ten Trading Corporations would have ensured a complete coverage of China's trade. The number of trading corporations increased to over 1000 by 1984, and it is very costly for an individual firm to establish trade links with the mushrooming number of Chinese trading corporations. Intermediation emerges to economize on the fixed cost of establishing trade links, and this demand for intermediation is channelled to Hong Kong due to its comparative advantage in intermediation. It should be noted that China's foreign trade decentralization came in three waves: in 1979, 1984 and 1988. It is also noteworthy that the shares of Hong Kong re-exports to China in China's total imports jumped from 0.5 per cent to 1.7 per cent from 1977 to 1979; jumped again from 7.8 per cent to 13.1 per cent in 1984 and jumped again in 1988 (Table 2.4). The share stagnated in 1989, which was a year of retrenchment of foreign trade decentralization. The figures strongly suggest the important impact of decentralization on inter-mediation. The market composition of China's indirect trade via Hong Kong is analysed in detail in Chapter 7. The results again confirm the overwhelming importance of trade decentralization on intermediation.

It is interesting to note that a Spanish company named Incoteco, involved in exporting chemicals to China, went straight to Beijing and set up an office there in 1981 instead of using Hong Kong as a springboard to the China market. However, after the decentralization of China's trading system, Incoteco found it advantageous to open an office in Hong Kong in 1986 (*South China Morning Post* 24 Oct. 1988). Mr Sancho, the Manager of the Hong Kong office, explained that decentralization has put more decision-making at the regional level and more travel is thus required for the individual buyers. Mr Sancho spent at least half of his time visiting clients in different cities. He said:

> We can't be in every province and now that there are so many Hong Kong companies trading with all areas of China we found that it was necessary to collaborate.

Mr Sancho's remarks highlight the importance of decentralization and search costs in China's trade. His remarks also confirm that it is advantageous to set up a trading office in Hong Kong due to the economy of agglomeration in big trading centres.

The rapid jump in the share of China's loans syndicated in Hong Kong in 1987 (Table 2.2) appears to be related to the decentralization of China's financial system. Starting from 1986, selected provincial governments and enterprises were allowed to raise foreign loans without central approval. The rapid drop in the share of China's loans syndication in Hong Kong in 1988–89 can be attributed to the recentralization of the power to borrow foreign funds during the period. Decentralization appears to have a major effect on intermediation.

As for tourism, the China Travel Service used to have a monopoly in organizing tours for foreign tourists, but in 1984 the management of the tourist trade was partially decentralized to provincial and local governments. It is noteworthy that the shares of foreign tourists going to and departing from China via Hong Kong increased in 1984–85. This development is consistent with the theory of intermediation.

Hong Kong tour operators organize many tours to China, including one-day tours of Shenzhen, for which the tour operator applies for group visas as individual visas are not required.

The prospects for Hong Kong as middleman

As both the theoretical and empirical analyses indicate, the prospects for Hong Kong's growing role in China's trade are bright. China plans to decentralize its economy further, implying a further multiplication in the number of trade links and a greater demand for intermediation.

At present, Chinese import–export firms compete with Hong Kong firms, but many of these Chinese firms are inefficient state enterprises hampered by administrative controls. In the very long run, with successful economic reforms, efficient, profit-maximizing Chinese trading firms may emerge. However, given economies of scale and economies of agglomeration in the production of intermediary services, Hong Kong does not have to fear competition from Chinese trading firms.

Even in the very long run, Shanghai is likely to be the only Chinese city capable of challenging the position of Hong Kong in intermediation, but even so, Shanghai's transport and communication facilities lag considerably behind Hong Kong and its service industries are rudimentary. China's commodity trade will shift towards less bulky and more heterogeneous goods and this will enhance the demand for intermediation. The open-door policy led to the development of services trade and investment in addition to traditional commodity trade, and this will enhance the need for intermediation, as the products of services tend to be more heterogeneous. Moreover, the secular decline in travel and transportation costs implies that the locational advantage of Shanghai will become less important, while proficiency in trading skills will grow in importance.

The Chinese themselves are establishing many trading companies in Hong Kong, showing that they recognize the established efficiency of Hong Kong in trading. Some Hong Kong traders fear competition from Chinese trading companies in Hong Kong. However, the situation is not a zero-sum game because of economies of agglomeration: the arrival of Chinese trading companies further enhances the position of Hong Kong as a trading centre.

China's economic reforms and open-door policy suffered severe blows during the 1988 recentralization and the 1989 Tiananmen incident. Further economic decentralization was halted, at least temporarily. However, with China's economic isolation after the Tiananmen incident, China may be even more dependent on Hong Kong for investment, loans, and export promotion. The impact of the Tiananmen incident on Hong Kong's role in China's open-door policy is analysed in the last chapter.

3

The institutional setting

Under the open-door policy, the traditional Chinese system of foreign trade proved to be inadequate for meeting the demands of an increasing variety of economic interactions. Organizational changes and new incentive structures were thus adopted from 1979 onwards.

Prior to 1979, international trade had been monopolized by nine National Foreign Trade Corporations (NFTCs) under the control of the Ministry of Foreign Trade. The Foreign Trade Corporations operated according to mandatory plans, purchasing fixed quantities of domestic goods at fixed prices for export and importing fixed quantities of foreign goods for domestic distribution at fixed prices. All foreign exchange earnings had to be remitted to Beijing. Because the renminbi was overvalued, corporations usually incurred losses on exports but earned profits on imports. However, this was not a matter of concern since the Ministry of Foreign Trade bore the losses and siphoned off the profits.

The system enabled planners to enforce their priorities at the cost of inhibiting international trade. Buyers and sellers could only conduct business through an intermediary. This lack of direct contact between producers and end-users also obstructed the transfer of technology that usually occurs between foreign producers and end-users. Moreover, such a rigid system could not respond to rapid changes in the international market.

The first reform drive and retrenchment (1979–81)

In 1979, new central agencies for trade and investment were created by the State Council in response to the need for functional specialization in implementing the open-door policy. These included the Foreign Investment Administrative Commission (FIAC), the Import–Export

Administration Commission (IEAC), the State Administration of Foreign Exchange Control (SAFEC), and the China International Trust and Investment Corporation (CITIC). The functions of FIAC and SAFEC were self-evident. IEAC was responsible for special trade not involving direct foreign investment. CITIC was a ministerial-rank multinational company formed to court foreign investment and finance. It had unprecedented autonomy in the communist world and was led by an old-style millionaire, Rong Yiren, who had refused to leave China during the communist takeover in 1949. In March 1982, the FIAC and IEAC were merged with the Ministry of Trade and the Ministry of Foreign Economic Relations into an umbrella organization called the Ministry of Foreign Economic Relations and Trade (MOFERT).

In addition to the creation of new agencies at the central level, powers of trade and investment have been widely decentralized. Industrial ministries under the State Council are allowed to establish their own import–export corporations. Ministerial Foreign Trade Corporations (MFTCs) usually export the Ministry's own products and handle imports required by the Ministry. The reforms facilitated direct technical contacts between Chinese and foreign enterprises.

Beginning with Guangdong, Fujian and the three central municipalities, an increasing number of provinces have set up provincial import–export corporations since 1979. A handful of producer enterprises have also achieved autonomy in exports. These include export enterprises established by the NFTCs, enterprises jointly established by industrial ministries and NFTCs, large enterprises under ministerial control, and some enterprises under provincial control (mainly in Fujian and Guangdong). Several hundred corporations and enterprises had achieved rights to export by 1980.

Despite these reforms, the Chinese trading system was still highly centralized with official approval required for all exports and imports. Exports were classified into three categories: Category I commodities, under the control of the Ministry of Foreign Trade (e.g. grain, coal, crude oil and finished steel), continued to be handled by the NFTCs and accounted for 80 per cent of China's total exports in 1980–81 (at the height of the first decentralization drive) (Kueh & Howe 1984:832); less important Category II commodities were handled by local authorities under central guidance, and locally established export prices were within centrally stipulated ranges; Category III goods were usually outside the plan, allowing local authorities to issue licences, set the prices, and handle exports (Ho & Huenemann 1984:41–4). Imports were even more centralized than exports because of strict foreign exchange controls.

The 1979–80 decentralization did, however, cause some confusion. Local authorities cut export prices to compete, especially in the

Hong Kong market (Xue 1986:4). The prices of native products in which China had a monopoly fell appreciably, and China reacted by instituting an export licensing system in 1981 (Sung 1985:6). The recentralization measures were part of the retrenchment program of the second readjustment, though export decentralization remained basically intact.

The second reform drive and retrenchment (1983–85)

The second reform drive of 1983–84 led to the opening of Hainan island and fourteen coastal cities as well as the radical proposal to decentralize foreign trade to foreign trade corporations. The reform package, approved by the State Council in September 1984, called for the separation of the functions of government and enterprises; i.e. the MOFERT and local trade authorities would concentrate on the overall management of foreign trade without interfering in the business of foreign trade corporations (NFTCs, MFTCs, and provincial foreign trade corporations), and the foreign trade corporations would gradually become independent of their administrative superiors, assuming responsibility for their own profits and losses. Furthermore, an agency system would be introduced, whereby foreign trade corporations would function as intermediaries in foreign trade for producers and users, collecting service charges in the process. The producers and users would be responsible for the profits and losses involved. Lastly, foreign trade plans would be simplified. Mandatory planning would be restricted to key commodities, and guidance planning would be used for secondary commodities (Zheng 1984:27–33).

The 1984 reform, if fully implemented, would have revolutionized the Chinese foreign trade system. The 1979–80 reform gave trading authority to ministerial and provincial authorities which could easily be controlled by administrative means, whereas the 1984 reform sought to make foreign trade corporations independent of administrative controls.

A prime objective of the 1984 reform proposal was to cut the huge subsidies on exports. As the renminbi was overvalued, the state had to subsidize exports according to their costs. Though the renminbi had been devalued repeatedly against the US dollar since 1979, the 'cost of earning foreign exchange' (COEFE) or the *Huanhui Chengben* (the cost in renminbi of earning one unit of foreign exchange) often exceeded the official exchange rate. Table 3.1 shows the average COEFE of China's exports and the official exchange rate in recent years. Though the 1979–80 reforms partially decentralized

Table 3.1 China's 'average cost of earning foreign exchange' in exports

Year	Average cost of earning US$1		Official exchange rate[a] (Yuan/US$)
	Yuan	Growth rate (%)	
1980	2.31	—	1.50
1981	2.48	7.4	2.80
1982	2.67	7.7	2.80
1983	3.07	15.0	2.80
1984	2.80	−8.8	2.80
1985	3.24	15.7	2.94
1986	4.25	31.1	3.46
1987	—	—	3.70

[a] The internal settlement rate is used for the official exchange rate in 1981–84.

Sources: 1980–84 data came from Wang (1986:46); 1985–86 data were estimated from the COEFE of Guangdong obtained from interviews with Guangdong officials, and it is assumed that the rate of growth of the COEFE nationwide was the same as that in Guangdong.

the power to trade, the financial responsibility was still centralized, i.e. exports were subsidized up to their costs. The system encourages foreign trade corporations to procure goods for export at high prices to meet mandatory export targets, leading to a rapid rise in the COEFE.

To lower costs, Chinese planners have been using the COEFE in well-run enterprises as an efficiency norm. Due to China's irrational price structure, different norms of the COEFE are established for different industries. Enterprises in which the COEFE is above the norm would be urged to increase efficiency or even to stop exporting. In view of the rapid rise of the COEFE in 1983, the State Council established ceilings of COEFE for different goods and banned the export of goods that cost more than the stipulated ceilings in December 1983 (Chan 1986:14). The COEFE declined temporarily in 1984, but shot up again in 1985. Given mandatory export targets and soft budget constraints, administrative controls on the COEFE failed to hold down the cost of exports.

The 1984 reform proposal attempted to shift the financial responsibility from the state treasury to enterprises, so that foreign trade corporations, producers of exports and users of imports would assume responsibility for their own profits and losses. Producers and foreign trade corporations would thus be encouraged to be cost-conscious, and end-users would be forced to economize on the use of imports.

The 1984 reform proposal was stalled by the severe macroeconomic imbalance of 1984–85. The price of export procurement was lowered in 1984 following the ban on high cost exports in December 1983, but domestic inflation was rapid due to the macroeconomic imbalance. Many export producers thus diverted their production capacity to the domestic market (Zhao & Liu 1986:36). From March to July 1985, China's exports declined by 5 per cent over the same period in 1984, though the decline was halted in August 1985 following stabilization measures that were taken in March 1985. Imports rose by 54 per cent in 1985 and China ran a huge trade deficit. The renminbi was devalued several times against the US dollar in 1985 and 1986, but the devaluations were not big enough to keep pace with the rapid rise of the COEFE. The state treasury had to continue to assume most of the financial responsibility in foreign trade (Tian et al. 1986:37), and the 1984 reform proposal remained largely unimplemented.

One aspect of the 1984 reform that was more widely adopted was the agency system, which permitted direct contact between producers and end-users. This is especially important for the import of appropriate technology. However, though the agency system was implemented quite fully on the import side, it covered only 10 per cent of exports; since exports were still heavily subsidized. Moreover, the role of the NFTCs is more prominent than the usual intermediary because the producers have little experience in exporting, and export prices are negotiated by the NFTC and the end-user (*Ta Kung Pao* 30 May 1987). The total number of corporations and enterprises with autonomy to export continued to grow, reaching 3000 by 1986.

The 1984 reform did lead to a reduction in the role of mandatory planning. Before 1985, the export plan included both mandatory procurement targets and export targets, and both procurement and export prices were fixed. In 1985, mandatory procurement plans for exports were abolished mainly because enterprises were given the autonomy to sell their output after the 1984 reform of the domestic sector (*Wen Hui Pao* 2 May 1987). However, in 1986, mandatory export targets still accounted for 70 per cent of all exports (*Wen Hui Pao* 6 June 1987). NFTCs, which handle the key commodities controlled by MOFERT, still handled 80 per cent of all imports and 90 per cent of all exports in 1986.[1] Decentralization of foreign trade has not made much headway since 1980–81 as NFTCs then handled only 80 per cent of China's exports.

With the restoration of external balance in 1987, China took another step towards the goal of the 1984 reform proposal. The contract responsibility system, which was introduced nationwide in 1987 to reduce losses and improve efficiency in state-owned enterprises, was also applied to the foreign trade sector in the same year.

---

[1] Information obtained in interview with Chinese trade officials.

Under this system, the ten NFTCs were assessed on the basis of three targets specified in a contract: value of exports, cost of exports, and profits. As two NFTCs would not be able to make profits, owing to the overvaluation of the renminbi, they would be assessed on the basis of planned losses. NFTCs would be allowed to retain part of the above-plan profits (or beneath-plan losses), and also retain part of the above-plan foreign exchange (*Wen Hui Pao* 30 May 1987). NFTCs would gain if they managed to lower the cost of exports below the planned level, and they would have to fund losses from their resources if the cost of exports rose above the planned level. However, the local branches of the NFTCs were still administrative appendages of their head offices in Beijing. The reforms have fallen far short of the goals of the 1984 reform in which all FTCs (including local branches of NFTCs) were meant to be financially independent.

The third reform drive and retrenchment (1988)

The third reform drive led to the opening of more coastal cities and coastal areas, including the establishment of Hainan as a province and as a SEZ. In March 1988, MOFERT started to restructure the foreign trade system and power was decentralized from the head offices of the NFTCs in Beijing to local foreign trade corporations (LFTCs), which had formerly been local branches of the NFTCs. The LFTCs became financially independent companies. The reform represented a further application of the contract responsibility system in foreign trade (*South China Morning Post* 10 Oct. 1988). Under the new system, each province or municipality must sign an annual contract with MOFERT specifying three targets, namely, foreign exchange earnings, amount of foreign exchange to be turned over to the state, and profits (or losses). To meet these obligations, the provincial or municipal governments will enter into contracts with the LFTCs which act as import and export agents for the local enterprises. The role of NFTCs was greatly diminished and the number of commodities subject to exclusive trading by NFTCs was limited to a few items.

Along with the decentralization of power, financial responsibility was also decentralized from the state to provincial governments and foreign trade corporations (NFTCs, MFTCs and LFTCs) which were required to be financially independent. To enable provincial governments and foreign trade corporations to cover the losses from exports, they were allowed to retain 80 per cent of their foreign exchange earnings that exceeded planned targets. This was in addition to the customary 25 per cent retention of within-target foreign exchange earnings which had been allowed since 1979. As the renminbi was overvalued, the right to retain foreign exchange served as a powerful incentive. The restrictions on the sale of foreign exchange earnings at prices above the official rate were also relaxed in early 1988. The foreign exchange retention scheme and restrictions on transfer of such foreign exchange are complicated subjects that will be discussed in greater detail in the next section. The generous foreign exchange retentions together with other economic incentives, such as the exemption of domestic taxes for exports, have enabled foreign trade corporations to become financially independent, and China came closer to the goals of the 1984 reform proposal. However, as the problem of soft budget constraint is deeply rooted in socialist economies (including marketized socialist economies), the complete financial independence of state enterprises in China has to await the full implementation of the bankruptcy law passed in 1988.

The macroeconomic imbalance of 1988 was mainly confined to the domestic sector. Though the trade deficit rose slightly in the second half of 1988, it was 10 per cent of total exports and was relatively much smaller than the deficit of 1985, which was 54 per cent of exports. Severe controls were imposed on investment and credit, and there was a crackdown on economic crimes and corruption, including a crackdown on illegal practices in foreign trade. However, as the external balance was not severe, there was no drastic recentralization of trade and the 1988 trade reforms remained basically intact.

Incentives to promote trade

Starting in 1979, incentives were adopted to promote trade, especially exports. Measures adopted included: devaluation of the renminbi; permission for local governments, ministries and export enterprises to retain a portion of the foreign exchange earned in exports; tariff exemption for imported inputs used in producing exports; and rebates on indirect taxes for exports. These new measures were introduced in addition to the established practice of priority allocation of scarce materials to export enterprises.

In 1979–80, the official exchange rate of roughly 1.5 yuan per dollar could not cover the costs of exporters, as the average COEFE was around 2.5 yuan per dollar (Table 3.1). The variation of the COEFE among localities and goods was large. In 1979, 77.2 per cent of Guangdong exports incurred losses, and the COEFE of some goods was 10 times the official rate (Kueh & Howe 1984:854). A dual rate system was adopted at the beginning of 1981. Commodity trade was settled at the internal rate of 2.80 yuan per dollar, and the official rate of 1.53 yuan per dollar continued to apply to non-commodity transactions. Table 3.1 shows the COEFE and exchange rate of China in recent years. From the period 1980–81 onwards, the internal settlement rate exceeded the COEFE. The dual rate system was strongly criticized by the United States as an export subsidy. As the United States dollar appreciated against other currencies in 1981–84, the renminbi was gradually devalued against the United States dollar, and the official exchange rate approached the internal rate. The dual rate system was abolished on 1 January 1985, when the official exchange rate was 2.84 yuan per dollar. By then, the COEFE of Chinese exports was 4.00 yuan per dollar and huge subsidies were still required for exports.

From 1 January to 30 September 1985, the renminbi was gradually devalued by a total of 12.5 per cent to 3.2 yuan per dollar, and remained steady at this level for 10 months until 4 July 1986, when it was further devalued by 14 per cent to 3.70 yuan per dollar. The yuan was still overvalued, but the continued weakness of the United States dollar in 1986–87 helped to ease the extent of overvaluation.

The foreign exchange retention scheme was first introduced in 1979. All foreign exchange earned through exports must be sold to the Bank of China at the official exchange rate, but the provincial government and the export enterprise are entitled to purchase a share of the foreign exchange at the official rate for later use on approved items that require the use of foreign exchange. It should be noted that the entitlement does not confer a secure right to use foreign exchange. In the 1985 crisis, enterprises seldom got approval to use their entitlements due to the tight foreign exchange situation. Provincial governments sometimes requisition the entitlements of enterprises under their control without compensation (Zhao & Liu 1986:28). However, with the improvement in the balance of payments since 1986, the right to foreign exchange entitlements have become more secure.

Before the 1988 trade reforms, provincial authorities and export enterprises gained from increased exports due to the foreign exchange retention scheme, but they did not assume financial responsibility, which remained with the central government. Provincial authorities thus did not hesitate to procure goods at high prices and dump them overseas at a loss (Xue 1986:4), which led to a rapid rise in the COEFE.

There is a wide variation in foreign exchange retention ratios. Before the 1988 trade reforms which raised the retention ratios, the usual ratio was 25 per cent, half going to the provincial and local

governments and half going to the export enterprises. The Guangdong and Fujian provincial governments were allowed to retain an
extra 5 per cent, giving a total retention ratio of 30 per cent. The
scheme was used as a means of regional redistribution, and the ratio
was usually higher in less developed and mountainous areas, and even
higher in the SEZs and open areas (World Bank 1988:24). The ratio
was 100 per cent for products made in Shenzhen and in Hainan
island. The ratio also differs for different products, and is higher for
exports which exceed planned targets (Tian et al. 1986:33).

The regional variation in retention ratios implies that regions with
high retention ratios, e.g. Hainan island and Shenzhen, can afford to
procure products from other regions at high prices for dumping
overseas. The artificial diversion of products to SEZs for exports is
irrational, as it results in greater transport and handling costs. It also
exacerbates the rise in the COEFE.

After 1980, enterprises were allowed to swap their foreign exchange entitlements to renminbi with other enterprises through the
Bank of China, and the price was allowed to rise a maximum of 10
per cent above the official rate (Wu 1987:9). The maximum prices in
1986 and 1987 were respectively 4.7 yuan and 5.7 yuan per US
dollar,[2] appreciably higher than the official rate of 3.7 yuan per
US dollar.

A significant liberalization of foreign exchange control has occurred with the development of 'foreign exchange adjustment centres', where enterprises with foreign participation can buy and sell
foreign exchange at prices higher than the official rate. The first
foreign exchange adjustment centre was established in Shenzhen in
December 1985, but trading was not active due to an imposed price
ceiling. The price ceiling was raised in December 1986 and trading
increased (*Wen Hui Pao* 23 Feb. 1987). Such centres have also been
established in Shanghai and other 'open' cities.

In the 1988 trade reforms, the retention ratios were raised and the
restrictions on the sale of foreign exchange entitlements were relaxed
to enable foreign trade corporations to become financially independent. Three industries, namely light industrial goods, textiles, and arts
and crafts, were selected for experimentation with the new system,
and they could retain 70 per cent of their within-target foreign
exchange earnings. As mentioned before, the retention ratios for
above-target foreign exchange earnings were generally raised to 80
per cent. The retention ratios were generally lower for primary
products and higher for products that involved a greater degree of

[2]Information obtained in interview with Chinese trade officials.

processing. Selected export enterprises were allowed 100 per cent foreign exchange retention on an experimental basis (*Ta Kung Pao* 3 Dec. 1987).

In October 1988, the State Council decided to lower the retention ratio for SEZs from 100 per cent to 80 per cent, starting in 1989, as a result of diversion of exports from other areas to SEZs (*Hong Kong Economic Times* 18 Oct. 1988). The lowering of the retention ratio in SEZs and the rise in retention ratios elsewhere imply a shrinking of the wide dispersion of retention ratios and should lead to fairer competition between SEZs and other areas.

In May 1988, the State Administration of Foreign Exchange Control (SAFEC) relaxed the restrictions on the trading of foreign exchange. Domestic enterprises can trade their foreign exchange entitlements in the foreign exchange adjustment centres at negotiated rates and they can also trade foreign exchange with foreign investment ventures at negotiated rates. The SAFEC planned to establish foreign exchange adjustment centres in all the thirty provinces, autonomous regions, and municipalities throughout China, giving rise to a national market in foreign exchange (*Ta Kung Pao* 12 May 1988). Though the price of foreign exchange is not strictly controlled, restrictions are still imposed on the source and use of foreign exchange. The seller is required to specify that the foreign exchange is obtained from a legal source, and the buyer has to specify a legitimate use of foreign exchange. Trading for speculation is strictly prohibited. A buyer may rely on the service of the centre to find a willing seller, but the process is slow as there is a long waiting list of potential buyers. In most cases, the buyer finds the seller through his own efforts and then legalizes the transaction at the centre by paying a service fee, usually fixed at 0.15 per cent of the total transaction. Individuals are generally not allowed to participate in trade, but they have been allowed to trade at the centre in Shenzhen since December 1986 (*Wen Hui Pao* 18 Aug. 1988).

In May 1988, at the Beijing foreign exchange adjustment centre, the average price of US currency was 6.1 yuan per dollar and the average price of foreign exchange entitlement was 5.47 yuan per US dollar (*Wen Hui Pao* 13 Sept. 1988). The price of US currency at the centre was only a few per cent lower than the black market rate, showing that the restrictions on the trading of foreign exchange at the centres were not very severe. However, the price of foreign exchange entitlements was appreciably lower than that of foreign currency, showing that there were significant restrictions on the use of foreign exchange entitlements. In 1987, a total of US\$4.2 billion was legally swapped in China and the share accounted for by foreign investment ventures was US\$0.33 billion (*Ta Kung Pao* 12 May 1988).

Part of the financial loss on exports is misleading because of the heavy tariffs on imported inputs used in producing exports and also because of heavy indirect taxes. In the period 1981–84, industry and commercial taxes accounted for 14 per cent of China's national income. The significance of tariffs and other indirect taxes might also be substantial, but they cannot be quantified due to lack of data. Tax rebates for exports have been proposed since the early 1980s, but provincial governments are unwilling to give tax rebates because of the adverse impact on provincial treasuries. Many taxes in China are collected by provincial authorities and then shared between Beijing and the provinces. Manufacturing usually involves intermediate inputs produced in different regions, and the precise geographical incidence of indirect tax is difficult to determine. Tariff exemption for imported inputs used in producing exports has been implemented because tariff exemption involves only the central treasury. From 1985 to 1987, the central government rebated domestic taxes on the final stage of production, which represented only one-third of the total taxes paid through all stages of production.[3]

The 1988 trade reform blueprint proposed a rebate of indirect taxes through all stages of production. For products procured for exports by FTCs, the rebates would be given to the FTCs. For products exported through the agency system, the rebates would be given to the production enterprises (*Ta Kung Pao* 3 Dec. 1987).

Organization and incentives for foreign investment

Special trade arrangements that have been practised by Eastern Europe in East–West trade were adopted by China in 1979. The Chinese definition of foreign investment is broader than the conventional one: all special trade arrangements are regarded as 'foreign investment' because foreign funds are involved. The Chinese distinguish five types of special trade, which are listed here in ascending order of complexity.

(i) Processing/assembling

This is also known as contractual manufacturing–processing. The foreign partners subcontract their manufacturing–processing operations to their Chinese partners, and pay a processing/assembling fee.

---

[3]Information obtained in interview with Chinese trade officials.

The foreign partners provide the necessary materials or components and design specifications, and sell the finished product. The foreign partners usually provide some equipment, which is paid for by instalments of the processing/assembling fee. If the foreign partners provide equipment, processing/assembling overlaps with compensation trade. Manufacturers from Hong Kong dominate processing/assembling operations, as these are only profitable with low transportation costs.

(ii) Compensation trade

The foreign partner provides China with equipment and receives products in return. The Chinese distinguish between direct compensation, where the products are produced by the equipment supplied, and indirect compensation (also known as 'counter trade'), where the foreign partner is compensated with other products. The foreign partner does not participate in the management of the Chinese enterprise though he is often involved in quality control, as he usually markets the product.

(iii) Cooperative venture

This is a flexible form of cooperation which covers arrangements outside China's joint venture law. The arrangement may or may not involve the formation of a limited company. The rights and duties of both partners are stipulated in a contract. The arrangement may take any form as long as it is accepted by both partners. Usually the foreign partner contributes funds, equipment and technology while the Chinese partner supplies land, factory premises, labour and raw material. The Chinese partner manages the project and repays the foreign partner through output of the project or with cash. If a legal entity is formed, it is taxed in the same way as an equity joint venture. If no legal entity is created, the income received by the foreign partner is taxed at progressive rates of 20 to 40 per cent. The duration of the contract is similar to that of an equity joint venture and the assets of the project belong to the Chinese partner after the contract expires.

(iv) Cooperative development

This involves the joint exploration and development of natural resources and is regarded by the Chinese as a separate category of special trade. Conceptually, it is a form of cooperative venture where no separate legal entity is formed. Generally, the foreign partner bears all exploration risks and expenses, and is compensated from a portion of the goods produced after deducting production costs. Cooperative development is taxed in the same way as a cooperative venture.

(v) Equity joint venture

This refers to limited companies formed according to China's law on joint ventures promulgated in 1979. The partners manage the company jointly and profits are shared in proportion to capital participation. The duration of the cooperative period is generally 20 years for heavy industry, 10–15 years for light industry, and 5–10 years for service and tourist industry. At the end of the contract, the assets of the company can be sold to the Chinese partner at an agreed price, or the company can apply for an extension of the contract. Tax is 30 per cent of the profit, with local tax taking another 3 per cent.

The 33 per cent effective tax on profits of an equity joint venture is roughly comparable to that of East Asian countries (Ho & Huenemann 1984:82). However, profit tax is only 15 per cent for the SEZs, Hainan island, the open cities and special projects in non-open areas. The length of the tax holiday initially decreed in 1980 was less generous than those in other East Asian economies (Ho & Huenemann 1984:82), but the gap was narrowed through the extension of tax holidays in September 1983 (Ho & Huenemann 1984:82).

Of the five types of industrial cooperation agreements, the equity joint venture is the most promising for technology transfer, as it involves long-term commitment and close ties between Chinese and foreign parties. Processing/assembling and compensation trade tend to be small and labour-intensive operations which are important for employment. Fully foreign-owned enterprises are also allowed if they use advanced technology and equipment and if a large portion of their products is exported. Cooperative ventures, equity ventures, and fully foreign-owned enterprises are collectively referred to as 'the three types of foreign-funded ventures'.

The pace of foreign investment in the 1980–82 period was slow. The 1983 extension of tax holidays and the opening of the coastal cities in 1984 brought about an acceleration in foreign investment. However, the many problems of the Chinese investment environment soon discouraged the initial enthusiasm of investors, and the 1985 recentralization further hampered foreign investment. Foreign investment fell sharply in 1985–86, and the Chinese leadership was so alarmed that a 22-point investment enticement package was announced in October 1986. The package tried to limit the salaries of local staff and the arbitrary charges imposed by local governments. Taxes were lowered for 'the three types of foreign-funded ventures' exporting at least 70 per cent of output and for those that imported advanced technology. Foreign investment revived in 1987–88, but still fell short of the 1985 peak. The many problems of the Chinese investment environment are detailed in the next chapter.

The three-tier structure of open areas

The open areas form a three-tier structure in terms of increasing degrees of autonomy: coastal open areas, coastal open cities, SEZs. The SEZs used to have a tremendous competitive edge in terms of low taxes and high foreign-exchange retention ratios, but the edge has been eroded by the opening of other cities and areas. In order to maintain their lead, the SEZs have been forced to grant more and more concessions to foreign investors. The competition among different open areas to grant more concessions to foreign investors may not work in the national interest, but Beijing has not been able to prevent such competition as more and more economic power has been decentralized from Beijing to the provinces and municipalities.

Until 1984, the 15 per cent profit tax for foreign investors in SEZs had been quite attractive compared with the 30 per cent profit tax elsewhere in China. However, in 1984, twelve coastal cities, among the fourteen opened in 1984, established Economic and Technology Development Districts (ETDDs) in which the 15 per cent profit tax also applied. The 15 per cent profit tax was then applied to special enterprises outside the SEZs and ETDDs, including technology-intensive enterprises, enterprises with foreign investment over US$30 million, investment with a lengthy pay-back period, or investment in energy, transportation and harbour facilities. Hong Kong's practice of taxing foreign investors at 15 per cent, which was first adopted by Shenzhen, appears to be spreading throughout China. The coastal open areas also joined in the tax-reduction competition and offered a variety of tax cuts and tax holidays. For instance, the profit tax of the Liudong peninsula was fixed at 24 per cent instead of the standard 30 per cent.

Beijing consulted Hong Kong businessmen on the establishment of the Hainan SEZ. They proposed that the Hainan SEZ should allow the sale of land, and their proposal was adopted. To maintain its competitive edge, Shenzhen pre-empted the Hainan move by selling land before the establishment of the Hainan SEZ (Sha 1988:63). Other open cities in China also started to sell land. Shenzhen planned to adopt Hong Kong commercial laws (*South China Morning Post* 1 Nov. 1988), a move that was also contemplated in Hainan. Despite the moves of Shenzhen, it appears that Hainan will still be the most special SEZ in China. For instance, Hainan will be allowed to retain foreign exchange in the form of currency rather than in the form of entitlements in accounts controlled by the state. This will encourage the circulation of foreign currency in Hainan.

In March 1988, after the central work conference on the opening of the coastal areas, Vice-Premier Tian Jiyuan summed up the division of labour among the three different kinds of open areas (*Ta Kung Pao* 19 Mar. 1988):

the coastal open areas are expected to export labour-intensive manufactures and agricultural products; the coastal open cities should rely on their strength in technology and industry to upgrade traditional exports, promoting the export of electrical machinery in particular; and the SEZs should be a model of an externally-oriented economy with advanced technology.

Tian's statement was little more than a retrospective rationalization of the confusion that emerged in the competitive drive of various open areas to grant preferential terms to foreign investors. Since Tian's speech, various inland areas, including Hubei, Anhui, Kiangsi, Gansu, Honan, Shenshi, Beijing and Sicheun, have also granted preferential terms to foreign investors (*Hong Kong Economic Times* 15 June 1988). Chinese economists started to talk about a four-tier structure of open areas, with inland open areas as the first tier. The distinction between each tier is not sharp. Many inland open areas have granted preferential terms that are as attractive as or even exceed those of the coastal open areas. For instance, the Loyang ETDD in Honan exempts all profit tax for a period of three years. The four SEZs and the ETDDs in the fourteen coastal cities only exempt profit tax for a period of two years (*Hong Kong Economic Times* 15 June 1988).

The SEZs initially tried to attract technologically advanced industries and turned away processing/assembling operations. However, the SEZs managed to attract only very few high-technology ventures and eventually were forced to accept processing/assembling operations. Counties in the Pearl River delta (a coastal open area) such as Dongguan, Zhongshan, and Foshan have been able to attract foreign investment in industries that are as sophisticated as those in the SEZs. Though SEZs have a better infrastructure, they are less flexible in their policies because they have been pushed into the limelight and thus suffer from the attention and meddling of Beijing. The obscure counties mentioned above can afford to ignore central directives and pursue more flexible policies. The planned division of labour among the different types of open areas exists more on paper than in reality.

The impact of Hong Kong on the decentralization of China's external sector

Hong Kong plays a catalytic role in the reform of China's external sector. As mentioned before, Hong Kong lowers the transaction cost of China's trade and facilitates China's interaction with the external world. However, the catalytic role of Hong Kong also goes beyond that of middleman and facilitator. Hong Kong activates market forces in China and adds to the pressures that push China down the path of liberalization and decentralization. Hong Kong expands the intended scope of China's trade decentralization because Chinese enterprises and local authorities can easily establish trading corporations in Hong Kong without approval. Beijing has been forced to accept the competition from these unofficial corporations and even recognized some of them as official. Hong Kong also acts as the offshore base for China's thriving black market in foreign exchange, and, in order to compete, Beijing has relaxed its foreign exchange controls and established a grey market through the Bank of China and foreign exchange adjustment centres.

From 1979–81, the number of Chinese Trading Corporations officially approved to operate in Hong Kong totalled fifty-one (*The Nineties* Feb. 1982:32). However, the number of unofficial traders was estimated to be about 300 (*Hong Kong Economic Times* 4 Oct. 1988). A popular form of unofficial representation is as a joint venture with Hong Kong traders. Since the trading firm is nominally operated by a Hong Kong trade, approval from Beijing is not necessary. Local authorities in China have been encouraging people who have relatives in Hong Kong to emigrate and to promote trade and investment, and some of them operate as one-person operations after their arrival in Hong Kong. One Hong Kong trader had come across seven 'one-person operators' claiming to represent various local authorities in China (Sung 1985:53). By 1988, the number of Chinese corporations in Hong Kong was estimated to total 3200, most of them unofficial (*Hong Kong Economic Times* 4 Oct. 1988).

In the 1988 retrenchment and crackdown on irregular economic practices, it was reported that Deng Xiaoping was of the opinion that one-third to two-thirds of the Chinese corporations in Hong Kong should be closed (*Hong Kong Economic Times* 11 Oct. 1988), and it was rumoured that Guangdong would close some 100 'underground' enterprises in Hong Kong (*Hong Kong Economic Times* 24 Oct. 1988). However, there was no significant shake-up of Chinese corporations in Hong Kong owing to the fact that China cannot close enterprises registered in Hong Kong. Moreover, many managers of these enterprises originally entered Hong Kong on the grounds that they had relatives in Hong Kong. They thus acquired residency rights in Hong Kong and Beijing cannot recall them. Instead of closing such enterprises, the Guangdong provincial government proceeded to check the financial conditions of such enterprises and allowed them to register with the provincial government as official overseas enterprises (*Hong Kong Economic Times* 4 Nov. 1988).

Hong Kong abets the thriving foreign exchange black market and illicit exports of China in many ways.[4] Hong Kong tourists supply foreign currency on the black market, and they carry native products, such as herbal medicine, to Hong Kong. Hong Kong firms in China producing for the Chinese market receive Chinese currency which they cannot remit. They sell Chinese currency on the black market or buy Chinese products for export, legally or illegally. Joint venture companies in China have the right to export their products, but this right may be abused. For example, Hong Kong farmers investing in vegetable farms in Shenzhen have bought vegetables from local vegetable farmers for export. Hong Kong provides a contact point and off-shore operation base for the black market. For example, Hong Kong residents sending remittances to relatives in China can sell Hong Kong dollars to a Hong Kong enterprise that has unconvertible yuan in China. They pay Hong Kong dollars to the Hong Kong enterprise in Hong Kong. The enterprise pays the relatives in yuan in China, and there is no need to smuggle currency across the border. The black market is so rampant that people in Hong Kong now remit money to their relatives in China mostly through the black market. Remittances through official channels have dwindled to negligible amounts.

Since late 1984, the black market rate for the yuan has dropped to about half the official rate. As mentioned before, China began to establish foreign exchange adjustment centres in late 1985 and a nationwide grey market for foreign exchange was established in 1988. Once again, Hong Kong has activated market forces that press China towards liberalization.

---

[4] Part of this information was obtained from *The Nineties*, Feb. 1985:37–42 and June 1985:46–52. The rest was gleaned from interviews with China traders.

4

Evaluation of the open-door policy

More than ten years have elapsed since the inauguration of the open-door policy. Commodity trade, services trade and foreign investment in China have increased by leaps and bounds, but thorny problems remain. Unsustainable trade deficits have emerged in the liberalization phase of each of the three reform cycles, and the reforms suffered setbacks as a result of administrative measures taken to stabilize the economy. The growth of foreign investment has been below expectations and symptoms of economic inefficiency abound in both trade and investment. The achievements and deficiencies of the open-door policy in the areas of trade and investment are detailed below.

The rapid increase in trade

The increase in exports and imports since 1979 has been extremely rapid. From 1978 to 1988, China's exports (imports) have grown at the average annual nominal rate of 17 (18) per cent in terms of the US dollar, increasing slightly less (more) than fivefold in the ten-year period. Due to the repeated devaluation of the yuan, the US dollar provides a more reliable yardstick with which to measure the growth of China's trade. Though the US dollar appreciated strongly against major currencies from 1978 to early 1985, this has been largely offset by its subsequent depreciation. Measuring the growth of China's trade by the US dollar or by a trade-weighted basket of currencies gives similar results over the period 1978–88 (Sung 1988:19).

The ratio of China's exports (imports) to its GDP has also risen rapidly since 1978. Table 4.1 shows the ratio of China's exports and imports to its GDP, and the ratio of India's exports to its GDP is included for comparison. India is chosen for comparison because the ratio is usually lower for large economies and higher for more developed economies; India is comparable to China in size and level of development.

61

Table 4.1 *Ratio of exports and imports to GDP in China* (per cent)

	China		India	
Year	Exports	Imports	Exports	Imports
1978	4.8	5.4	5.6	6.6
1979	5.5	6.3	5.9	7.5
1980	6.3(9.7)[a]	6.9	5.3	9.2
1981	7.9(11.8)	7.9	4.5	8.4
1982	8.2(11.8)	7.1	5.0	7.5
1983	7.8(12.1)	7.5	4.5	6.7
1984	8.6(10.8)	9.2	4.9	6.2
1985	9.7(10.6)	15.1	4.4	6.2
1986	11.4(13.9)	15.8	4.1	6.6
1987	13.3 —	14.6	4.4	6.5
1988	12.8 —	14.9	4.7	6.8
1989	12.6 —	14.1	—	—

[a] Figures in brackets represent the ratio obtained from using the true value of exports instead of the official data. The true value of exports is obtained by multiplying the value of exports in US dollars by the average cost of earning foreign exchange.
Sources: China's exports and GDP are obtained from the *Statistical Yearbook of China*, and India's exports and GDP are obtained from the IMF *International Financial Statistics;* the average cost of earning foreign exchange is obtained from Table 3.1.

In the ten years of reform and open-door policy from 1978 to 1989, China's ratio of exports to GDP rose sharply from 5 to 13 per cent, according to official data, while the same ratio for India decreased from 6 to 5 per cent in the period 1979–88. China's imports grew even faster than exports, and the ratio of imports to GDP rose from 5 per cent in 1978 to 14 per cent in 1989. Chinese data in fact understate the openness of the Chinese economy because the official data on the renminbi value of exports and imports are biased downwards to avoid charges of dumping. The Chinese data are obtained by converting the US dollar value of exports or imports at the official exchange rate, which is substantially lower than the true cost of exports or imports. Data on the COEFE of China's exports (Table 3.1) can be used to estimate the true renminbi cost of exports, and the adjusted data give a ratio that is appreciably higher than the official ratio. In 1986, India's ratio was only 4 per cent whereas China's adjusted ratio was 14 per cent. China's economy is thus much more open than that of India and China's export drive has been remarkably successful. No data are available on the true cost of imports. Since the official exchange rate is much lower than the black market rate, the value of imports is also understated.

Though China's official data on exports and imports are seriously biased downwards, they have been used in numerous research projects and policy papers and might have misguided policy makers.

China's exports (imports) are heavily subsidized (taxed), and the official exchange rate is grossly overvalued. In the analysis of China's trade, the relevant variable is not the official or the nominal exchange rate but the effective exchange rate (EER), which is defined as the amount of local currency actually received (paid) by the exporter (importer) per unit of foreign currency of goods exported (imported). The COEFE (Table 3.1) is a convenient proxy for the export EER. It is not a perfect proxy, as the producer may earn a profit over and above cost, but it is difficult to find a better proxy given the limitation of data. It should be noted that a rise (fall) in the EER represents depreciation (appreciation) of the renminbi.

It is very difficult to estimate the import EER, as there is very little data on China's complicated system of import charges, indirect taxes, and subsidies. However, as taxes and subsidies are usually levied on an *ad valorem* basis, the index of the official foreign exchange rate can be taken as a very crude index of the import EER.

The official exchange rate of the renminbi and the COEFE are usually denominated in terms of the US dollar. Due to the sharp fluctuation of the US dollar against major currencies since 1980, the exchange rate of the renminbi and the COEFE should be measured against a basket of currencies rather than against the US dollar. The chosen basket includes the currencies of the six major trading partners of China, namely Hong Kong, Japan, USA, UK, West Germany and Singapore. Their average shares in China's exports (imports) to (from) these six economies in the period 1983–86 are used as weights in the export (import) weighted index.

The base period is to be January 1980, and the indices belong to the Laspeyres type of index, as fixed sets of weights are used. This facilitates comparison between two dates. The Paasche type of index is not used because (i) comparison between two dates is difficult and (ii) the weights are not up-to-date (as China's trade figures are published with a considerable time-lag).

The six economies chosen accounted for 75 per cent (65 per cent) of China's exports (imports) in the period 1983–86, and the remaining portions were mostly accounted for by countries of the Comecon bloc. Since trade with the Comecon bloc and the exchange rate of the renminbi against the currencies of the Comecon bloc are not mainly determined by market forces, the currencies of the Comecon bloc were not included in the currency basket. The six economies chosen in this study accounted for over 90 per cent of China's trade with market economies.

The real exchange rate, which is a measure of the exchange rate that is adjusted for changes in purchasing power between China and the rest of the world, can be computed from the EER. The export (import) real EER, which is a proxy for the real exchange rate, is defined as follows:

$$\text{export (import) real EER} = \text{export (import) EER} \times \frac{PW}{PD}$$

where PW is the index of the world price level, and is taken to be the export (import)-weighted consumer price index of the six countries in the currency basket; and, PD is the index of the domestic price level and is taken to be China's GDP deflator.

Table 4.2 shows the nominal exchange rate indices of the yuan denominated in terms of the US dollar and in terms of the currency baskets. The export-weighted exchange rate index of renminbi rose from 100 points to 179 points in 1981 due to the adoption of the internal settlement rate. However, the index fell back to 148 points in 1984 due to the sharp appreciation of the US dollar against other currencies. Thereafter, the index rose sharply to 230 points in 1987 as a result of (i) the devaluation of the renminbi against the US dollar, and (ii) the sharp depreciation of the US dollar against major currencies. The movement of the import-weighted index is broadly similar to the export-weighted index. However, in comparison with the export-weighted index, the fall of the import-weighted index from 1981 to 1984 was less substantial, and its rise thereafter was more dramatic, the weight of the Japanese yen being higher in the import-weighted index than in the export-weighted index.

Table 4.2 *Indices of the nominal exchange rates of the renminbi*

| Year | Nominal exchange rate index | | |
| | Y/US$ | Y/basket of currencies | |
		Export-weighted	Import-weighted
1980	100	100	100
1981	187	179	181
1982	187	165	166
1983	187	154	163
1984	187	148	158
1985	195	154	164
1986	229	203	235
1987	249	230	280

Sources: The nominal exchange rates of the renminbi are annual averages, and the internal settlement rate is used in 1981–84. The values of exports and imports used in the currency basket come from *Chinese Customs Statistics*, and the exchange rates are taken from the IMF *International Financial Statistics*.

The export and import EER indices are given in Tables 4.3 to 4.4. The depreciation of the export real EER of renminbi was quite moderate during the period 1980–85 (from 100 points to 123 points or a depreciation of 19 per cent), but very rapid from 1985 to 1986. Rapid depreciation in this latter period is attributable to the rapid rise in COEFE and the sharp depreciation of the US dollar. The import real EER depreciated sharply between 1980 and 1981 due to the adoption of the internal settlement rate. It appreciated slightly in the period 1981–85 due to the appreciation of the US dollar, and it has depreciated sharply again since 1986 due to the depreciation of the US dollar. The depreciation of the real import EER was much more marked than the depreciation of the real export EER. This is partly because of the larger change in the nominal exchange rate (which is taken as proxy for the import EER) in comparison with change in the COEFE, and partly because the weight of trade with Japan was higher in imports than in exports, and the depreciation of the US dollar against the Japanese yen was particularly sharp.

The incentive to export as measured by the export real EER increased significantly from 1980 to 1986. We have no data on the COEFE beyond 1986, but we do know that in the 1988 trade reforms, foreign exchange retention ratios were raised significantly (up to 80 per cent in major export industries) and the restrictions on the swapping of foreign exchange were eased. Thus the incentive to export should have continued to rise from 1986 to 1988.

As mentioned before, the price of foreign exchange at the Beijing foreign exchange adjustment centre in May 1988 was quite close to black market rates. It is clear that there have been very significant depreciations in the import and export real EERs in the period 1980–88, and China came quite close to setting a realistic exchange rate in mid-1988 through the mechanism of foreign exchange adjustment centres. International studies indicate that setting a realistic exchange rate is a prerequisite of successful trade liberalization (Krueger 1978: ch. 10). The depreciation of China's export EER since 1980 is an important factor behind the rapid expansion of China's exports.

Import liberalization and bias reduction

Under exchange controls, imports are constrained by administrative means, and the nominal price of imports (price paid by users) is usually lower than their scarcity price, resulting in a premium for import licences. Devaluation is usually not large enough to absorb the entire premium (otherwise administrative controls of imports would be redundant). Devaluation would thus increase the nominal price,

Table 4.3 *China's export effective exchange rate (EER)*

Year	Nominal foreign exchange rate (Y/$US)	Cost of earning foreign exchange (Y/$US)	EER index in terms of:		Export-weighted CPI of six countries	China's GDP deflator index	China's real EER
			US$	Currency baskets			
1980	1.50	2.31	100.0	100.0	100.0	100.0	100.0
1981	2.80	2.48	107.4	101.5	108.2	101.8	110.2
1982	2.80	2.67	115.6	100.9	113.8	101.7	117.1
1983	2.80	3.07	132.9	108.4	118.1	102.8	131.2
1984	2.80	2.80	121.2	94.8	122.5	108.2	114.6
1985	2.94	3.24	140.3	109.0	105.7	110.1	123.0
1986	3.46	4.25	184.0	161.5	127.3	123.3	178.9
1987	3.70	—	—	—	129.7	132.5	—

Sources: The nominal exchange rate and the 'cost of earning foreign exchange' come from Tables 4.2 and 3.1 respectively; the consumer price indices of the six importing countries are taken from the IMF *International Financial Statistics*, the GDP deflator is obtained from the *Statistical Yearbook of China*, and the estimation of the various EER indices have been described in the text.

Table 4.4 *China's import effective exchange rate (EER)*

Year	EER index in terms of: US$	EER index in terms of: currency basket	Import-weighted CPI of six countries	China's GDP deflator	Import real EER index
1980	100	100	100.0	100.0	100.0
1981	187	181	108.2	101.8	192.5
1982	187	166	113.8	101.7	185.4
1983	187	163	118.1	102.8	187.7
1984	187	158	122.5	108.2	178.8
1985	196	164	125.7	119.1	173.5
1986	231	235	127.3	123.3	240.1
1987	247	280	129.7	132.5	274.9

Sources: China's GDP deflator is obtained from the *Statistical Yearbook of China*; the CPI of the six countries is obtained from the IMF *International Financial Statistics*; and the computation of the various EER indices have been described in the text.

but not the scarcity price, of imports, absorbing part of the premium, and so lead to a 'liberalization' of imports (Krueger 1978:87). The benefits of 'liberalization' or premium absorption include improved efficiency in the allocation of imports, decrease in rent-seeking activities and a more equitable income distribution as the windfall gains of importers are partly wiped out.

Devaluation under foreign exchange controls usually does not affect the scarcity price of imports. As the international prices of exports are given in the world market (except for the few commodities in which China has monopoly power), devaluation would raise the domestic price of exports. The price of import-competing goods relative to exports, or the bias of trade, would thus decrease. Resources would then flow from import-competing industries into export industries.

We do not have enough data to detail the change in liberalization and the bias of trade, but the crude data we do have indicate significant import liberalization and bias reduction. The depreciation of China's import EER since 1980 has been very marked, indicating a substantial rise in the nominal price of imports and import liberalization. The rise in the import EER should curb import demand implying that import controls and foreign exchange controls can be eased. We do observe a relaxation of foreign exchange controls with the institution of foreign exchange retention schemes and foreign exchange adjustment centres, and these developments are consistent with import liberalization.

As mentioned before, China's imports have grown very rapidly. The ratio of imports to GDP stayed close to 7 per cent from 1980 to 1983, but rose to 9 per cent in 1984 and jumped to 15 per cent in

1985 (Table 4.1). The ratio stayed at about 15 per cent in the period 1985–88. The jump in imports and the relaxation of foreign exchange controls point to a decrease in the scarcity price of imports. This, together with the large rise in the export EER, implies a significant reduction in the bias of trade. International empirical studies indicate that bias reduction is a key variable in stimulating exports (Krueger 1978:298).

Open-door policy and economic decentralization

In the Hua Guofeng era of 1976–78, China attempted to pursue an open-door policy without reforming its centralized command economy. As mentioned before, a program of massive plant imports was grafted onto the Stalinist strategy of extensive and unbalanced growth characterized by forced savings and neglect of efficiency. The rate of export growth was quite high, but the rate of import growth was even higher, resulting in an unsustainable trade deficit (Table 1.1). Moreover, the centralization of imports led to great inefficiency, as evidenced by the giant Bao Shan General Iron and Steel Works near Shanghai. Under the then highly centralized trading system, buyers and sellers could only conduct business through an intermediary. The lack of direct contact between producers and end-users was detrimental to export expansion as producers could not respond to the rapid changes in the international market. It impeded technology transfer and led to inefficiency in the use of imports because the end-user could not communicate directly with the foreign supplier.

Since 1979, China has attempted to pursue an open-door policy through the decentralization of the powers of trade and investment. Compared with Hua Guofeng's strategy, this represents a step in the right direction. However, decentralization of the external sector should not precede the economic reforms necessary to control and coordinate decentralized economic units. Such economic reforms include reforms to make enterprises sensitive to profit and loss, and also reforms in the system of economic coordination, replacing direct quantitative controls with indirect economic levers such as prices, taxes, and exchange rates. China has decentralized the power to trade without carrying through the necessary economic reforms, and this lack of coordination lies at the heart of China's trade problems. For example, China started to decentralize the power to trade in 1979, but foreign trade corporations were not required to be financially independent until 1988. The result was the rapid rise of the COEFE, because the system encouraged foreign trade corporations to procure goods at high prices for export to meet mandatory export targets. China has decentralized the power to trade, but the exchange rate is still overvalued despite repeated devaluations. The result is trade deficit as imports (exports) appear artificially cheap (expensive). Price reforms have not generally been carried out. The result is inefficient resource allocation; China may be exporting (importing) goods that appear to be cheap (expensive) to produce but which are really expensive (cheap).

Chinese enterprises, typical of enterprises in command economies, are not sensitive to profit and loss, and the effectiveness of economic controls is limited. Moreover, China's price structure is highly irrational, and control through the present price mechanism would be inefficient. Because exchange rate reforms, price reforms and enterprise reforms will take a long time to implement, import and export licences, quotas and foreign exchange controls will be useful interim administrative levers while China moves from a centralized to a decentralized system. In the long term, China should replace import–export licences and quotas with price instruments such as tariffs and subsidies. Instead of being carefully planned, such administrative controls on China's external sector have been haphazard, as will be detailed later.

Both politics and the technical difficulty of coordinating reform measures accounted for the failure of China to institute adequate economic and administrative controls in conjunction with the decentralization of economic power. Efficient economic controls imply price reforms which are technically complicated and politically unpopular. Given the arbitrary price system in China, price reforms would involve massive income redistribution and also kindle fears of open inflation.

The use of administrative controls would appear to be relatively simple in an economy such as China's. However, Chinese politics and administration have long been characterized by a highly personal style and *ad hoc* approach. The Chinese bureaucracy has been noted neither for its impartiality nor for its efficiency in administering sophisticated controls. The cost of administering controls is high because China is a vast and diversified country. Central planners appear to have been overconfident of their ability to restrain and check subordinate units through traditional *ad hoc* methods.

Unlike the institution of adequate economic and administrative controls, the decentralization of economic power to subordinate units is politically popular. In the case of the decentralization of the external sectors, provinces, ministries and selected enterprises are enabled to break the state's monopoly on foreign trade and investment. Regionalism has always been a problem due to China's size and geographical diversity. It should also be noted that China launched its open-door policy and reform drive immediately after the Cultural Revolution, at a time when the party and central government were politically weak and vulnerable to regional pressures. A Chinese trade official admitted:

> The management and regulating system of foreign trade are very much imperfect. We have inadequate experience and we have under-estimated the change in the external sector following the reforms . . . the lift of rigid control of foreign trade has only contributed to a situation in which each does things in its own way without coordinating with others. At one time, Hong Kong and Macau were flooded with smuggled goods. The cause of this is that effective control and adequate management measures have not been introduced following the relaxation of control (Li 1987:7).

Problems with China's foreign trade

The problems with China's foreign trade can be grouped under three headings: (i) macroeconomic imbalance, (ii) commodity overconcentration, and (iii) ineffectiveness and inefficiency of trade controls. As mentioned earlier, the third problem is fundamental, and it interacts with the first two.

(i) Macroeconomic imbalance

Macroeconomic imbalance has been a recurring problem and China has undergone three stop–go cycles since 1979. The inflationary bias of the Chinese economy since 1979 can again be attributed to the lack of coordination in reform measures. As mentioned before, while economic power has been decentralized, the interest rate has remained centrally fixed and has been kept at an artificially low level. This has led to runaway credit expansion and inflation. The rate of inflation was over 20 per cent in 1988, but deposit rates were a meagre 9 per cent, rising to only 12 per cent in early 1989. The 'soft budget constraint' of state enterprises also contributes to inflation. State enterprises are likely to over-invest as the state will bail them out of unprofitable investments.

The adverse impact of inflation on the trade balance can be softened to some extent with the adoption of floating exchange rates, but rampant inflation will inhibit trade liberalization. The exchange rate will depreciate rapidly under rampant inflation, and rapid depreciation will heighten inflationary expectations, which will lead to expectation of further depreciation and capital flight. These developments will generate a vicious cycle of inflation and depreciation

(World Bank 1985b:15). The government will be forced to adopt quantitative restrictions on imports to restore the balance of trade, thus reversing the trend towards liberalization. Good macroeconomic management is a prerequisite for the successful reform of the external sector.

(ii) Commodity overconcentration

The commodity composition of China's exports is shown in Table 4.5. China's trade data computed by the United States Central Intelligence Agency (CIA) is used instead of *Chinese Customs Statistics* because the latter source assigns all exports from processing/ assembling operations into Division 9 (not classified elsewhere) of the Standard International Trade Classification (SITC) without further breakdown into different commodities. The share of Division 9 in China's exports has risen from 4 per cent in 1981 to 19 per cent in 1987, reflecting the rapid growth of processing/assembling operations involving mainly Hong Kong investors. China's data on imports since 1984 are affected by the same problem. The CIA statistics estimate China's exports and imports by using the trade statistics of importing countries. This gives a better picture of the commodity composition of China's trade because the exports and imports of processing/assembling operations are classified into detailed commodity categories instead of lumped together in Division 9. In this study, CIA statistics will be used for all analyses involving the commodity composition of China's trade.

China's exports are heavily concentrated in textiles and oil: the 1985 shares of textiles (including textile fibre, fabric, and clothing) and fuels in China's exports were 30 per cent and 23 per cent respectively. Textiles and fuels thus accounted for over 53 per cent of China's exports in 1985.

In 1986, the share of fuels dropped sharply to 12 per cent due to falling oil prices, but the textile share rose to 35 per cent. The growth of textile exports is limited by the Multi-Fibre Arrangement (MFA), and oil exports are limited externally by world oversupply, and internally by supply constraints and rising domestic demand. It should be noted that in 1987, the share of oil dropped further to 9 per cent and the share of textiles declined marginally by 0.4 per cent. The World Bank has recommended diversification of exports into other manufactures, including machinery and metals (World Bank 1985a:146). China has a large and diversified manufacturing sector and the range of potential Chinese exports is wide. However, some economists have stressed that countries with a comparative advantage in labour-intensive products have been able to expand textile exports rapidly despite the MFA, although success in textiles would

Table 4.5 Commodity composition of China's exports (per cent)

Year	Food	Crude materials (2, 3, 4)			Manufactures (5, 6, 7, 8, 9)						Total
		Textile fibre	Fuels	Sub-total	Chemicals	Textile fabric	Machinery	Clothing	Others	Sub-total	
	(0, 1)[a]	(26)	(3)		(5)	(65)	(72)	(84)	(9)		(0–9)
1970	31.6	4.9	2.7	21.3	5.4	18.2	0.9	4.7	0.1	47.0	100.0
1975	29.7	3.3	14.3	26.6	4.8	14.5	1.1	5.1	0.3	43.6	100.0
1977	24.9	3.9	14.2	27.4	4.9	15.2	1.4	7.2	0.3	47.8	100.0
1979	20.1	3.7	17.9	30.1	5.7	16.6	1.4	7.7	0.3	49.9	100.0
1981	16.2	2.4	22.2	32.3	6.2	14.2	1.6	9.8	0.4	51.5	100.0
1982	15.1	2.5	22.8	30.9	5.7	12.5	1.4	10.5	5.9	54.0	100.0
1983	14.3	3.1	20.3	29.4	5.4	13.6	1.7	11.6	6.9	56.3	100.0
1984	13.0	3.7	20.8	30.5	5.0	14.4	2.0	12.1	6.3	56.5	100.0
1985	13.3	4.2	23.4	33.6	5.1	12.9	1.9	12.4	4.4	53.1	100.0
1986	14.6	3.6	12.0	21.3	5.4	14.6	2.9	16.6	5.3	64.1	100.0
1987	12.1	3.5	9.5	18.3	5.2	14.3	4.6	16.5	5.8	69.6	100.0

[a] Figures in brackets are SITC commodity divisions.

Sources: United States Central Intelligence Agency; National Foreign Assessment Centre; *China: International Trade*, various issues.

require quality-upgrading. Since China has only a small share of the world textile market and possesses considerable bargaining power in world trade, diversification away from textiles may be premature (Findlay & Xin 1985:12). The arguments about diversification are, in any case, something of a red herring. The key to good export performance, whatever the product mix, lies in successful microeconomic policy and the decentralization of China's trade regime. Only thus can an appropriate product mix emerge. The World Bank emphasized that, for successful machinery exports,

> an extensive and flexible network of subcontracting and other cooperative agreements between China and foreign enterprises would therefore be vital, but would be hard to establish through China's present airlock of administrative intermediation (World Bank 1985a:146).

Improving the quality of clothing and textiles to circumvent restrictions would need direct enterprise contacts with foreign buyers to alert producers to changing fashion. Without the flexibility provided by direct contact in a decentralized setting, successful exports of high fashion clothing is unlikely. Chinese exports are often competitive in price but deficient in style, design, quality, packaging, and punctuality.

(iii) Ineffectiveness and inefficiency of trade controls

This is a vast subject that deserves detailed study. China has not yet been able to devise satisfactory trade controls a decade after the inauguration of the open-door policy, and microeconomic problems are likely to plague China's trade for many years to come.

Trade decentralization under irrational prices, rigid exchange rates and inadequate controls give rise to gross inefficiencies. For example, Chinese enterprises competed among themselves to export pig iron despite the fall in the export price from US$180 per tonne in autumn 1981 to US$98 per tonne in autumn 1982; energy is the main input in the manufacture of pig iron and Chinese energy prices were artificially low because rent was not included in the cost of production (Du 1985:65). It is very difficult to determine rent without a market mechanism. Enterprises are in fact exporting cheap energy. Another obvious case of inefficiency is the over-expansion of native product exports in which China has a monopoly; prices have fallen so much that less foreign exchange has been earned for some exports. The prices of vegetables, meat and fish in Hong Kong fell by 30–50 per cent in early 1985 due to overexpansion of exports (*Economic Reporter* 22 Apr. 1985:8). Even for manufactures in which China is a small exporter, the earning of more foreign exchange through more exports may be deceiving: the domestic resource cost of some exports is so high that China's national income may in fact be lowered by more exports. Controls are also circumvented through rampant smuggling, illicit trade, and false invoicing, as will be detailed later. Although the reimposition of centralized administrative controls in late 1988 suppressed some of the symptoms of poor economic management, it can only be a stop-gap measure because recentralization increased effectiveness at the cost of efficiency. Cutting off direct contacts between producers and foreign buyers is detrimental to long-run export performance.

Ideally the result of careful planning, controls on China's foreign trade were implemented haphazardly in response to the confusion that emerged after the partial decentralization of China's foreign trade in 1979. Export licences were instituted in 1981, two years after the first steps toward decentralization were taken, and largely in response to the over-expansion of those native products in which China had a monopoly. From 1981 to 1985, the system of export licences was adjusted about twenty times (*Wen Hui Pao* 14 Nov. 1985) in response to particular circumstances. It was only in late 1985 that China held a national conference to discuss a comprehensive system of export licences. Even after the conference, action to establish a comprehensive system of export licences was slow. It was not until late 1988 that the MOFERT established a bureau to manage export–import licences. The number of its local offices was planned to increase from five to thirty to prevent over-issue of licences. Provincial governments tended to license more than their allocated quota of exports because they benefit from more exports under the foreign exchange retention scheme (*Ta Kung Pao* 12 Dec. 1988). The impact of these measures cannot yet be evaluated because these local offices are still to be fully established.

This *ad hoc* approach to export licences was evident in the notorious case of raw silk exports (*Wen Hui Pao* 15 Nov. 1985). Export licences for raw silk were first granted by provincial authorities. This, however, did not stop 'parallel trade', that is, trade outside regular channels, including smuggling and legal licences obtained through corruption and influence. When the granting of export licences was centralized through the MOFERT, it was discovered that the total exports licensed by provincial authorities amounted to four times the annual raw silk production of China. There are numerous reports of corruption in the granting of export/import licences, particularly to influential institutions such as the army (*The Nineties* Dec. 1985:63–4). Centralization of export licences under the MOFERT did not stop parallel trade. In the first half of 1988, parallel trade accounted for 48 per cent of China's silk exports. The price of raw silk through parallel trade was only US$43–48 per kilogram, whereas the price through regular channels was US$60–70 per kilogram. China thus lost US$20 million in foreign exchange as a result of parallel trade in raw silk over this period (*Ta Kung Pao* 5 Nov. 1988).

Perhaps the best known case of Chinese mismanagement of exports is the overshipment of textiles to the United States and the European Communities (EC). The overshipment was so serious that the United States had put an embargo on thirteen Chinese quota categories by June 1987 (*South China Morning Post* 22 June 1987). Many provincial authorities had granted licences in excess of their quotas, and the forging of false export licences by Hong Kong businessmen exacerbated the situation. In 1988, China established direct links with the computer network in major ports in the USA, in order that the validity of each textile export licence would be confirmed with China before admitting the goods. In 1988, instances of overshipment of textiles to the USA have decreased (*Hong Kong Economic Times* 3 Oct. 1988).

The frequent changes to the export licence system have been the object of bitter complaint among those who trade with China. For example, the MOFERT prohibited the export of selected non-ferrous metals starting in January 1989 due to domestic shortages, but then released in March 1989 a new list of commodities for which export licences were required, including the prohibited items. In mid-1988, a MOFERT official pledged to Hong Kong traders that export licences were only a temporary measure, and that their use would decrease in 1989. However, the number of commodities for which export licences were required increased from 130 in 1987 to 140 in 1988, and then to 159 in January 1989 and to 166 in March 1989. Traders sometimes get caught by the frequent changes, and goods already licensed under the old system have been held at ports because they have to be re-licensed under the new system (*Wen Hui Pao* 22 Mar. 1989).

On the import side, the lack of coordination and market information has led to excessive imports of assembly lines for popular consumer products, such as refrigerators, television sets and washing machines, resulting in chronic excess capacity. Hainan island alone imported more than twenty assembling lines for colour televisions in the period 1984–85, and the number of plants manufacturing refrigerators mushroomed to 116 by 1985. In mid-1985, the State Council ordered the closure of 76 refrigerator plants due to excess capacity (*The Nineties* Aug. 1985:61–2). Strong administrative controls were imposed on imports in mid-1985, but banned items, including luxury consumer goods, continued to make their way into the Chinese market through irregular channels (*Ming Pao* 6 July 1987).

Mistakes in planning also led to tremendous wastes. For example, China imported around 20,000 Japanese trucks in 1985, but the trucks could not be sold because of the sales drive of China's largest domestic truck producer to get rid of its old models. The Japanese trucks were allowed to rust for two years in the open air before state agencies mounted a sales drive to sell them in October 1987 (*Ta Kung Pao* 29 Nov. 1987).

The 1985 import surge and the Hainan scandal

The crudeness of China's trade controls is exemplified by the policies leading to the 1985 import surge and the Hainan scandal. The latter began in October 1983, when Hainan was allowed to use locally retained foreign exchange earnings to import 17 centrally controlled items. Beijing did not specify that these imports could not be resold to the mainland. There was also no stipulation that the 'locally retained foreign exchange earnings' had to originate on Hainan island itself. The looseness of Beijing's policy permitted Hainan to buy 'locally retained foreign exchange earnings' and import controlled goods for resale to the mainland. Before Beijing tightened the controls in March 1985, Hainan imported 79,000 automobiles and over 10,000 had been resold to the mainland.

Besides the Hainan scandal, the import surge of 1985 was abetted by the premature relaxation of foreign exchange controls. After the second readjustment at the end of 1980, China's trade balance had improved rapidly, and by the end of 1984, China had accumulated a foreign exchange reserve of US$16 billion, enough to pay its imports bill for eight to nine months. The reserves were regarded as too high, and in late 1984, Beijing relaxed its trade controls in the following ways (Qi 1985a:49–50).

- The list of centrally controlled imports was reduced from 17 to 11 items. The six deregulated items were popular products in high demand including calculators, video tapes, recorder components, bikes, radios and electric fans.
- Import controls were relaxed when the importing enterprise was able to raise its own foreign exchange. This led to widespread black market activity in foreign exchange, even involving provincial governments.
- The Bank of China was permitted to extend foreign exchange loans to domestic enterprises to import foreign equipment; the enterprises could repay the loan in renminbi. The policy was intended to encourage the use of foreign exchange, but it was annulled in April 1985 when China's foreign exchange reserves plummeted to a low level.

The relaxation of trade controls led to a surge of imports (imports grew by 28 per cent in 1984). Despite the imposition of Draconian measures in March 1985, imports grew by 54 per cent in 1985. The actual degree of decentralization went far beyond that intended by planners because provinces and enterprises exploited every opportunity to circumvent state controls. A popular form of such circumvention was the establishment of a trading firm through implicit cooperation with Hong Kong traders. Since the firm was nominally operated by a Hong Kong trader, approval from Beijing was not necessary. For local authorities and enterprises that could not operate in Hong Kong, establishing a trading firm in Shenzhen was a common substitute, as Shenzhen had easy access to Hong Kong intermediaries. Industrial cooperation agreements with foreign investors were also used as an informal channel. Foreign investors in China have rights to import new materials tariff-free and to export their products; such rights can easily be abused. Some industrial cooperation agreements turned out to be mere shelters for trading activities.

Regional approach to trade decentralization

China's regional approach to trade decentralization complicates the task of trade controls. While export-processing zones with relatively liberalized trade regimes are common in developing countries, the regional approach to trade decentralization in China has not only been applied to the five SEZs but also to provinces and cities that are not export-processing zones.

Because China is a vast country with substantial regional differentiation, there is an economic rationale for a regional approach to decentralization. Administratively the Chinese are not experienced in managing decentralization. It may therefore be wise to choose particular regions, such as Shenzhen and Xiamen, for decentralization experiments.

The regional approach can, however, create problems. In the event that the liberalized region enjoys special privileges in trade, e.g. tariff exemption or higher foreign-exchange retention ratios, the flow of goods between liberalized and non-liberalized regions must be regulated. Furthermore, the ensuing supervision costs can be extremely high if there are many liberalized regions. The presence of liberalized regions will make it easier to evade controls elsewhere in the country, with the result that such controls will become more complicated. The spreading of the developmental process from the cities to the hinterland will be hampered by regional barriers. The creation of liberalized regions also raises the question of regional inequality: the non-liberalized areas will press for similar special status.

Evasion of controls

The crux of the illegal trade problem is that local authorities and enterprises have vested interests in circumventing central controls. The enforcement of detailed administrative controls in a country as vast as China is a problem, and the cost of supervising administrative controls increases with the degree of decentralization.

Evasion of controls takes many forms, including bribery in licensing, fake invoicing and smuggling. Imports are over-invoiced and exports are under-invoiced for capital flight. Imports and exports may also be under-invoiced to evade tariffs and export taxes.

A great deal of evasion occurs through Hong Kong because of its proximity and its flexible and versatile market system. Parallel trade was particularly strong in the Hong Kong market in 1985. Hawkers selling herbal medicines congregated at the doorstep of the official distributor of Chinese medicine in Hong Kong because it was cheaper for the distributor to buy herbs from the hawkers than through official channels (*The Nineties* Feb. 1985:40).

False invoicing is reported to be serious among Hong Kong investors in China (*Ta Kung Pao* 7 Jan. 1989). In the case of imports, the connivance of an outside party is not even necessary in false invoicing. Enterprises and local authorities in China can covertly establish trading companies on paper in Hong Kong. The paper company can over-invoice by legally charging a commission over and above the import price. The foreign exchange thus earned by the paper company can be deposited overseas (Ma 1985:104). China gives high priority to imports of technology and equipment, and detection of over-invoicing in these imports is particularly difficult.

False invoicing and smuggling can sometimes be detected by using the statistics of trade partners. Table 4.6 compares China's exports to Hong Kong as recorded in Chinese and Hong Kong statistics from 1981 to 1989. Comparison of import statistics is not very useful because, in the Chinese statistics, part of Hong Kong's re-exports to China are classified as imports from Hong Kong instead of from the country of origin. For total Chinese exports to Hong Kong, the gap between Chinese and Hong Kong statistics widened appreciably in 1984 and 1985, probably indicating under-reporting in Chinese statistics. It should be noted that some smuggling presumably escaped both the Chinese and Hong Kong customs. Native products, for example, carried into Hong Kong in fishing junks are frequently not recorded. In Guangdong province alone, Chinese goods can be transported to Hong Kong from some 300 locations. In October 1988, a car racket that had smuggled at least several hundred cars into China was exposed. The racket involved the army, public security and postal departments (*South China Morning Post* 11 Oct. 1988).

Table 4.6 *China's exports to Hong Kong: comparisons of Chinese and Hong Kong statistics (US$m)*

		1981	1982	1983	1984	1985	1986	1987	1988	1989
Total exports	(i)	5,293	5,186	5,818	6,689	7,168	9,778	13,762	18,269	21,916
	(ii)	5,276	5,424	5,888	7,131	7,568	10,462	15,050	19,938	25,215
		(100.3)ᵃ	(95.6)	(98.8)	(93.8)	(94.7)	(93.5)	(91.4)	(91.6)	(86.9)
Major exports (2 digit SITC)										
00 Live animals for food	(i)	—	345	319	294	—	—	—	—	—
	(ii)	—	339	298	306					
			(101.7)	(107.0)	(95.9)					
33 Petroleum	(i)	—	404	386	269	—	—	—	—	—
	(ii)	—	397	369	300					
			(101.8)	(104.6)	(89.6)					
65 Textile yarn and fabrics	(i)	—	978	1,292	1,637	—	—	—	—	—
	(ii)	—	968	1,237	1,678					
			(101.0)	(104.4)	(97.6)					
34 Clothing	(i)	—	504	596	815	—	—	—	—	—
	(ii)	—	776	885	1,188					
			(64.9)	(67.4)	(68.6)					
89 Manufactures n.e.s.	(i)	—	452	461	606	—	—	—	—	—
	(ii)	—	259	278	415					
			(174.5)	(165.8)	(146.2)					

(i) Data from China Customs Statistics.
(ii) Data from Hong Kong Trade Statistics.
ᵃ Figures in brackets represent ratios of Chinese data to Hong Kong data (per cent).
Sources: Chinese Customs Statistics; Hong Kong Trade Statistics.

The 'trade partner statistics' technique is usually used for disaggre-gated commodity groups instead of total exports. Although China has reported its trade by two-digit SITC since 1982, trade involving processing/assembling operations is classified under Division 9 in China's customs statistics from 1985 onwards and such trade has formed a significant part (over 30 per cent) of China–Hong Kong trade since 1985. Comparisons of two-digit categories are thus not shown after 1984 in Table 4.6. The 1982–84 comparisons suggest that China's clothing exports to Hong Kong have been under-report-ed. The over-reporting of miscellaneous manufactures is due to classification rather than false invoicing: China groups all handicrafts (regardless of materials or manufacture) in SITC 89 because handi-crafts are a major export item.

Foreign loans and investment

Before 1980, China classified some forms of commercial credit, namely compensation trade, processing/assembling and leasing, as direct foreign investment. After 1985, commercial credits were sepa-rated from direct foreign investment. In this study, 'foreign invest-ment' refers to direct foreign investment and the three types of commercial credit listed above, and the total of direct and indirect foreign investment is referred to as 'foreign loans and investment'.

Chinese statistics on foreign loans show a dramatic decline from 1979 to 1983. This is because the statistics on foreign loans include the foreign currency loan from the Bank of China to pay for the equipment of the Bao Shan General Iron and Steel Works (*Maoyi Nianjian* 1982:2095). For the purposes of the present study, such loans are excluded from foreign loans because the Bank of China is not a foreign entity. Table 4.7 shows that, with the exclusion of the loans from the Bank of China, both contracted and utilized foreign loans have risen rapidly since 1979.

From 1979 to 1988, utilized foreign loans and investment have increased 8.7 times while utilized foreign investment has risen 10 times and utilized foreign loans 8.1 times. However, as China did not allow any foreign investment before 1979, and did not borrow foreign loans until 1977, the rates of foreign loans and investment are bound to be high.

As mentioned before, Hong Kong accounted for close to 60 per cent of the foreign investment in China in the period 1979–89, and there is no sign of a decrease in this share. In 1989, pledged invest-ment from Hong Kong was 7 times that of Japan and 6.6 times that of

Table 4.7 *China's utilization of foreign capital (US$m)*

	Contracted					Utilized				
	Loans[a]		Contracted foreign investment	Total		Loans[a]		Utilized foreign investment	Total	
	(i)	(ii)		(i)	(ii)	(i)	(ii)		(i)	(ii)
1979–81 (average)	—	—	—	—	—	797 (68.1)	3,030	374 (31.9)	1,171 (100.0)	3,404
1979–82 (average)	1,240 (47.3)	3,131	1,384 (52.7)	2,624 (100)	4,514	864 (66.2)	2,531	442 (33.8)	1,306 (100.0)	2,981
1982	—	—	—	—	—	923 (58.7)	1,783	649 (41.3)	1,572 (100.0)	2,432
1983	1,513 (44.1)		1,917 (55.9)	3,430 (100.0)		1,064 (53.7)		916 (46.3)	1,980 (100.0)	
1984	1,916 (40.0)		2,875 (60.0)	4,791 (100.0)		1,286 (47.5)		1,419 (52.5)	2,705 (100.0)	
1985	3,534 (35.8)		6,333 (64.2)	9,867 (100.0)		2,506 (56.2)		1,956 (43.8)	4,462 (100.0)	
1986	8,407 (71.6)		3,330 (28.4)	11,737 (100.0)		5,014 (69.1)		2,244 (30.9)	7,258 (100.0)	
1987	7,817 (64.4)		4,319 (35.6)	12,136 (100.0)		5,805 (68.7)		2,647 (31.3)	8,452 (100.0)	
1988	9,814 (61.2)		6,189 (38.7)	16,002 (100.0)		6,487 (63.4)		3,740 (36.6)	10,226 (100.0)	
1989	5,185 (45.2)		6,294 (54.8)	11,479 (100.0)		6,286 (62.5)		3,773 (37.5)	10,059 (100.0)	

[a] (i) and (ii) represent totals which respectively exclude and include foreign currency loans from the Bank of China that were extended to pay for the equipment for Bao Shan Steel Works before 1983.
[b] Bracketed figures represent the percentage share in total contracted or utilized capital (excluding the foreign currency loan from the Bank of China).
Source: Almanac of China's Foreign Relations and Trade, various issues.

the United States. In 1987, Japan's investment in China was only one-fifth of its investment in Hong Kong. China's leaders were disappointed with the low level of foreign investment, especially that of the Japanese.

The fast rates of growth of utilized investment conceal the many problems of China's investment environment. Figures on contracted investment are used as they are more sensitive to changes in this environment. Contracted foreign investment fell by 47 per cent in 1986 when the enthusiasm of foreign investors was chilled by the many problems of China's investment environment. Contracted foreign investment recovered somewhat between 1986 and 1988, but the 1988 figure was still appreciably lower than the peak in 1985. Despite the fall in contracted investment, utilized investment continued to rise in 1986 and 1987. This was partly due to investment from past commitments, and partly due to an improvement in the rate of utilization of contracted capital as a result of better investment control in China since 1986. The 1984–85 boom in contracted investment concealed investment projects of dubious quality, for example, industrial processing agreements are merely shelters for importing tariff-free raw materials. To make up for the fall in investment, there was a sharp rise in contracted bank loans between 1985 and 1986. However, from 1986 to 1987, contracted bank loans declined slightly due to concern about debt servicing. Foreign investment hit a record high in the first half of 1989, but the Tiananmen incident led to a dramatic slump in both foreign loans and investment in the second half of 1989. For the year as a whole, contracted loans fell severely and utilized loans fell slightly. Both contracted and utilized foreign investment stagnated.

Problems of foreign investment

China's problems in foreign investment are similar to but more complicated than those in foreign trade. China has decentralized the power to solicit foreign loans and investment without devising appropriate economic and administrative instruments of coordination. For instance, the overvaluation of the yuan means that the prices of China's resources are artificially high for the foreign investor. Low energy and raw material prices mean that investment in such sectors is unprofitable, though these sectors constitute the worst bottlenecks in China's economic growth. Investment is attracted instead to sectors where prices are artificially high, e.g. to the manufacture of consumer durables protected by high tariffs. The regional approach to liberalization implies that different regions vie with each other to grant more concessions to the foreign investor.

China's problems in foreign investment are more complicated than those in foreign trade because investment represents a lengthy commitment whereas trade is a 'one-shot' deal. Trading with China implies learning to live with lengthy negotiations and slow bureaucratic decision-making, at least until the deal is concluded. For the investor, concluding the deal merely represents the beginning of his nightmares. The investor has to learn to operate in a command economy where essential raw materials are rationed rather than sold in the market, and delays and defects in raw material supply are very common. The labour system in China also constrains the autonomy of the foreign investor in hiring and firing workers.

As the problems of investment are more complicated than those in trade, the demand for intermediation in investment should also be higher than that in trade, and this has already been confirmed by the data presented in Chapter 2.

Tables 4.8 and 4.9 show contracted and utilized foreign investment by different types of foreign venture. The fall in contracted investment in joint exploration reflected the evaporation of the initial high hopes of prospecting for off-shore oil in the South China Sea. The sharp rise in contracted investment in joint ventures and cooperative ventures from 1983 to 1985 reflected some success in attracting foreign investment, as these two types of foreign investment involve closer cooperation with foreign parties and have greater potential for technology transfer. The drastic slump of these two types of foreign investment in the period 1985–86 was a severe setback. It should be noted that contracted investment in compensation trade and processing/assembling continued to grow, reflecting the tendency of Hong Kong manufacturers to move labour-intensive operations over the border to avoid high labour costs in Hong Kong. Investments involving compensation trade and processing/assembling tend to be simple operations with short recoupment periods and they are more sensitive to conditions in the international market than to conditions in China's investment environment. The 1986 fall in direct foreign investment and rise of investment in compensation trade and processing/assembling indicates a shift from high-technology to low-technology investment.

The size distribution of foreign investment also suggests limited potential for the transfer of industrial technology which is stressed by planners. From 1979 until 1983, 46 per cent of the pledged investment in equity joint ventures, cooperative ventures and foreign-owned ventures came from investment with a value of less than US$1 million per project. Though investment of over US$9 million per project accounted for 41 per cent of the total pledged investment, 75 per cent of this was investment in hotels, real estate and services (Kueh 1986:30–1). In 1984, 58 per cent of the contracts involved investment of less than US$0.5 million (Xie 1987).

Table 4.8 Types of contracted foreign investment (US$m)

Year	Direct foreign investment					Commercial credit				Total
	Joint venture	Cooperative venture	Full foreign-owned firms	Joint exploration	Total	Compensation trade	Processing/assembly	Leasing	Total	
1979–82 (average)	32 (2.3)[a]	682 (49.3)	83 (6.0)	355 (25.7)	1,152 (83.2)	182 (13.2)	49[b] (3.5)		231 (16.7)	1,384 (100)
1983	188 (9.8)	503 (26.2)	40 (2.1)	1,000 (52.2)	1,731 (90.3)	102 (5.3)	83[b] (4.3)		185 (9.7)	1,917 (100)
1984	1,067 (37.1)	1,484 (51.6)	100 (3.5)	0 (0.0)	2,651 (92.2)	162 (5.6)	63[b] (2.2)	(2.2)	225 (7.8)	2,875 (100)
1985	2,030 (32.1)	3,496 (55.2)	46 (0.7)	360 (5.7)	5,932 (93.7)	260 (4.1)	98 (1.5)	44 (0.7)	402 (6.3)	6,333 (100)
1986	1,375 (41.3)	1,351 (40.6)	20 (0.6)	81 (2.4)	2,834 (85.1)	313 (9.4)	140 (4.2)	43 (1.3)	496 (14.9)	3,330 (100)
1987	1,950 (45.1)	1,283 (29.7)	471 (10.9)	4.7 (0.1)	3,709 (85.9)	428 (9.9)	165 (3.8)	18 (0.4)	610 (14.1)	4,319 (100)
1988	3,134 (50.6)	1,624 (26.2)	481 (7.8)	57 (0.9)	5,295 (85.6)	532 (8.6)	205 (3.3)	156 (2.5)	894 (14.4)	6,189 (100)
1989	2,659 (42.2)	1,083 (17.2)	1,654 (26.3)	204 (3.2)	5,600 (89.0)	475 (7.5)	148 (2.4)	72 (1.1)	694 (11.0)	6,294 (100)

[a] Bracketed figures represent the percentage share in total contracted foreign investment.
[b] Processing/assembly and leasing were not disaggregated before 1984.
Source: Almanac of China's Foreign Relations and Trade, various issues.

Table 4.9 Types of utilized foreign investment (US$m)

Year	Direct foreign investment					Commercial credit				Total
	Joint venture	Cooperative venture	Full foreign-owned firms	Joint exploration	Total	Compensation trade	Processing/ assembly	Leasing	Total	
1979–81 (average)	22 (5.9)[a]	118 (31.6)	0.33 (0.1)	106 (28.3)	246.33 (65.9)	94 (25.1)	34[b] (9.1)		128 (34.2)	374 (100)
1982	34 (5.2)	178 (27.4)	39 (6.0)	179 (27.6)	430 (66.3)	122 (18.8)	97[b] (14.9)		219 (33.7)	649 (100)
1983	74 (8.1)	227 (24.8)	43 (4.7)	292 (31.9)	636 (69.4)	197 (21.5)	83[b] (9.1)		280 (30.6)	916 (100)
1984	255 (18.0)	465 (32.8)	15 (1.1)	523 (36.9)	1,258 (88.7)	98 (6.9)	63[b] (4.4)		161 (11.3)	1,419 (100)
1985	580 (29.7)	585 (29.9)	13 (0.7)	481 (24.6)	1,659 (84.8)	169 (8.6)	98 (5.0)	31 (1.6)	298 (15.2)	1,956 (100)
1986	804 (35.8)	794 (23.4)	16 (0.9)	260 (6.9)	1,875 (87.4)	181 (8.4)	140 (3.4)	48 (0.8)	269 (12.6)	2,244 (100)
1987	1,486 (56.1)	620 (23.4)	25 (0.9)	183 (6.9)	2,314 (87.4)	222 (8.4)	91 (3.4)	20 (0.8)	333 (12.6)	2,467 (100)
1988	1,975 (52.8)	779 (20.8)	226 (6.0)	213 (5.7)	3,194 (85.4)	317 (8.5)	69 (1.8)	161 (4.3)	546 (14.6)	3,740 (100)
1989	2,037 (54.0)	752 (19.9)	371 (9.8)	232 (6.1)	3,393 (89.9)	261 (6.9)	56 (1.5)	64 (1.7)	381 (10.1)	3,773 (100)

[a] Bracketed figures represent the percentage share in total utilized foreign investment.
[b] Processing/assembly and leasing were not disaggregated before 1984.
Source: Almanac of China's Foreign Relations and Trade, various issues.

Red tape, stringent foreign exchange controls, inadequate infrastructure and arbitrary charges and fees imposed by local governments have been the chief complaints of investors. On three occasions in 1982 and 1983, Beijing ordered local authorities to stop levying arbitrary charges on foreign investors, but to little avail. The 22-point investment enticement package of October 1986 again banned arbitrary charges. The package specified that for joint ventures that either export at least 70 per cent of output or transfer advanced technology, the fee for land use should be decreased from US$5–$30 per square metre to US$5–$20 per square metre. However local authorities vie with each other to decrease fees for land use; the fees were decreased to US$1–$15 in Quanzhou and to US$0.50–$1.00 in Zhuhai. In fact, Zhangzhou annulled land charges altogether for five years (Qi 1986:33). The rush to decrease land prices can hardly instil confidence in the Chinese investment environment. It emphasizes the fact that Chinese society has been run by administrative decrees rather than law and due process for nearly four decades; in investment as well as in trade, the administrative controls devised by Beijing are crude and inefficient.

The 22-point investment enticement package of October 1986 addressed the problem of red tape. The package stipulated that relevant officials must process investment applications (a process which has been known to take a year or more) within three months. The package also marginally relaxed stringent foreign exchange controls such that foreign enterprises were allowed to swap yuan for foreign currency among themselves in the foreign exchange adjustment centres. As mentioned before, the restrictions on foreign exchange swapping was further relaxed in 1988, and foreign enterprises can now trade foreign exchange with domestic enterprises.

Although the 22-point package specified that foreign enterprises have the power to hire and fire employees, foreign investors often have to hire workers through local labour bureaus. Working for foreign enterprises is lucrative; workers often have to bribe local officials before they can be recommended for recruitment. Local officials therefore frown upon dismissal of workers in foreign enterprises. Moreover, because the local labour bureau is responsible for finding new jobs for dismissed workers, local officials would do their best to prevent such dismissals (Qi 1986:35).

It must not be assumed that more foreign investment necessarily benefits China. Given China's arbitrary policies and the import-substitution policy in particular, more foreign investment can make China worse off. This is known in the economic literature as 'immiserizing foreign investment'. The paradox happens because an import-substitution policy distorts resource allocation and makes import-competing industries artificially profitable. Foreign investment will be attracted to such industries, exacerbating the distortion in resource allocation. The recipient of foreign investment then ends up worse off (Bhagwati 1983:296). One way to avoid immiserizing foreign investment is to insist that foreign investors should export instead of catering to the highly protected domestic market. This is in fact the Chinese policy, but it is not welcomed by foreign investors who are attracted to China by the vast domestic market. In establishing export operations, the Chinese investment environment is less attractive than the export-processing zones in many developing countries. Foreign investors seem to have numerous ways of circumventing the Chinese insistence on exporting. The contract of a camera assembling operation, for example, specified that 30 per cent of the products had to be exported, and the remainder could be sold in China. However, the exported cameras were taken apart in Hong Kong and shipped back to China as components. Another case is the manufacture of lounge suits which were exported to Hong Kong and sold by hawkers at US$3 per suit; the price did not cover the cost of materials (Yuan 1985b:56). The profit of the operation came mainly from internal sales from the illegal sale of raw materials (which were exempt from tariffs as they were supposedly imported for use by the foreign enterprise). A lot of compensation trade agreements have turned out to be merely shelters for importing tariff-free raw materials. The foreign partner can avoid investing any money because the Chinese partner can over-invoice the value of the imported equipment by around 20–30 per cent, and the foreign partner then supposedly contributes capital up to the over-invoiced portion of the agreement (Yuan 1985b:56). The authority to approve foreign investment has often been decentralized to provincial and local authorities, and local officials are ready targets for bribery.

Shenzhen before 1985 is perhaps the best known case of investment mismanagement. Shenzhen was planned as an export-oriented economy and was heralded as a model in the open-door drive of 1984. However, it was revealed in the 1985 recentralization that Shenzhen managed to export only one-third of its products and the rest were sold in China. During the period 1980–84, utilized foreign investment in Shenzhen totalled 1.6 billion yuan. Infrastructural costs, however, totalled 3.5 billion yuan, most of which was funded from the state budget or from state bank loans (Qi 1985b:53). Moreover, in the period 1984–85, Shenzhen had become a focus of black market foreign exchange dealings and illegal trade. Deng Xiaoping revised his earlier positive appraisal of Shenzhen in July 1985, saying

The Shenzhen Special Economic Zone is an experiment. Whether or not the course is right remains to be proved. No matter what, it is a new phenomenon of socialism. We hope it will succeed. But if it fails, we can draw lessons from it.

For a while, the future of Shenzhen was clouded by investigation of economic crimes and the 1985 recentralization. However, the Shenzhen experiment was politically too important to be thrown away; it remains an important lure to entice Hong Kong and Taiwan to rejoin mainland China. Beijing continued to support Shenzhen and the huge infrastructural investment gradually bore fruit. By 1988, utilized foreign investment totalled US$2 billion and Shenzhen's exports increased rapidly, surpassing those of Beijing in 1987.

Table 4.10 shows the distribution of contracted foreign investment by industry. The industrial classification since 1985 is not identical to that of 1983 and 1984, but rough comparisons can be made. The earlier classification distinguishes between energy (mainly coal and oil) and manufacturing whereas the 1985–87 classification combines them under 'industry'. Investment in energy has dwindled since 1984 as hopes for large strikes of off-shore oil have evaporated. The bulk of investment in 'industry' since 1985 is thus largely investment in manufacturing industry, and the share of investment in this sector has been rising. There appears to be substantial overlapping between the item 'tourism' (1983–84) and 'real estate and public utilities' (1985) because the building of hotels has been a major item of foreign investment.

Table 4.10 *Distribution of contracted foreign investment by industry, 1983–85* (per cent)

	1983	1984	1985	1986	1987	1988	1989
Agriculture	0.9	2.7	2.0	3.1	4.0	4.1	2.1
Industry	66.9	21.9	43.3	37.1	52.3	77.6	84.5
manufacturing	13.6	21.4	—	—	—	—	—
energy	53.3	0.5	—	—	—	—	—
Communications and posts	3.1	2.9	1.7	1.0	0.4	1.5	0.8
Tourism[a]	5.0	32.7	—	—	—	—	—
Real estate & public utilities[a]	—	—	35.9	48.6	34.1	8.6	8.3
Building & building materials	3.0	2.7	2.1	1.6	1.3	1.9	1.1
Others[b]	21.1	37.0	15.0	8.6	7.9	6.3	3.2
Total	100.0	100.0	100.0	100.0	100.0	100.0	100.0

[a] The classification from 1985 onwards does not list the share of tourism. However, the bulk of investment in tourism involves the construction of hotels, which is included in 'Real estate & public utilities'.
[b] Others include commerce, catering, finance and services.
Source: *Almanac of China's Foreign Economic Relations and Trade*, various years.

China desires investment in manufacturing geared for the export industry rather than services, partly because services are more oriented towards the domestic market than the international market, and partly because China values hard technology more than soft technology. The increase in the share of investment in manufacturing industry is in line with official policy.

Though China has not been able to go beyond its Hong Kong connection in attracting foreign investment, China's investment environment has improved in recent years. Pledged investment has recovered gradually from the 1986 slump, and there has been a shift from cooperative venture to joint ventures, which have a higher potential for technology transfer. The dramatic increase in fully foreign-owned firms in 1987 also indicates an improvement in the investment environment.

Problems of loans

China's problems in foreign loans are similar to those in foreign investment and foreign trade. China has decentralized the power to borrow without devising appropriate economic and administrative instruments of coordination. Table 4.11 shows the breakdown of China's loans. In 1986, as contracted foreign investment halved, contracted bank loans more than doubled and commercial loans nearly quadrupled. Most of the increase in bank loans was due to an increase in commercial loans.

The rapid jump in commercial loans in 1986 was related to the decentralization of China's financial system in the same year. By the end of 1986, over 1700 agencies in China were able to borrow from external sources (*Economist* 19 Mar. 1988). China did not have comprehensive statistics on the loans of subordinate units and the Chinese estimates of foreign debt reported to the IMF were several billion dollars lower than estimates drawn from overseas. China's debt management was extremely crude and China lacked adequate systematic projections of external loans (He 1988:99–100).

The debt service ratio of China in 1987 was only 7 per cent, which compares very favourably with the average ratio of 22 per cent in developing countries in 1986. However, China has so far only been paying interest on its loans. The repayment of principal will be bunched together in 1991–93 due to poor debt management. Moreover, yen debt accounted for 46 per cent of China's foreign loans at the end of 1986, and China is paying heavily for the appreciation of the yen (*South China Morning Post* 16 Mar. 1988).

Enterprises and local governments tend to overborrow, as they are only subject to a soft budget constraint and the central government has to shoulder the financial responsibility if the investment projects

Table 4.11 Types of external loans ($USm)

	Contracted					Utilized				
	Commercial loans	Soft loans	Bank of China loans	Total[a] (i)	(ii)	Commercial loans	Soft loans	Bank of China loans	Total (i)	(ii)
1979–81 (average)	—	—	—			178 (22.3)[b]	619 (77.7)	2,233	797 (100)	3,030
1979–82 (average)	252 (20.3)	989 (79.8)	1,891	1,240	3,131	203 (23.5)	661 (76.5)	1,890	864 (100)	2,539
1982	—	—	—			366 (39.7)	556 (60.2)	860	923 (100)	1,783
1983	173 (11.4)	1,340 (88.6)		1,513 (100)		275 (25.8)	789 (74.2)		1,064 (100)	
1984	442 (23.1)	1,474 (76.9)		1,916 (100)		380 (29.5)	906 (70.5)		1,286 (100)	
1985	1,382 (39.1)	2,152 (60.9)		3,534 (100)		1,415 (56.5)	1,091 (43.5)		2,506 (100)	
1986	5,138 (61.1)	3,269 (38.9)		8,407 (100)		2,831 (56.5)	2,183 (43.5)		5,014 (100)	
1987	4,400 (52.3)	3,417 (43.7)		7,817 (100)		4,292 (73.9)	1,513 (26.1)		5,805 (100)	
1988	4,739 (48.3)	5,074 (51.7)		9,814 (100)		4,185 (64.5)	2,302 (35.5)		6,487 (100)	
1989	2,858 (55.1)	2,327 (44.9)		5,185 (100)		3,052 (48.6)	3,233 (51.4)		6,286 (100)	

[a] (i) and (ii) are totals which respectively exclude and include the foreign currency loans from the Bank of China that were extended to pay for the equipment for Bao Shan Steel Works before 1983.

[b] Bracketed figures represent the percentage share in total contracted or utilized foreign loans (excluding the foreign currency loan from the Bank of China).

Source: Almanac of China's Foreign Relations and Trade, various issues.

of subordinate units go sour. As a result, loans may not be efficiently used and some local enterprises have not been able to repay their external loans on schedule (*Hong Kong Economic Times* 5 Dec. 1988). The debt service ratio of Fujien province (calculated on the foreign exchange retention of the province) had already reached 39 per cent in 1987 (He 1988:102).

To strengthen control over its foreign loans, China severely recentralized the power to borrow external loans in February 1989. Only ten organizations are now permitted to borrow foreign commercial loans. They include three banks (Bank of China, Communications Bank and China Investment Bank), the CITIC and six provincial/municipal international trust and investment corporations (Quangdong, Fujian, Hainan, Shanghai, Tianjin, and Dalian). All other agencies have to apply for foreign commercial loans through the People's Bank of China, and all foreign loans have to be registered with the SAFEC (*South China Morning Post* 27 Feb. 1989). The centralization is likely to have adverse impacts on Hong Kong, as Hong Kong is an important centre for syndication of commercial loans to China.

Problems of and prospects for the open-door policy

Despite the many problems of China's open-door policy, China is close to having effective controls on trade, foreign investment, and foreign loans in 1989. In late 1988, the MOFERT established a bureau to manage export/import licences and a computer network linking the major ports of China was being considered (*Ta Kung Pao* 12 Dec. 1988). In February 1989, the power to borrow foreign loans was recentralized and China was reported in March 1989 to be setting up a Debt Management Office under the Ministry of Finance to centralize debt management (*South China Morning Post* 16 Mar. 1988). As mentioned earlier, China's investment environment has improved since 1987. Moreover, China has already achieved considerable success in its reform of commodity trade. The incentive to export has increased considerably with the rise of the export EER, import liberalization has occurred with the rise in import EER, and the bias of trade has been reduced. The ratio of exports to GDP is high and increasing.

Effective controls, however, do not imply efficient controls. Recentralization achieves effectiveness at the expense of efficiency. Instituting efficient controls on foreign transactions will take a very long time. To achieve efficiency, China has to accomplish three difficult tasks, namely, exchange rate reform, price reform, and enterprise reform. Of these, exchange rate reform will probably be easiest. In 1988, total retained foreign exchange in China was close to US$19 billion, or nearly 40 per cent of the value of China's exports, and the amount of foreign exchange traded in the adjustment centres totalled US$6.3 billion. A 100 per cent retention ratio with freedom of transfer would be equivalent to a system of a floating exchange rate for commodity trade. Though retained foreign exchange was 40 per cent of China's exports in 1988, China's exchange rate reform can be said to be more than 40 per cent complete. The retention ratios for above-target foreign exchange earnings were generally raised to 80 per cent in 1988 (which means that the marginal foreign exchange retention ratio is 80 per cent). In economic decision-making, it is the marginal rather than the average ratio which is relevant. China's foreign exchange reform can be said to be 80 per cent complete as far as commodity trade is concerned. However, it is difficult for China to complete its exchange rate reform under severe inflationary pressures. As mentioned before, deregulating the exchange rate in an inflationary environment may lead to a vicious cycle of inflation and depreciation.

Price reform and enterprise reform are much more difficult than exchange rate reform for the simple reason that they involve the whole economy and not just external transactions. While China has had little success with price reform, it has achieved partial success in enterprise reform with the contract responsibility system. Foreign trade enterprise also implemented the contract responsibility system in 1988 and exporting below cost has largely disappeared because the foreign trade corporations have become financially independent and have to bear their own losses (*Wen Hui Pao* 11 May 1988). However, the contract responsibility system is only a half-way house to fully autonomous enterprises because the latter have to renegotiate the relevant targets with the supervising agency every time the contract expires, and this gives the supervising agency an opportunity to meddle with the enterprise. Moreover, the problem of soft budget constraint is deeply ingrained in socialist economies and the hardening of budget constraints has to wait for long-term reform in property rights.

The recent inflationary pressures have hampered both exchange rate reforms and price reforms. There is no quick way to end inflation owing to the severity of the macroeconomic imbalance in the period 1988–89. Reforms of the external sector are thus likely to be held up for at least a couple of years. Though further reform of China's external sector is likely to be a long and arduous task, Hong Kong can be of considerable help. Given the efficiency and versatility of the Hong Kong economy, the effects of Chinese policies on trade and investment will be manifested quickly. For instance, the lack of adequate controls on China's exports of native products had a direct impact on the Hong Kong market in 1985 when prices there dropped by 30–50 per cent. Chinese planners can avail themselves of this rapid feedback mechanism of the Hong Kong economy to gauge the effectiveness and efficiency of their policies.

5

Hong Kong as financier

The role of Hong Kong as financier is briefly surveyed in Chapter 2 with particular reference to foreign investment and loans. This chapter analyses this aspect in greater detail and also examines Hong Kong's contribution to the development of financial expertise and financial markets in China. In addition, this chapter studies the link between Hong Kong investment and the development of export industries in China, particularly in the Pearl River delta in Guangdong.

Foreign loans

According to Chinese statistics (presented in Chapter 2), Hong Kong is the predominant source of foreign investment in China, but Hong Kong's share in total contracted loans was only 5 per cent in 1987 (Table 2.2). China's statistics, however, grossly understate the contribution of Hong Kong for two reasons. First, as is mentioned in Chapter 2, Hong Kong is the major centre of loan syndication to China. It is very difficult to trace the source of funds for such loans and the funds may not come entirely from Hong Kong banks. Second, Hong Kong banks also lend to foreign enterprises in China, and such loans are not recorded in China's statistics unless the Chinese government is involved in the borrowing. Statistics on syndicated loans in Hong Kong and Hong Kong loans to customers in China can be obtained from Hong Kong statistics.

Table 5.1 shows the liabilities and claims between the Hong Kong banking system and China. Liabilities to China's banks, claims on China's banks, and especially claims on non-bank customers have all grown rapidly. The growth reflects the increasingly important role of Hong Kong as a financier. Hong Kong banks had net claims on China

94

from the beginning of 1979 to the end of 1981, and the net claims arose mainly from the claims on China's banks. This was the period marking the beginning of the open-door policy and the first readjustment (which failed to rectify the internal and external imbalances following Hua Guofeng's over-ambitious plan of modernization). China borrowed heavily, especially from the Bank of China, to finance its imports. The net claims of Hong Kong banks on China's banks reflected the active role of Hong Kong in financing China's external deficit. The claims of Hong Kong banks on non-bank customers in China were quite small until 1985.

From the beginning of 1982 to mid-1985, Hong Kong banks had net liabilities to China. This was the period when China accumulated sizable foreign exchange reserves after the second readjustment. This was also the period of political uncertainty over the future of Hong Kong, leading to economic and monetary crises. The Hong Kong branch of the Bank of China joined with the Hong Kong and Shanghai Bank in mid-1985 to lend to a failing Hong Kong bank. The substantial Chinese loans to Hong Kong banks undoubtedly stabilized the Hong Kong monetary system during this critical period (Jao 1988:43).

From mid-1985 onwards, the loans of Hong Kong banks to non-bank customers increased rapidly, and the net claims on China's banks were quite small. This was a period of trade deficit and foreign exchange difficulty in China, whereas the economy of Hong Kong was booming after the signing of the Sino-British agreement in September 1984.

The claims of Hong Kong banks on non-bank customers understate the amount of Hong Kong bank loans to China, as part of the loans had been repaid. However, the increase in claims of Hong Kong banks to non-bank customers in 1988 was US$2379 million. This is a lower limit for loans extended by Hong Kong banks to customers in China in 1988, and it amounted to 60 per cent of total foreign commercial loans borrowed by China in 1988. Claims of Hong Kong banks on non-bank customers in China declined in the last quarter of 1989 as a result of the Tiananmen incident.

Table 5.2 summarizes Hong Kong's contribution to foreign loans borrowed by China in terms of (i) direct lending according to Chinese statistics, (ii) loan syndication and (iii) increase in claims of Hong Kong banks on non-bank customers in China. The total of the first two items is also shown in Table 5.2, but the third item is kept separate as it partly overlaps with the first two items. The third item represents a combination of direct lending recorded in Chinese statistics and of funds for syndicated loans originating in Hong Kong.

Hong Kong's loans to China are expressed as percentages of China's total foreign loans borrowed and total commercial loans

Table 5.1 *The liabilities to China and claims on China of Hong Kong banks*
(US$m)

Year	Quarter	Liabilities to China's banks	Claims on China's banks	Claims on non-bank customers	Net liabilities (−) or claims (+)
1979	I	84	1,048	0.40	+964
	IV	43	1,177	22	+1,156
1980	IV	191	1,389	98	+1,297
1981	IV	950	1,166	130	+346
1982	I	1,250	1,047	81	−122
	IV	1,779	836	105	−838
1983	IV	2,374	1,089	110	−1,175
1984	IV	2,962	1,366	233	−1,363
1985	I	3,047	1,999	248	−801
	II	2,628	1,976	329	−323
	III	2,737	3,137	449	+848
	IV	2,821	3,116	803	+1,098
1986	I	2,766	3,212	1,218	+1,664
	II	3,007	3,469	1,416	+1,878
	III	3,123	3,923	1,260	+2,060
	IV	3,482	3,926	2,083	+2,527
1987	I	4,312	4,392	1,474	+1,554
	II	5,018	4,934	1,936	+1,852
	III	5,856	5,401	2,171	+1,716
	IV	5,978	5,428	2,673	+2,123
1988	I	5,279	5,984	2,866	+3,571
	II	6,271	6,489	3,555	+3,773
	III	7,130	7,013	4,422	+4,305
	IV	7,574	7,760	5,052	+5,238
1989	I	7,366	7,826	5,432	+5,892
	II	6,364	5,491	5,979	+5,105
	III	7,874	4,431	6,313	+2,870
	IV	10,144	5,481	6,231	+1,568

Source: *Hong Kong Monthly Digest of Statistics*, various issues.

borrowed. From 1979 to 1983, Hong Kong's shares in China's total foreign loan were only about one to two per cent. However, Hong Kong's shares in commercial loans were a few times higher. This is because soft loans, including loans from governments and international agencies, represented a major part of China's foreign loans until 1985 (Table 4.11), and Hong Kong's loans to China were exclusively commercial loans.

Beginning in 1984, Hong Kong contributed a substantial share of foreign loans, especially commercial loans. The combined shares of direct loans and syndicated loans from Hong Kong ranged from one-

Table 5.2 *Hong Kong's contribution to foreign loans borrowed by China* (US$m)

Year		Hong Kong as:			Increase in claims of Hong Kong banks on non-bank customers in China
		lender	centre of syndication	total	
1979–82 (average)		19	75	94	26
	(i)	(1.5)	(6.0)	(7.6)	(2.1)
	(ii)	(7.5)	(30.0)	(37.3)	(10.3)
1983		9	104	113	5
	(i)	(0.6)	(6.9)	(7.5)	(0.33)
	(ii)	(5.2)	(60.1)	(65.3)	(2.9)
1984		51	250	301	123
	(i)	(2.7)	(13.0)	(15.7)	(6.4)
	(ii)	(11.5)	(56.6)	(68.1)	(27.8)
1985		73	513	586	570
	(i)	(2.1)	(14.5)	(16.6)	(16.1)
	(ii)	(5.3)	(37.1)	(42.4)	(41.2)
1986		244	1,538	1,782	1,280
	(i)	(2.9)	(18.3)	(21.2)	(15.2)
	(ii)	(4.7)	(29.9)	(34.7)	(24.9)
1987		401	2,400	2,801	590
	(i)	(5.1)	(30.7)	(35.8)	(7.5)
	(ii)	(9.1)	(54.5)	(63.7)	(13.4)
1988		580	1,945	2,525	2,186
	(i)	(5.9)	(19.8)	(25.7)	(22.3)
	(ii)	(12.2)	(41.0)	(53.3)	(46.1)
1989		488	718	1,206	1,179
	(i)	(9.4)	(13.8)	(23.2)	(22.7)
	(ii)	(17.1)	(25.1)	(42.2)	(41.3)

(i)   As percentage of total foreign loans borrowed by China.
(ii) As percentage of total commercial loans borrowed by China.
Sources: Tables 2.2, 4.11 and 5.1.

third to two-thirds of China's commercial loans in the period 1984–87. Hong Kong is thus not only the foremost source of foreign investment, but is also one of the biggest sources of commercial loans since 1984.

It should be noted that, besides foreign loans, China has utilized substantial foreign currency loans from the Bank of China, amounting to US$7560 million contracted during the period of 1979–81. The Bank of China has a huge deposit base in Hong Kong, large enough to finance a loan several times this size. However, the Bank of China also has substantial operations outside Hong Kong. Jao (1983:72) estimated that 50 per cent of the profits of the Bank of China originated from its Hong Kong operations. If it is assumed that half of the loans of the Bank originated from Hong Kong, then the estimate of indirect loans from Hong Kong to China would be US$3780 million, or a share of 27 per cent of total external loans (foreign loans plus the foreign currency loans from the Bank of China) during 1979–83. As mentioned before, Hong Kong banks had net claims on China's banks of over US$1 billion from 1979 to 1980 (Table 5.1), and part of these net claims might have been the source of the foreign currency loan from the Bank of China. If one takes into account the foreign currency loan from the Bank of China, Hong Kong was a major source of loans even in the 1979–83 period.

Besides bank loans, China has also issued bonds and commercial papers in Hong Kong. The China International Trust and Investment Corporation (CITIC) raised HK$300 million (US$38.5 million) through bond issues in Hong Kong in 1985, and Guangdong Enterprises, the trading arm of Guangdong province, issued commercial paper worth HK$250 million (US$32 million). Since 1985, China-owned banks have issued certificates of deposit worth HK$6800 million (US$872 million). However, China has made greater use of the bond markets in Japan, Singapore and Frankfurt than in Hong Kong because the Hong Kong bond market, particularly the secondary market, is less active (*South China Morning Post* 18 June 1987).

Financial expertise and development of financial markets

In Hong Kong, the Bank of China and its thirteen 'sister banks' have expanded rapidly since 1979 and accounted for one-quarter of the total deposits in Hong Kong in the mid-1980s. Moreover, they have diversified into merchant banking. The Hong Kong Bank of Communications, one of the thirteen sister banks of the Bank of China, was the first foreign bank to offer comprehensive banking services in China. The competition of foreign banks has had a considerable impact on banking reforms in China.

In 1988, China was seriously considering launching experimental futures markets in China to meet the hedging and price discovery needs of agricultural commodities traded within China. The Hong Kong Futures Exchange and authorities in China were reported to be considering launching futures contracts in Hong Kong for major Chinese export commodities. This would reduce price risks for traders and help China to plan the supply and demand of its exports (*South China Morning Post* 1 Aug. 1988). However, the plans for futures markets in China and Hong Kong were shelved with the recentralization in late 1988.

In 1987, China-backed companies, including Tian An China Investment Co., Guangdong Enterprises and Yue Xiu Enterprises began to raise funds on Hong Kong's stock market through share placements or listings (*South China Morning Post* 18 June 1987). Market capitalization of the Hong Kong stock market was HK$55 billion in mid-1987, or only 1.5 per cent of the world total, but Hong Kong is capable of raising large amounts of capital: in the first five months of 1987, HK$16.3 billion had been raised. The ability to issue securities would enable entrepreneurs to roll over their profits and reinvest in new business. However, a listing on the Hong Kong stock market requires a five-year earnings track record. Joint ventures in China do not usually show early profits, though their long-term prospect may be promising (*South China Morning Post* 17 June 1987). The needs of such ventures may be better met in the proposed secondary market, which has been favourably considered since the mid-1980s. However, the international stock market crash of November 1987 exposed the many weaknesses of the Hong Kong stock market, and the introduction of the secondary market was shelved.

Chinese enterprises have found it difficult to meet the accounting and disclosure rules required by the Hong Kong stock exchange. However, China has conducted studies on the possibility of allowing Chinese enterprises to go public in Hong Kong (*South China Morning Post* 18 June 1987). This development was held up by the 1987 stock market crash and China's recentralization in late 1988.

Hong Kong is potentially very useful to China in developing its financial markets and institutions, though this potential can only be realized after the rectification of the present macroeconomic imbalance in China.

Foreign investment

Hong Kong's predominant share of contracted foreign investment in China is discussed in Chapter 2. In Table 5.3, the contribution of Hong Kong to contracted and utilized investment in China is compared with that of the USA and Japan, which are respectively the second and third largest investors in China. From 1979 to 1989, contracted foreign investment in China totalled US$38 billion. Hong Kong contributed close to US$22 billion or 59 per cent of the total. The USA was a poor second with US$4.1 billion or 11 per cent of the total, and Japan ranked third with US$2.5 billion or 7 per cent of the total.

Throughout the period 1985–87, the utilized investment from Hong Kong exhibited healthy growth whereas utilized investment

Table 5.3 *Contribution of Hong Kong, USA and Japan to contracted and utilized foreign investment in China* (US$m)

Year	Contracted investment from			Utilized investment from		
	Hong Kong	USA	Japan	Hong Kong	USA	Japan
1979–82 (average)	919 (66)[a]	96	215	—	—	—
1983	642 (34)	478	95	—	—	—
1984	2,175 (76)	165	203	748 (53)	256	225
1985	4,134 (65)	1,152	471	956 (49)	357	315
1986	1,773 (53)	541 (16)	283 (8.5)	1,329 (59)	326	263
1987	2,331 (54)	361	386	1,796 (68)	271	267
1988	4,033 (65)	382 (6.2)	370 (6.0)	2,395 (64)	244 (6.5)	598 (16)
1989	3,645 (58)	646 (10)	515 (8.2)	2,295 (61)	288 (7.6)	408 (10.8)
1979–1989	22,409 (59)	4,109 (11)	2,538 (6.6)	—	—	—

[a] Figures in brackets represent percentage share of total contracted or utilized foreign investment.
Source: Almanac of China's Foreign Relations and Trade, various issues.

from the USA and Japan declined. Hong Kong's share in utilized investment thus rose from 49 per cent in 1985 to 68 per cent in 1987. The investment slump of 1985 appears to have affected mainly the foreign investors rather than the Hong Kong investor. This shows again that the Hong Kong investor is better adapted to China's investment environment than foreign investors. Between different types of foreign investment, Hong Kong's shares in contracted commercial credit (mainly compensation trade and processing) and direct foreign investment were 63 per cent and 53 per cent respectively in 1988. This suggests that Hong Kong's share in compensation trade and processing is about as high as its share in foreign investment.

Hong Kong industries are moving to the Pearl River delta in Guangdong due to high labour costs in Hong Kong, and Hong Kong investment is the major force behind the rapid industrialization of Guangdong. Commentators have speculated that Guangdong and Thailand will vie for the title of the fifth dragon of East Asia. According to Chinese estimates, since 1979 Hong Kong enterprises

have employed two million workers in Guangdong. Sixty per cent of
the enterprises involved in industrial processing are located in the
countryside, and this is a great boost to rural development in Guangdong. The Pearl River delta is so short of labour that over 100,000
workers have had to be recruited from elsewhere, including neighbouring provinces (*Wen Hui Pao* 5 Aug. 1987). Although industrial
processing does not involve high technology, technology transfer is
still significant because Hong Kong has accumulated considerable
skills in its main export industries, namely clothing, textiles, toys,
plastics and electronics. These are the industries that are emphasized
in China, and Chinese exports from these industries have grown
rapidly. In addition to production skills, China has also gained
marketing experience and access to world markets. Hong Kong's gain
from such arrangements is also substantial. The payroll per worker in
Shenzhen is 50–70 per cent lower than in Hong Kong, and the wage
level is even lower in the neighbouring areas of Shenzhen. In the
Shenzhen SEZ, factory rent is only one-third that of Hong Kong, and
rents are even lower outside the Shenzhen SEZ (*Hang Seng Economic
Monthly* Apr. 1987). Hong Kong firms are moving their labour-
intensive production facilities to China where they are concentrating
on the more skill-intensive processes of product design, testing,
marketing, and technical support (*Sung* 1985:63).

The rapid growth of industrial processing is an important reason
for the growth of China's total trade as well as trade between China
and Hong Kong. Beginning in 1985, the imported raw materials and
exports of industrial processing operations were separately listed in
the *Chinese Customs Statistics*. Unfortunately, no statistics on the
trade involving industrial processing through Hong Kong were released. However, as Hong Kong is the predominant investor in
industrial processing, and most industrial processing operations are
located in the coastal open areas close to Hong Kong, the bulk of the
trade involving industrial processing is likely to go through Hong
Kong. Table 5.4 shows China's trade involving industrial processing
from 1985 to 1989, and this trade forms a substantial and rising
portion of China's trade as well as the trade between Hong Kong and
China. In 1987, the exports (imports) of industrial processing represented 12 (11) per cent of China's total exports (imports) and 32 (43)
per cent of China's exports to (imports from) Hong Kong. Hong
Kong investment in industrial processing in China thus contributed
significantly to China's export drive and import expansion. Table 5.5
shows that Hong Kong's domestic exports of raw materials and
components to China from 1978 to 1986 have grown 97 times, or at
an average annual growth rate of 66 per cent. Such exports may be
used in Chinese enterprises not involved in industrial processing.
However, since Hong Kong is noted for its comparative advantage in

producing finished light consumer goods rather than raw materials and components, Chinese enterprises are not likely to import large quantities of Hong Kong-made raw materials and components unless the Chinese enterprises involved are Hong Kong firms that have moved to China. Vertical division of labour is taking place between Hong Kong and Guangdong as Hong Kong firms move part of their operations to China. It is thus reasonable to assume that the major part of such exports is used in industrial processing.

Table 5.4 *China's trade arising from industrial processing*

Year	Imports for industrial processing			Exports of industrial processing		
	US$m	Percentage share of China's imports from		US$m	Percentage share of China's exports to	
		All countries	Hong Kong		All countries	Hong Kong
1985	1,974	4.7	25.1	2,368	8.7	31.3
1986	2,981	6.9	39.5	3,417	11.0	32.7
1987	4,874	11.3	48.2	4,740	12.0	31.5
1988	6,664	12.1	39.1	6,486	13.6	33.4
1989	7,002	11.8	37.2	8,230	15.7	32.6

Sources: Chinese data: *Chinese Customs Statistics*, various issues; Hong Kong data: *Hong Kong Trade Statistics*, various issues.

Table 5.5 *Hong Kong's domestic exports of raw materials and components to China*

Year	US$m	Share in total domestic exports to China (%)
1978	11.5	69.1
1981	195.6	37.4
1984	434.7	30.1
1985	362.4	18.6
1986	675.5	29.3
1987	—	—
1988[a]	3,580	73.4
1989	4,098	76.0

[a] Data from 1988 onwards refers to Hong Kong's domestic exports for processing in China. This includes raw materials, semi-manufactures and near finished goods for assembly and packaging. The coverage of the data from 1988 onwards is thus wider than before.
Sources: 1978–86 data, *Hang Seng Economic Monthly*, Apr. 1987; 1988 and after, *Hong Kong External Trade*, various issues.

Hong Kong's domestic exports of raw materials and components accounted for 29 per cent of Hong Kong's domestic exports to China in 1986, declining from the high of 69 per cent in 1978. This shows that China's imports of Hong Kong-made consumer goods and machinery have grown even faster than raw materials and components. Although assembling/processing operations do not involve transfer of high technology, Hong Kong is also dominant in other forms of foreign investment which have potential for technology transfer, namely cooperative ventures, equity ventures and fully foreign-owned enterprises. The 22-point investment enticement package of October 1986 offered privileged treatment for two types of foreign ventures: (i) those exporting at least 70 per cent of their output and (ii) those that involved advanced technology. By August 1987, 702 foreign enterprises, or 8.2 per cent of all foreign enterprises, were officially recognized as belonging to these two categories, with 513 enterprises in the first category and 205 enterprises in the second category. Although precise numbers are not available, Chinese officials made it known that Hong Kong and Macau enterprises were most numerous in both categories. Japanese and US enterprises ranked second and third respectively in the first category, and US enterprises ranked second in the second category (*Hong Kong Economic Journal* 6 Aug. 1987).

To summarize, Hong Kong is the foremost foreign investor in China and also the biggest, or one of the biggest, sources of foreign loans. Hong Kong's role in financing is closely connected to its role in trade. Hong Kong has invested heavily in export-oriented enterprises in China, financing China's export drive from the production side. Besides Hong Kong's investment in industrial processing, a substantial portion of Hong Kong's direct foreign investment in China also went to export-oriented enterprises because China strongly discouraged sales in the domestic market. Besides extending loans to China, loans extended by Hong Kong banks to Hong Kong traders also played an important role in China's trade. In 1987, 80 per cent of Hong Kong's entrepôt trade involved trade between China and other countries, and this trade was heavily financed by Hong Kong banks because of Hong Kong businesses being involved in exporting or importing. Hong Kong banks also advanced loans to finance 'trade not touching Hong Kong', mostly Chinese trade in which Hong Kong firms have played a brokerage role. Such loans increased from US$168 million in 1980 to US$1485 million in 1988, increasing nearly ninefold in eight years.

6

Hong Kong as trading partner

The role of Hong Kong as a trading partner is discussed broadly in Chapter 2. This chapter will examine the relative participation of Hong Kong in China's exports and imports by commodity categories. The role of Hong Kong in helping China to circumvent barriers to trade will be examined, as will the future prospects of China's direct exports to Hong Kong and Hong Kong's domestic exports to China.

Hong Kong's share in Chinese trade by commodity

Table 6.1 summarizes Hong Kong's share of Chinese exports by commodity. Chinese exports to Hong Kong are divided into exports retained in Hong Kong and exports re-exported through Hong Kong. Hong Kong does not publish statistics on the commodity composition for re-exports by country of origin, but they can be obtained from the Census and Statistics Department. Such statistics are necessary to compute the commodity composition of Chinese exports (i) retained in Hong Kong, and (ii) re-exported through Hong Kong. The many studies on the significance of Chinese exports in the Hong Kong market have unfortunately tended to estimate the commodity composition of Chinese merchandise retained in Hong Kong instead of obtaining correct data from the Census and Statistics Department; such estimates are inaccurate. In the Appendix, Census and Statistics Department data are compared with the estimates of two well-known studies, the first by Hsu (1983) and the second by Hsueh and Woo (1981). Hsueh and Woo made an unacceptable assumption that the fraction of Chinese imports retained is constant across commodity categories. Hsu assumed that Hong Kong's foodstuff re-exports came

104

entirely from China, and that Hong Kong's re-exports of raw materials and chemicals (SITC groups 2, 3, 4 and 5) are minimal and negligible. In fact, according to the 1984 data of the Census and Statistics Department, as much as 52 per cent of Hong Kong's foodstuff re-exports were of non-Chinese origin. From Table 6.1 it can be seen that, of Chinese exports to the world, the share of food fell from 32 per cent in 1970 to 12 per cent in 1987. The share of crude materials rose from 1970 until 1985, largely as the result of oil exports. However the 1986 fall in oil prices led to a drastic reduction in the share of crude materials. The share of manufactures rose from 42 per cent in 1970 to 64 per cent in 1987. The Hong Kong share in Chinese food exports is large, ranging from 24 to 41 per cent. As a result of Engel's Law and rising affluence in Hong Kong, the share of China's food exports retained in Hong Kong stagnated at around 30 per cent from 1970 until 1984, and then fell rapidly to 15 per cent by 1987. Besides growing affluence, the switch from traditional foods to western foods also contributed to the rapid fall since 1984. The fall of the share of Chinese food exports retained in Hong Kong from 29 per cent in 1984 to 20 per cent in 1985 was particularly abrupt. This was due to rampant parallel trade in 1985 when local authorities in China competed to export, leading to export over-expansion. Parallel trade diminished with the institution of export licences and quotas to Hong Kong and Macao in 1985, but the problem was not entirely solved. At the first national meeting on the management of export quotas for Hong Kong and Macao in 1987, it was revealed that China had still not instituted a system of information storage, retrieval and feedback to administer export quotas; instances of export licences exceeding quotas were still occurring (*Wen Hui Pao* 25 Feb. 1987). In contrast to the decline in the share of food retained in Hong Kong, the share of food re-exported through Hong Kong rose from 2 per cent of China's total food exports in 1975 to 9 per cent in 1987.

The Hong Kong share in the Chinese export of manufactures rose from 17 per cent in 1975 to 40 per cent in 1987. The share of manufactures retained in Hong Kong rose from 10 per cent in 1975 to 19 per cent in 1984, but declined to 13 per cent in 1987. The share of manufactures re-exported through Hong Kong rose from 7 to 26 per cent between 1975 and 1987. Since 1985, the volume of Chinese re-exports of manufactures through Hong Kong exceeded the volume retained in Hong Kong. Hong Kong's shares in China's exports are very high in some important export items. In 1987, the shares for textile fabric, machinery, and clothing were 46 per cent, 87 per cent, and 62 per cent respectively. Hong Kong's share of Chinese exports is high with good growth potential, namely manufactures, particularly textiles and machinery. Hong Kong's share is low in oil, which has

Table 6.1 *Hong Kong's share in Chinese exports by commodity* (SITC numbers)

Year		Food	Crude materials (2, 3, 4)		
			Textile fibre	Fuels	Sub-total
		(0, 1)	(26)	(3)	
1970	(i)	31.6	4.9	2.6	21.3
	(ii)	35.3	1.7	1.2	6.4
	(iii)	32.3	1.2	1.2	4.4
	(iv)	3.0	0.5	—	2.1
1975	(i)	29.7	3.3	14.3	26.6
	(ii)	31.3	16.9	5.5	10.2
	(iii)	29.0	16.4	5.4	8.0
	(iv)	2.3	0.6	0.1	2.2
1979	(i)	20.2	3.8	18.1	30.5
	(ii)	33.2	4.3	11.9	12.1
	(iii)	28.6	2.1	11.3	9.3
	(iv)	4.6	2.3	0.6	2.8
1981	(i)	16.6	2.3	22.2	32.2
	(ii)	36.0	13.4	8.7	11.3
	(iii)	30.0	2.6	8.3	7.2
	(iv)	6.0	10.8	0.5	4.1
1983	(i)	14.3	1.2	20.3	29.4
	(ii)	40.9	36.8	7.9	11.1
	(iii)	29.9	13.0	7.6	7.5
	(iv)	8.1	23.8	0.3	3.6
1984	(i)	13.0	3.7	20.8	30.5
	(ii)	36.8	26.2	5.1	9.5
	(iii)	28.9	8.6	4.8	5.7
	(iv)	7.9	17.7	0.2	3.8
1985	(i)	13.3	4.2	23.4	33.6
	(ii)	26.9	20.6	3.5	7.5
	(iii)	19.5	5.7	3.2	3.9
	(iv)	7.4	14.8	0.2	3.6
1986	(i)	14.6	3.6	12.0	21.3
	(ii)	26.0	15.5	5.3	10.1
	(iii)	17.1	3.2	4.4	4.7
	(iv)	8.9	12.3	0.9	5.4
1987	(i)	12.1	3.5	9.5	18.3
	(ii)	23.8	17.7	4.2	8.6
	(iii)	14.9	2.3	3.5	3.0
	(iv)	9.0	15.4	0.7	5.6

(i) Distribution of Chinese exports to the world by commodity (per cent).
(ii) Chinese exports to Hong Kong (as percentage of Chinese exports to the world).
(iii) Chinese exports retained in Hong Kong (as percentage of Chinese exports to the world).
(iv) Chinese exports re-exported via Hong Kong (as percentage of Chinese exports to the world).

Table 6.1 *continued*

Chemicals	Textile fabric	Machinery	Clothing	Sub-total	Total
		Manufactures (6, 7, 8, 9)			
(5)	(65)	(7)	(84)		(0–9)
5.5	18.2	3.5	4.7	41.5	100.0
11.2	20.4	12.3	21.0	20.3	21.6
8.2	10.5	7.4	15.3	12.9	17.1
3.0	9.8	4.8	5.7	7.4	4.5
4.8	14.5	3.8	5.1	38.5	100.0
16.0	18.9	13.4	12.1	17.4	19.3
11.0	10.8	7.1	6.1	10.4	15.2
4.9	8.1	6.3	6.0	7.0	4.3
5.6	16.6	3.1	7.8	43.3	100.0
19.9	27.6	21.4	20.9	25.5	22.6
10.8	15.0	12.2	9.2	14.4	15.5
9.1	12.6	9.2	11.7	11.1	7.1
6.1	14.2	3.8	9.7	44.7	100.0
17.7	33.9	32.5	31.7	31.4	24.7
6.8	20.5	18.1	18.4	18.1	15.7
11.0	13.4	14.5	13.3	13.3	9.1
5.5	13.6	3.5	11.6	44.0	100.0
20.3	38.5	36.4	32.1	34.2	24.9
9.0	25.0	24.4	14.8	18.6	15.1
11.3	13.6	12.0	17.3	15.6	9.7
5.0	14.4	4.0	12.1	51.5	100.0
19.3	44.5	30.6	43.7	36.1	25.0
7.1	27.8	21.6	20.9	18.8	14.3
2.2	16.7	9.1	22.8	17.3	10.8
5.1	12.9	3.3	12.4	48.0	100.0
20.8	45.1	63.4	58.4	37.9	24.5
7.0	24.5	48.0	24.7	17.1	12.2
13.9	20.7	15.4	33.7	20.8	12.4
5.4	14.6	4.5	16.6	58.7	100.0
22.0	47.7	81.5	63.6	38.1	29.5
7.9	25.5	59.1	22.1	16.5	13.5
14.1	22.3	22.4	41.6	21.8	15.9
5.2	14.3	6.8	16.5	64.4	100.0
22.9	46.3	86.7	62.0	39.5	31.1
7.3	22.7	43.8	20.0	13.3	11.8
15.7	23.6	42.8	42.0	26.2	19.3

Sources: Chinese data came from United States Central Intelligence Agency, National Foreign Assessment Centre, *China: International Trade*, various issues; Hong Kong data were obtained from Census and Statistics Department, Hong Kong.

a low growth potential due to supply bottlenecks and increasing domestic demand. Thus, the share of Hong Kong in Chinese exports is likely to increase further.

Table 6.2 shows Hong Kong's share of Chinese imports by commodity. Hong Kong's share is higher in manufactures than in food and raw materials, and this points to a greater future role for Hong Kong in China's imports. Hong Kong's shares were high and rising in some important items of light manufacturing: textile fabrics (SITC no. 65), electrical machinery (SITC no. 72) and miscellaneous

Table 6.2 *Hong Kong's share in Chinese imports by commodity* (SITC numbers)

Year		Food and crude materials (0–4)	Chemicals (5)
1979	(i)	28.2	10.1
	(ii)	1.5	1.5
	(iii)	0.4	0.1
	(iv)	1.1	1.3
1981	(i)	36.4	11.3
	(ii)	2.9	4.5
	(iii)	0.7	1.3
	(iv)	2.1	3.3
1983	(i)	27.4	12.2
	(ii)	6.3	6.1
	(iii)	1.8	1.1
	(iv)	4.5	5.0
1984	(i)	24.1	13.7
	(ii)	7.3	7.5
	(iii)	2.1	1.4
	(iv)	5.2	6.1
1985	(i)	13.0	9.4
	(ii)	11.5	11.8
	(iii)	3.8	1.7
	(iv)	7.7	10.1
1986	(i)	14.4	9.3
	(ii)	13.6	15.2
	(iii)	3.8	2.4
	(iv)	9.8	12.8
1987	(i)	17.0	12.2
	(ii)	14.1	20.0
	(iii)	3.8	3.8
	(iv)	10.2	16.2

(i)   Distribution of Chinese imports by commodity (per cent).
(ii) Hong Kong exports to China as percentage of Chinese imports.
(iii) Hong Kong domestic exports to China as percentage of Chinese imports.
(iv) Hong Kong re-exports to China as percentage of Chinese imports.

manufactured articles (SITC no. 89). In 1987, Hong Kong's shares in China's imports of the above commodities were 78 per cent, 42 per cent, and 58 per cent respectively. The shares of these commodities in China's imports have also risen markedly since 1979, partly because China was more willing to allow the importation of light manufactures for consumption, and partly because of the increased importation of textile fabrics and electronic components for the production of clothing and consumer electronics. Because Hong Kong's shares are high and rising in the commodities that are increasingly important

Table 6.2 *continued*

	Manufactures (6, 7, 8, 9)			Total
Textile fabric (65)	Electrical machinery (72)	Miscellaneous manufactures (89)	Sub-total	(0–9)
2.1	3.8	0.5	61.7	100
28.4	9.1	20.9	3.4	2.7
13.5	3.3	14.6	1.2	0.8
14.9	5.8	6.3	2.2	1.8
8.8	7.7	1.0	52.3	100
42.6	27.9	46.8	17.3	10.8
7.1	8.8	32.5	4.8	2.9
35.5	19.0	14.3	12.6	7.9
5.5	6.5	2.2	60.4	100
65.2	37.7	47.5	18.6	13.8
22.0	13.6	31.0	6.7	4.7
43.2	24.1	16.5	11.9	9.1
6.1	9.6	3.1	62.2	100
71.1	55.2	42.6	27.6	20.0
16.9	17.9	24.9	8.1	5.7
54.3	37.3	17.6	19.5	14.3
5.7	13.0	2.7	77.6	100
67.5	40.7	42.4	22.3	20.0
12.2	11.1	25.5	5.6	5.0
55.3	29.6	16.9	16.8	15.1
6.8	11.2	2.4	76.3	100
74.6	32.1	54.6	21.8	20.1
18.3	11.2	39.0	7.1	6.1
56.3	20.8	15.5	14.7	14.0
8.2	12.3	3.2	70.8	100
78.3	42.4	57.8	32.4	27.8
21.0	15.6	40.9	10.8	8.8
57.3	26.8	16.9	21.6	19.0

Sources: Chinese data: United States Central Intelligence Agency, National Foreign Assessment Centre, *China: International Trade*, various issues; Hong Kong data: *Hong Kong Trade Statistics*, various issues.

in China's imports, it is more than likely that they will increase further. This rise reflects partly Hong Kong's increasing investment in assembling/processing operations, and partly Hong Kong's efficiency in intermediation.

Circumventing barriers to trade

In recent years, Hong Kong manufacturers have moved labour-intensive processes to China, while usually keeping the finishing stages of production in Hong Kong. Such moves are generally due to the comparative advantages of capital- or skill-intensive processes, such as the dyeing and finishing of grey cloth. However, such moves can also be due to trade barriers. For example, surplus textile quotas available in Hong Kong, and Hong Kong's qualification for the United States General Scheme of Preferences (GSP), enable Hong Kong to help China circumvent trade barriers. The best known example is knitwear manufacture; panel knitting is usually done in China, and the linking and looping of panels into sweaters carried out in Hong Kong, despite the fact that this latter stage is not particularly capital- or skill-intensive. An examination of the 6-digit SITC trade statistics of Hong Kong reveals that the import of semi-manufactured garments (mostly knitted panels) into Hong Kong has increased rapidly, and this partly explains the rapid rise in the share of Chinese clothing in Hong Kong's retained imports (Table 6.3). This activity has caught the attention of importing countries. The United States Government unilaterally declared, on August 1984, that, while the processes of linking and looping would no longer confer country of origin status, the process of panel knitting would. For texile fabrics, dyeing and finishing would also no longer confer country of origin status, while the weaving of fabrics would. Although the United States action removes the distortion of comparative advantage in knitwear, it introduces a fresh distortion by inducing the development of dyeing and finished (capital- and skill-intensive processes) in China.

Hong Kong's domestic export of finished fabrics to the United States is not large: in 1983 it was US$47 million, or 5.9 per cent of the value of retained imports of textile fabrics from China. Most finished fabrics are used for clothing manufacture in Hong Kong. Thus the United States rule on finished fabrics did not have a large impact on imports of Chinese fabric to Hong Kong. The impact of the United States rule on knitwear was more significant. In 1983, Hong Kong's domestic exports of knitwear to the United States totalled US$259 million or 42 per cent of all Hong Kong's domestic exports of

Table 6.3 *Hong Kong retained imports of Chinese and non-Chinese clothing*
(US$'000)

Year	Chinese clothing			Non-Chinese clothing
	All clothing	Semi-manufactured	Completed clothing	
1977	66,160	—	66,160	81,340
	(0.76)[a]		(0.76)	(0.93)
1978	73,016	44	72,972	119,900
	(0.66)	(0.00)	(0.66)	(1.08)
1979	96,080	3,071	93,009	140,620
	(0.57)	(0.02)	(0.68)	(1.03)
1980	238,354	28,031	210,323	191,882
	(1.41)	(0.17)	(1.24)	(1.14)
1981	383,090	92,327	290,763	216,510
	(2.09)	(0.50)	(1.59)	(1.18)
1982	396,196	121,180	275,016	245,462
	(2.29)	(0.70)	(1.59)	(1.42)
1983	406,680	143,436	363,244	229,220
	(2.33)	(0.82)	(1.51)	(1.31)
1984	569,600	204,622	364,978	230,200
	(2.93)	(1.05)	(1.88)	(1.18)
1985	572,000	215,261	356,739	270,900
	(3.16)	(1.19)	(1.97)	(1.50)
1986	736,100	198,819	537,281	332,700
	(3.36)	(0.91)	(2.45)	(1.52)
1987	910,700	234,267	676,433	435,900
	(3.19)	(0.82)	(2.37)	(1.53)
1988	907,213	33,941	873,272	505,787
	(2.68)	(0.10)	(2.58)	(1.49)
1989	1,019,372	21,104	998,268	618,102
	(2.96)	(0.06)	(2.90)	(1.80)

[a] Figures in brackets represent percentage share of total retained imports.
Sources: Census and Statistics Department, Hong Kong; *Hong Kong Trade Statistics*, various issues.

knitwear. Hong Kong manufacturers switched to automated panel knitting to comply with the new United States rules, a move expected to reduce the retained imports of knitting panels from China. However, non-United States markets continued to grow, softening the impact of the change. Hong Kong's retained imports of semi-manufactured garments from China stagnated from 1984 to 1986 and fell sharply in 1988.

The United States General Scheme of Preferences (GSP) does not seem to have had a significant impact on Hong Kong's imports from China. For most major markets, China qualifies to GSP. The only exception is the United States, and the tariff is only 6 per cent for countries that do not qualify for GSP. The differential is not large enough to have a major impact. Moreover, no more than 15 per cent of Hong Kong's domestic exports to the United States enjoyed GSP benefits in 1986. Most of Hong Kong's major exports including clothing, textiles, footwear and watches, have already 'graduated' (*Economic Reporter* 26 Nov. 1984:10–11). In January 1988, the United States Government decided to abolish all GSP benefits for Hong Kong, Taiwan, Singapore and South Korea as from 1989.

Circumventing trade barriers illegally

The share of Chinese clothing in the retained imports of Hong Kong is high even after the exclusion of semi-manufactures (Table 6.3). The ratio of retained imports of Chinese clothing relative to foreign clothing was about 67 per cent in 1979, but the ratio jumped to 109 per cent in 1980. In the Hong Kong market, non-Chinese imported clothing occupies the high quality end of the market, and Chinese clothing is regarded as inferior both to other imports and to Hong Kong clothing. The share of non-Chinese clothing in Hong Kong's retained imports rose gradually from 1977 to 1987, with increasing expenditures on high fashion goods due to prosperity. The sharp increase in the share of Chinese clothing is difficult to explain; the influx of 500,000 Chinese immigrants during the period 1977–81, and the improved quality of Chinese clothing and marketing strategy employed, probably account for part of the increase. Another explanation for the sharp rise in the market share of Chinese clothing is that it conceals illicit exports of Chinese clothing under the Hong Kong quota. According to Hong Kong clothing manufacturers, there are two main channels of illicit trade: (i) completed Chinese clothing which is concealed beneath semi-manufactured clothing in containers in shipments from China to Hong Kong, and (ii) completed Chinese clothing which is imported by retailers of Chinese clothing in Hong Kong, so as not to arouse suspicion. Such clothing is then resold to Hong Kong manufacturers who label it as their own product (Sung 1985:18). In both cases, manufacturers will present false production records to claim Hong Kong origin.

The first of the above schemes does not appear to be important in illicit trade. Although imports of semi-manufactured clothing grew rapidly (Table 6.3), Hong Kong's retained import of semi-manufactured clothing (mostly knitted panels) was US$143 million in 1983, or 23 per cent of the value of the domestic exports of knitwear. The imports of semi-manufactured clothing do not appear to be excessive. Moreover, the first illicit scheme involves more risk than the second: there is always the possibility that customs inspectors will examine a whole container.

The second method of illicit trade involves less risk and could account for part of the sharp rise in the import of completed Chinese clothing. The extent of illicit trade is estimated as follows. In the eight years 1972–79 (the period before the sharp rise in the share of Chinese clothing), the share of Chinese clothing in Hong Kong's retained imports was 62 per cent of that of non-Chinese clothing. During the period 1980–88, this ratio jumped to 144 per cent. If we assume that the ratio stayed at 62 per cent during 1980–88, all of the excess (82 per cent of non-Chinese clothing imports) represented illicit trade. Such a figure would, however, overstate illicit trade because the ratio of retained imports would have risen with improved Chinese marketing strategy since 1979. If we assume that the ratio rose to 144 per cent there would be no illicit trade. Taking a middle course, assume the ratio has risen to 103 per cent, and the excess is illicit trade. From 1980 until 1988, the total estimated amount of illicit trade was US$1090 million, or 29 per cent of completed Chinese clothing imports. However, illicit trade was only 1.9 per cent of Hong Kong's domestic export of clothing. It appears that most firms involved in illicit trade are small because of the high penalty for keeping false production records.

Hong Kong as consumer of Chinese goods

As is mentioned in Chapter 2, Hong Kong became a significant consumer of Chinese exports during the 1960s. Just before the Cultural Revolution in 1966, Hong Kong's consumption of Chinese goods represented 17 per cent of Chinese exports and 26 per cent of Hong Kong's retained imports (Table 2.3). China was the largest supplier of retained imports to Hong Kong. However, as the Cultural Revolution progressed, China lost its pre-eminent position in the Hong Kong market to Japan and has not been able to regain its former position, despite its open-door policy.

From the point of view of the Hong Kong market, Chinese merchandise has been competing poorly. Table 2.3 shows that the Chinese share of Hong Kong's retained imports declined sharply from 26 per cent in 1966 to 15 per cent in 1970. There was a partial recovery of the Chinese share to 19 per cent in 1975, but thereafter the Chinese share stagnated and declined to 15 per cent in 1977. Starting with the open-door policy of 1979, there was a temporary recovery until 1986, but China's share stagnated between 1984 and 1986 and fell abruptly from 22 per cent in 1986 to 14 per cent in 1989. As a share of Chinese exports, Hong Kong's consumption of Chinese goods declined from 17 per cent in 1970 to 14 per cent in

1987 and then fell abruptly to 9 per cent in 1989. The poor performance of Chinese exports in the Hong Kong market calls for a more detailed analysis.

Table 6.4 summarizes China's share of the retained imports of Hong Kong by SITC groups from 1970 until 1989. It can be seen that retained imports of beverages and tobacco (1), crude materials (2), and oils and fats (4) from China were relatively insignificant. Food (0), fuels (3), and manufactures (6, 7 and 8) dominated retained

Table 6.4 *China's share of the retained imports of Hong Kong by commodity* (SITC numbers)

Year		Food	Beverages and tobacco	Crude materials	Fuels	Oils & fats	Chemicals
		(0)	(1)	(2)	(3)	(4)	(5)
1970	(i)	18.3	2.0	7.8	3.2	0.6	6.8
	(ii)	46.3	16.5	6.9	0.8	37.9	5.8
	(iii)	57.9	2.3	3.7	0.2	1.6	2.7
1975	(i)	20.5	2.0	7.4	7.4	0.7	6.3
	(ii)	51.4	15.6	19.5	13.2	14.2	10.6
	(iii)	56.8	1.6	7.6	5.1	1.2	3.5
1979	(i)	12.5	1.7	4.3	6.8	0.5	7.2
	(ii)	40.3	7.1	14.2	15.1	30.1	8.4
	(iii)	37.0	0.9	4.5	7.6	1.1	4.4
1983	(i)	12.4	1.5	3.3	8.7	0.4	6.9
	(ii)	44.0	20.1	24.8	23.9	23.2	9.6
	(iii)	26.6	1.5	4.0	10.2	0.4	3.2
1984	(i)	11.0	1.5	3.2	7.6	0.4	6.6
	(ii)	43.9	19.5	29.9	20.2	30.5	7.8
	(iii)	23.1	1.4	4.6	7.4	0.5	2.5
1985	(i)	11.2	1.8	3.0	7.2	0.4	6.6
	(ii)	39.1	20.1	30.5	19.8	21.3	8.8
	(iii)	21.2	1.8	4.4	6.9	0.5	2.8
1986	(i)	9.9	1.5	2.9	4.6	0.3	7.3
	(ii)	37.8	22.8	38.9	17.9	13.1	9.8
	(iii)	16.8	1.6	5.1	3.7	0.2	3.2
1987	(i)	8.6	1.6	3.2	3.8	0.2	7.9
	(ii)	32.3	22.1	16.6	17.6	14.7	8.7
	(iii)	15.3	2.0	2.9	3.7	0.2	3.8
1988	(i)	8.3	1.7	2.5	3.1	0.2	9.0
	(ii)	31.3	25.4	12.1	18.2	10.1	10.0
	(iii)	15.6	2.6	1.8	3.4	0.1	5.4
1989	(i)	8.7	2.1	2.6	3.9	0.2	8.5
	(ii)	27.9	26.9	9.2	16.7	13.3	10.7
	(iii)	17.7	4.2	1.7	4.8	0.2	6.7

(i) Distribution of Hong Kong's retained imports (per cent).
(ii) Share of Chinese merchandise in Hong Kong's retained imports (per cent).
(iii) Distribution of Hong Kong's retained imports from China (per cent).

imports from China. Within manufactures, textile fabrics (65), cloth-ing (84), and machinery (7) were most important. From 1970 until 1975, over half of Chinese exports retained in Hong Kong consisted of food, but the share of food fell sharply with increasing prosperity in Hong Kong from 1975 onwards. The importance of Chinese fuels rose rapidly in the period 1970–79, but declined abruptly in 1986 due to the fall in oil prices. The share of Chinese manufactures expanded rapidly.

Table 6.4 *continued*

Manufactures (6, 7, 8)				Total	Value of total retained imports (US$m)
Textiles (65)	Machinery (7)	Clothing (84)	Sub-total (6, 7, 8)		
17.7	17.6	1.5	61.2	99.9	2,500
9.4	2.3	40.8	7.6	14.7	
11.4	1.5	4.3	31.7	100.0	
15.0	17.3	1.2	55.5	99.8	5,561
13.3	2.0	32.1	9.1	19.2	
10.3	1.8	2.0	26.3	100.0	
13.8	22.2	1.7	66.5	99.5	13,744
17.9	1.7	40.6	9.1	13.7	
18.1	2.7	5.1	44.6	100.0	
13.6	21.8	3.6	66.5	99.7	17,543
33.5	5.4	64.0	16.7	20.7	
22.3	5.7	11.3	54.0	100.0	
14.4	24.5	4.1	69.3	99.6	19,492
37.3	6.9	71.2	18.1	20.8	
25.9	8.2	14.0	60.4	100.0	
14.1	23.1	4.6	69.1	99.3	18,219
34.8	9.8	67.9	18.6	20.8	
23.8	11.0	15.2	62.4	100.0	
14.8	24.7	4.9	73.1	99.6	22,016
37.5	13.7	68.9	21.0	22.2	
25.2	15.3	15.1	69.4	100.0	
14.9	26.7	4.7	74.0	99.3	28,562
37.4	12.1	67.6	17.7	18.3	
30.7	17.8	17.5	72.1	100.0	
12.8	29.4	4.2	74.8	99.6	33,910
33.0	11.9	64.2	15.3	15.9	
25.4	21.2	16.2	69.1	98.0	
13.5	28.8	4.8	73.0	99.3	34,402
29.2	10.6	62.3	11.5	13.4	
29.0	22.2	21.7	61.8	97.1	

Sources: Census and Statistics Department, Hong Kong; *Hong Kong Trade Statistics*, various issues.

In the early 1970s, Chinese products competed on the basis of low price rather than quality. Advertising and packaging were largely ignored. Such a strategy was ill-suited to the dynamic market of Hong Kong, although this weakness was masked by the recession of 1973–75. In those lean years, the share of expenditure on food rose, and relatively more was spent on goods at the lower end of the market. The Chinese share in imported food rose accordingly. There was also a rapid rise in the export of Chinese oil, partly the result of higher energy prices brought about by the increase in petroleum prices. Thus, the Chinese share of Hong Hong's retained imports rose to 19 per cent in 1975. However, economic recovery and prosperity revealed the weakness of the Chinese position; from 1975 until 1979 the Chinese share of Hong Kong's retained imports declined sharply. The decline was largely brought about by the high share of food in China's exports to Hong Kong. During the period 1975–79, the share of food in total retained imports declined. The Chinese share in the retained imports of food also declined, partly because of the switch from traditional to western food, and also because of the inferior quality of food supplied by China. The decline in China's overall share would have been even sharper had it not been for the rapid expansion of oil exports.

From 1979 there was a change in China's export and marketing strategy. Quality, advertising and packaging were emphasized. This accounted for the recovery in China's market share from 1979 to 1986. During this period the Chinese share of the retained imports of manufactures rose, and manufactures accounted for over 70 per cent of all retained imports in Hong Kong in 1986–87. Moreover, the share of manufactures in Hong Kong's retained imports was rising throughout the period 1970–87. The Chinese share of the retained imports of food also rose from 1979 to 1983, reflecting successes in marketing and quality upgrading. Despite the decline of China's share in fuels from 1983 onwards, China's success in manufactures resulted in a rise in China's share of Hong Kong's retained imports. China's success in manufactures was mainly in textiles, clothing, and transport equipment and machinery. China's export of transport equipment and machinery largely consisted of the export of electronic and electrical goods. However, because of the change in the SITC classification of electronic and electrical goods in the mid-1970s, it is very difficult to extract these products from trade data, and the catch-all category of 'transport equipment and machinery' is used instead.

However, China's success during 1979–89 in the export of manufactures to Hong Hong was narrowly based on textiles and clothing. The share of textiles in Hong Kong's retained imports from China rose sharply from 16 per cent in the early 1970s to 51 per cent in 1989 (Table 6.5). Chinese textiles had only a small share of the world textile market, but China's share of Hong Kong's total retained imports of textiles was large: 38 per cent for textile fabric and 69 per cent for clothing in 1986 (Table 6.4). China's small share of the world's textile market may enable her to increase her textile exports to the world through quality-upgrading, despite the restrictions of the Multi-Fibre Arrangement. However, the Hong Kong market is probably close to saturation with Chinese textiles, despite the absence of import restrictions, and China's shares of Hong Kong's retained imports of textile fabric and clothing have fallen since 1986.

Most of the imports of Chinese textiles into Hong Kong were used as intermediate inputs in Hong Kong's clothing industry, that is, textile yarn, fabric, and semi-manufactured garments. From 1970 to 1989, the share of these three items in Hong Kong's retained imports from China rose from 16 to 51 per cent. Since the export of Hong Kong clothing is subject to quotas, and the scope for quality upgrading is much greater for clothing than for fabrics, the Hong Kong market for Chinese yarn and fabrics is limited. In addition, the market for semi-manufactured garments is limited by the 1984 country-of-origin rule of the United States. The market for Chinese food is limited according to Engel's law, while the export of Chinese oil is subject to severe supply bottlenecks. From 1983 to 1989, the Chinese share in Hong Kong's retained imports of oil declined (Table 6.4). It is thus not surprising that China's share of Hong Kong's retained imports has fallen sharply since 1987.

Table 6.5 *Share of Chinese textiles in Hong Kong's retained imports from China*
(per cent)

Year	Textile fibre (26)	Textile fabric (65)	Clothing (84)	Total
1970	0.3	11.4	4.3	16.0
1975	3.6	10.3	2.0	15.9
1977	0.4	11.4	5.1	16.9
1979	0.5	18.1	5.1	23.7
1981	0.2	18.6	11.3	30.1
1983	0.7	22.3	11.3	34.3
1984	1.4	25.9	14.0	41.3
1985	2.0	23.8	15.2	41.0
1986	0.8	25.2	15.1	41.1
1987	0.7	30.7	17.5	48.9
1988	0.0	25.4	16.2	41.6
1989	0.0	29.0	21.7	50.7

Source: Census and Statistics Department, Hong Kong.

Hong Kong as supplier to China

Table 6.2 shows that Hong Kong's domestic exports to China have risen from virtually nil to 9 per cent of China's imports in 1987. In 1987, the share of Hong Kong's domestic exports was particularly high in the following SITC categories: 41 per cent in miscellaneous manufactured articles (89), 21 per cent in textile fabrics (65), and 16 per cent in electrical machinery (72). The major Hong Kong manufacturing industries that have invested in processing/assembling operations in China also fall into these categories. The supply of components and raw materials to such operations form an important part of Hong Kong's domestic exports to China. However, as mentioned before, China's imports of Hong Kong-made consumer goods and machinery have grown even faster than imports of raw materials and components.

Hong Kong has emerged as an important supplier of machinery to China in the 1980s. However, since Chinese trade statistics are only broken down by 2-digit SITC, it is not possible to compute Hong Kong shares in China's machinery imports, although Hong Kong's share in electrical machinery (SITC category 72) is high, as mentioned above. In the period 1980–85, Hong Kong's domestic exports of machinery to China grew at an average annual rate of 75 per cent (Hong Kong Trade Development Council 1986). Though China has a huge machine-building industry, it is geared towards heavy equipment and is ill-suited to the recent Chinese emphasis on the export of light industrial products. Hong Kong's machinery industry, which caters mainly to Hong Kong's export industries (textiles, plastics and electronics), suits China's priorities well. Moreover, Hong Kong's cultural and physical proximity to China is particularly important for the training of technicians in after-sales service which is important for machinery exports. The fact that Hong Kong cannot supply much in the way of high technology equipment has not proved a problem; in fact Hong Kong machines suit the Chinese environment rather better. Hong Kong has been able to provide machinery and after-sales service some 40 per cent cheaper than have Japan, West Germany, or Italy, and the appreciation of Japanese and European currencies has continued to enhance Hong Kong's competitiveness (Hong Kong Trade Development Council 1986).

The Chinese market is an important element in the diversification of Hong Kong's domestic exports. Traditionally, Hong Kong was an exporter of light consumer goods. The Chinese market, which has been the second largest market for Hong Kong's domestic exports since 1984, absorbed producer goods rather than consumer goods. Table 6.6 shows China's share of the domestic exports of Hong Kong by SITC commodity groups. Although the SITC classification does not show the distinction between consumer goods and producer goods, the table shows that the distribution of Hong Kong's domestic exports to China is very different from the distribution of Hong Kong's total domestic exports. In particular, the shares of food and crude materials (0–4), chemicals (5), and textile fabrics (65) in Hong Kong's domestic exports to China are much higher than the corresponding shares in total domestic exports. Clothing (84) is unimportant in Hong Kong's domestic exports to China. This confirms the conjecture that the Chinese market stimulates the growth of new exports instead of traditional ones. Chinese market shares in Hong Kong's domestic exports were high in the following SITC categories in 1989: 35 per cent in food and crude materials (0–4), 75 per cent in chemicals (5), 37 per cent in textile fabrics (65), and 41 per cent in telecommunications and sound-reproducing equipment (76). Moreover, these shares have risen rapidly since 1979, and domestic exports of these commodities should continue to grow rapidly.

As mentioned earlier, the stimulus of the Chinese market to Hong Kong's machinery industry was phenomenal. In 1985, the Chinese market dominated several categories of Hong Kong machinery exports: 67 per cent in plastics machinery, 81 per cent in textile machinery and 67 per cent in machinery-related packaging, printing, publishing, and food processing (Hong Kong Trade Development Council 1986). Imports of machinery are expected to be given high priority in China and exports of Hong Kong machinery to China will grow further.

The prospects for direct trade between Hong Kong and China

The domestic exports of Hong Kong to China have grown rapidly while Hong Kong's retained imports from China have declined. In 1989, the former exceeded the latter. Since 1967, China's position as the number one supplier of retained imports has been usurped by Japan: Japan's share of Hong Kong's retained imports is appreciably higher than China's — 24 per cent (Japan) and 15 per cent (China) in 1988. Japan has been investing in large department stores in Hong Kong. Given the Japanese dominance in vehicles, capital goods, consumer durables and consumer goods at the higher end of the market, China has to increase its efforts simply to retain its market share. The 1978–86 success was largely due to the rectification of past negligence in marketing and packaging, and the penetration of

Table 6.6 *China's share of the domestic exports of Hong Kong by commodity (SITC numbers)*

Year		Manufactures (6, 7, 8)								Sub-total	Total (0–9)	Value of domestic exports (US$m)
		$(0-4)^a$	$(5)^b$	$(65)^c$	$(76)^d$	$(77)^c$	$(84)^f$	$(88)^g$	$(89)^h$			
1979	(i)	2.9	0.8	7.3	7.3	5.8	36.0	9.2	16.9	95.4	100	11,176
	(ii)	5.0	2.5	4.9	1.2	0.6	0.04	0.9	0.6	1.0	1.1	
	(iii)	13.5	1.8	33.0	8.2	3.2	1.5	7.3	9.2	83.6	100	
1981	(i)	2.9	0.9	6.6	7.0	7.2	35.2	10.1	16.5	95.8	100	14,379
	(ii)	11.5	19.0	11.9	9.2	1.8	0.6	4.7	2.5	3.2	3.6	
	(iii)	9.1	4.9	21.5	17.6	3.6	5.6	13.1	11.2	85.0	100	
1983	(i)	3.7	1.0	6.8	8.1	7.9	33.0	9.0	15.9	94.6	100	14,355
	(ii)	17.5	17.3	22.6	9.1	3.6	1.0	3.9	5.4	5.3	6.0	
	(iii)	10.7	2.8	25.7	12.3	4.7	5.3	5.9	14.3	84.9	100	
1984	(i)	3.1	1.0	6.3	8.0	8.3	33.9	7.6	15.8	95.1	100	17,643
	(ii)	23.7	29.6	23.5	18.6	5.9	1.1	4.5	6.9	7.3	8.2	
	(iii)	9.0	3.5	18.0	18.2	6.0	4.5	4.2	13.3	85.3	100	
1985	(i)	3.4	1.0	6.0	6.9	7.7	34.6	8.3	15.8	94.4	100	16,671
	(ii)	34.6	37.6	27.1	25.7	10.4	1.1	8.3	10.0	10.4	11.7	
	(iii)	10.1	3.2	14.0	15.2	6.9	3.2	5.8	13.6	84.1	100	

(i) Distribution of Hong Kong's domestic exports (per cent).
(ii) Share of Chinese markets in Hong Kong's domestic exports (per cent).
(iii) Distribution of Hong Kong's domestic exports to China (per cent).

a Food and crude materials
b Chemicals
c Textile fabrics
d Telecommunications and sound reproducing equipment
e Electrical machinery
f Clothing
g Photographic equipment and optical goods
h Miscellaneous manufactures

Table 6.6 *continued*

Year		(0–4)[a]	(5)[b]	(65)[c]	(76)[d]	(77)[e]	(84)[f]	(88)[g]	(89)[h]	Sub-total	Total (0–9)	Value of domestic exports (US$m)
							Manufactures (6, 7, 8)					
1986	(i)	2.9	1.0	7.1	7.6	7.3	33.9	8.5	16.5	94.9	100	19,734
	(ii)	35.8	42.6	33.3	20.7	9.2	1.5	8.5	10.7	10.4	11.7	
	(iii)	8.9	3.6	20.3	11.9	5.7	4.3	6.1	15.1	84.7	100	
1987	(i)	2.9	1.3	8.2	7.6	7.4	33.5	8.0	15.4	94.5	100	25,039
	(ii)	27.5	59.5	34.0	25.7	12.4	2.0	10.0	13.9	12.7	14.3	
	(iii)	5.6	5.4	19.5	13.7	6.4	4.7	5.6	14.9	84.0	100	
1988	(i)	3.2	1.9	7.1	8.0	8.0	30.9	8.9	13.7	93.7	100	27,906
	(ii)	38.2	70.6	34.1	33.4	17.0	2.3	11.4	16.3	15.4	17.5	
	(iii)	6.9	7.8	14.0	15.2	7.8	4.1	5.8	12.8	82.7	100	
1989	(i)	3.4	2.4	7.5	7.2	8.0	32.1	8.7	12.4	93.0	100	28,731
	(ii)	35.0	74.8	36.6	40.7	19.2	2.6	13.3	19.5	17.0	19.3	
	(iii)	6.1	9.2	14.2	15.1	7.9	4.3	6.0	12.6	81.9	100	

(i)   Distribution of Hong Kong's domestic exports (per cent).
(ii)   Share of Chinese markets in Hong Kong's domestic exports (per cent).
(iii) Distribution of Hong Kong's domestic exports to China (per cent).

a   Food and crude materials
b   Chemicals
c   Textile fabrics
d   Telecommunications and sound reproducing equipment
e   Electrical machinery
f   Clothing
g   Photographic equipment and optical goods
h   Miscellaneous manufactures

Source: Hong Kong Trade Statistics, various issues.

the Hong Kong clothing industry. It is difficult to see how further success can be attained so readily. Moreover, the potential for inputs into the Hong Kong clothing industry is limited by quotas. Unless China can upgrade quality and increase the export of electronics, electrical goods and other manufactures rapidly, its share of Hong Kong's retained imports will continue to decline.

7

Hong Kong as middleman

In Chapter 2 the argument is put forward that an increasing share of China's commodity trade, tourist trade and loan syndication is handled through Hong Kong, despite the fact that China now has many more direct links with the rest of the world. This paradox is explained by a theory of intermediation, which predicts a surge in demand for intermediation as the economy is decentralized.

In this chapter, the entrepôt function of Hong Kong is examined in detail because of its empirical and theoretical importance. The theory of intermediation developed in Chapter 2 is elaborated upon and applied specifically to entrepôt trade. Alternative explanations of entrepôt trade, such as historical and cultural factors, monopoly power, and economic distortions are also examined and applied to the analysis of the China–Hong Kong connection. China's indirect trade through Hong Kong relative to its total trade is analysed in detail by country and commodity.

The function of Hong Kong as a centre of trans-shipment will also be analysed. However, the data on trans-shipment are not as detailed as those available for entrepôt trade. Hong Kong trading firms performing a purely brokerage role in China's direct trade also appear to be important, but this part of the analysis will be brief as the data are fragmentary. The role of Hong Kong as a gateway for tourists to China is covered in Chapter 2 and is not repeated here.

Entrepôt trade
The significance of entrepôt trade

Since adoption of the open-door policy, an increasing proportion of China's trade is conducted via Hong Kong in the form of entrepôt trade. This is surprising because China has established direct commercial relations with most countries since emerging from its political and economic isolation.

Moreover, the growth of entrepôt trade in Hong Kong is not an isolated exception. Despite the advent of modern communications, which enable exporters and importers to trade directly, entrepôt trade continues to thrive in some places, notably Hong Kong, Singapore, Gibraltar, Bahrain, and Puerto Rico. The reasons for the resilience of entrepôt trade have received little attention in economic literature.

The study of entrepôt trade is not only important for China's open-door policy; the study has wider theoretical implications applicable to internal trade. Given the wealth of data on the movement of goods passing through customs, it is certainly much easier to study entrepôt trade than internal trade.

The nature of entrepôt trade

Although many studies of Hong Kong's 'middleman' role have been undertaken, only two distinguish between trans-shipment and re-exports; other authors erroneously assume that the re-export statistics of Hong Kong include trans-shipment.[1] As mentioned before, re-exports are classified into processed re-exports and pure re-exports, where processed re-exports refer to re-exports that have been physically treated (packaged, sorted and so on), and pure re-exports have not been changed in any physical way.

In the case of pure exports, an entrepôt supplies intermediation, transportation, finance and insurance services. According to the International Standard Industrial Classification (ISIC), intermediation (brokerage) is classified in division six, the trade sector; transportation is classified in division seven; and finance and insurance are classified in division eight. In this book, these services are collectively referred to as trading services because they are usually bundled together in trade.

There are many channels of international trade. As shown in Table 7.1, international trade can be conducted through three modes of transportation: direct shipment, trans-shipment, and entrepôt trade. International trade can be conducted with or without intermediation, and the intermediary may be a domestic firm (a firm of the producing country), or a foreign firm. Moreover, an intermediary can provide trading services directly or indirectly. When a trader (the intermediary) buys goods for resale, trading services are provided indirectly as they are embodied in the goods sold, and the trader assumes the risk of owning the goods temporarily. A firm can provide these services directly to another party through a service contact without either buying the goods involved or assuming the risks of owning the goods.

---

[1] The two studies that make the distinction are Y. C. Jao (1983:24) and Ronald Hsia (1984:3).

As shown in Table 7.1, there are five forms of intermediation: no intermediation (direct trade), direct intermediation by a domestic firm or by a foreign firm, and indirect intermediation by a domestic firm or by a foreign firm. The two modes of transportation, direct shipment and trans-shipment, and five forms of intermediation give rise to ten different channels of international trade. Entrepôt trade involves indirect intermediation by definition, and gives rise to two channels of international trade (channels 11 and 12).

The firm handling entrepôt trade is usually a foreign firm located at the entrepôt (channel 12), although the supplying country may also set up bases at the entrepôt to conduct its trade (channel 11), e.g. China has set up trading firms in Hong Kong to handle its trade.

From Table 7.1, it is apparent that entrepôt trade is the exception rather than the rule. A foreign trading firm at the entrepôt has to compete with direct trade, and also with domestic trading firms in the producing country. Moreover, instead of indirect intermediation through entrepôt trade, the foreign firm can (i) offer direct intermediation through a service contract (channels 3 or 8) or (ii) set up a local base of operation through direct foreign investment to take legal possession of the goods in the producing country and conduct trade through direct shipment or trans-shipment (channels 5 or 10). In the invisibles account of the balance of payments, activity (i) appears as 'export of services' and activity (ii) appears as 'income flows from investment in service activities'. Entrepôt services do not appear in the invisibles account because such services are embodied in goods. Statistics on entrepôt services are easier to obtain than statistics on the other two trade activities, largely because statistics on trade in goods are easier to collect.

The theory of pure re-exports and processed re-exports

As is explained in Chapter 2, a theory of international trade in intermediary services includes the following three elements: (i) an explanation of the need for intermediation, (ii) an analysis of the economy of scale and economy of agglomeration in supplying intermediary services and (iii) an analysis of the provision of intermediary services by a foreign firm (versus a domestic firm). The above elements can be readily used to analyse pure re-exports. In the Townsend model, the need for intermediation is explained in terms of the fixed transaction costs involved in establishing trade links. In this context, the greater need for intermediation in international trade

Table 7.1 *The channels of international trade*

Mode of shipment	No intermediation (direct trade)	Forms of intermediation[a] Intermediation through:			
		service contract by a		purchasing and selling by a	
		domestic firm	foreign firm	domestic firm	foreign firm
Direct shipment	1	2	3	4	5
Trans-shipment	6	7	8	9	10
Entrepôt trade				11	12

[a] Numbers are channel numbers referred to in text.

(versus internal trade) is evident: the fixed cost of establishing links in international trade is higher because of greater physical, cultural and sociological distance. The economy of scale and the economy of agglomeration in supplying trading services both increase the efficiency of intermediation. Besides the production of market information, which is mentioned in Chapter 2, many other facets of entrepôt activity also involve large fixed costs and small marginal costs, thus implying the existence of economies of scale. Transportation, facilities and arrangements made at ports of origin and destination involve large fixed costs and small marginal costs. Furthermore, trading companies can coordinate shipping times and locations to reduce the average costs of goods transported. Hedging against exchange risks in the forward exchange market is also characterized by fixed transaction costs and small marginal costs (Yamamura 1976:184–5). Although transport and financial services can be contracted separately, economies of scale in transport and financial services do enhance the demand for intermediation as trading companies can realize these economies of scale.

As is mentioned in Chapter 2, a foreign firm may have a comparative advantage over the domestic firm in providing intermediary services due to cultural heterogeneity and the relatively high skill intensity of intermediary services. Moreover, it may not be economical for the foreign firm to set up a local base of operation due to factor prices and the economies of scale of agglomeration in supplying intermediary services. In the context of pure re-exports, setting up a local base of operation to acquire legal possession of the goods in the supplying country implies direct shipment or trans-shipment. This may enable the producer to identify the final importer because the goods are consigned directly to the final consumer. Entrepôt trade gives better protection of market information. This factor is especially relevant in China's trade, as the shipping companies are owned by the state. Moreover, it may not be economical for foreign firms to keep stock for resale at local ports as the charges for storage, communication, and handling may be lower at the entrepôt due to economies of scale and economies of agglomeration.

Though this theory of intermediation can be readily applied to entrepôt trade, it does not explain why the foreign firm buys the goods for resale instead of offering intermediation directly through a service contract. It is quite common for trading firms to bear the risk of purchasing the goods for resale. There are at least three reasons for this. First, a trading firm usually has better market information than the producer and is in a better position to bear risks. Second, buying the goods for resale also protects the market information of the trading firm, because there is always the danger that the producer and importer can get together to cut out the middleman. Protection of market information does not imply, however, that the trading firm is exploiting its customers through its monopoly of information. It only implies that information is costly to acquire and protection is needed to maintain a competitive edge. Third, as Yamamura (1976:263–4) pointed out in his analysis of Japanese trading companies, a trading firm can reduce risks in a number of ways. It can reduce the risk of fluctuations in demand by trading in many commodities; it can also reduce the risk of fluctuations in exchange rates by dealing both in importing and exporting, thus reducing transactions across currencies to a fraction of total import and export business.

In addition to the above considerations, packaging and processing costs may be important in processed re-exports. Processed re-exports can be regarded as a special form of intra-industry trade, where the processes are confined to those that do not confer country-of-origin status. In addition to the theory of pure re-exports, standard trade theory and the theory of intra-industry trade can be used to explain processed re-exports.

Historical and cultural factors

Although the presence of trading companies and entrepôt trade can be explained by economic factors alone, historical and cultural factors also play an important role. In the West, cultural and geographical proximity combine to lower the transaction costs of international trade among Western trading partners, and indirect trade becomes the exception rather than the rule. Furthermore, the historical growth of Western countries has permitted the natural accumulation of skills and development of institutions for international trade. Countries in the Far East lacked the necessary institutions and skills for international trade at the time of first contact with the West. Transaction costs in international trade were extremely high and general trading companies emerged in Japan to bridge the gap. European merchant houses in Hong Kong and Singapore were similarly established for these reasons. Due to the economies of scale in the provision of trading services, trading firms tend to thrive once they become established. In Japan, general trading companies handle over half of Japan's international trade (Yamamura 1976:161). Similarly, the economies of agglomeration imply that once a city acquires a comparative advantage in trade or in entrepôt trade, that advantage will persist.

The significance of monopoly power

The rise of trading companies and entrepôts has sometimes been attributed to trade monopolies, which may be artificial, as in the case of the East India Company, or natural, as in the case of a deep-water port in a strategic location. However, the 'monopoly power' explanation of entrepôt trade is at odds with history. In fact, successful trading companies or entrepôts usually emerge when monopolies are broken.

Both Singapore and Hong Kong are renowned for their free-trade policy. McClellan (1971) emphasizes that Singapore grew because its free-trade policy broke the Dutch monopoly in the Malaysian archipelago. In Dutch trading centres, local traders of Straits produce had to pay heavy port taxes and deal with one buyer. Import prices were fixed and goods had to be carried on Dutch company boats. Dutch company officials even enforced controls on local production; they went out into the countryside and destroyed clove trees in order to restrict the supply of cloves. It is not surprising that local traders bypassed Dutch ports to trade in the tax-free port of Singapore where there were a large number of buyers.

Hong Kong also rose to prominence when independent opium traders tried to break the monopoly of the East India Company in the opium trade with China. Yamamura (1976:167) describes in detail how Japanese trading companies rose to break the monopoly of Western merchant houses in Japanese port cities. The rapid growth of free ports and stagnation of monopolistic trading centres is hardly surprising; economists since Adam Smith have not been impressed by the dynamism of monopolies.

In addition to artificial barriers to entry, the significance of natural factors such as a deep-water port and a strategic location have often been over-emphasized. With modern technology, it is not difficult to create a good port in a less-than-ideal environment. McClellan (1971) argues that, even in the nineteenth century, the free-port policy of Singapore was more decisive than its location. The Rhio Islands and the Dutch trading ports along the coast of Sumatra were just as strategically located as Singapore in relation to China trade. Furthermore, China trade was only important in Singapore for a few decades. The establishment of Hong Kong and the opening up of China's treaty ports in 1842 meant a loss of China trade for Singapore. The exchange of Straits produce for European and Indian goods came to dominate Singapore's trade, and

Singapore was certainly not a central location for distribution to and collection from the Archipelago. During the nineteenth century, Singapore

traders were quite worried about competition from other potential entrepôts in the region — particularly Kuching, Labuan, and Macassar.
However, these threats were never fully realized . . . The Bugis traders came
all the way from Moluccas and Celebes, bypassing Macassar as long as it
remained a protected port, to trade in Singapore. The economic policy of a
free port was far more important to the establishment of Singapore as an
entrepôt than its geographic location (McClellan 1971:180–1).

As for China trade, Hong Kong is less strategically situated than
Shanghai, but Hong Kong now surpasses Shanghai in its amount of
trade with China. This again confirms that location is not as decisive
as economic efficiency in the provision of trading services.

The observation that location is often not a decisive factor is
consistent with the theory of entrepôt trade. Location is closely
related to transportation costs, which explains trans-shipment rather
than entrepôt trade advantages. The free-port policy of Hong Kong
and Singapore has conferred upon these entrepôts an initial advantage that continues to grow due to economies of scale and economies
of agglomeration in the provision of trading services. Once a trading
centre grows, it can gain a decisive advantage, even if its location is
less than ideal.

The effect of distortion

In addition to economic efficiency in the provision of entrepôt
services, entrepôt trade can also be accounted for by distortions, both
internal and external. External distortions refer to barriers to direct
international trade and investment, including the absence of political
and commercial relations, restrictions in visits of foreign nationals
from unfriendly countries, quotas, tariffs and foreign exchange controls. Internal distortions refer to the rigidities of the domestic
economy that hamper international trade. Distortions generally increase the fixed costs of transactions, thus enhancing the demand for
intermediation and entrepôt services. Some distortions generate
asymmetric transaction costs that tend to favour entrepôt traders.
These distortions further enhance the demand for entrepôt services.

External distortions

Barriers to direct foreign investment in the trade sector are common
in many developing countries, and they undoubtedly promote entrepôt trade. Many countries used to trade indirectly with China

through Hong Kong because of the absence of political and commercial relations. As China gradually gained international recognition in the 1970s, the United States, Thailand, the Philippines, India and Indonesia established or re-established direct commercial links with China, and at present, only four economies (Taiwan, South Korea, South Africa, and Israel) do not officially trade with China directly. However, it is possible to ship goods directly between China and South Korea, though payment has to be arranged in Hong Kong due to the lack of official political and commercial links (*Hong Kong Economic Journal* 15 Mar. 1988). Such direct shipments have increased rapidly since 1987, but they are still officially classified as indirect trade. Though Taiwan outlaws direct trade with China, the value of illegal direct trade was reported to be over US$100 million in 1987 (*Wen Hui Pao* 8 Oct. 1988).

Trade controls, including quotas, tariffs and foreign exchange controls, generally raise the fixed costs of transactions in trade, and the demand for intermediation and entrepôt services is thereby increased. Entrepôt trade can also be a means (legal or illegal) of evading controls. Entrepôt trade, for example, has been a means of quota and tariff evasion, but importing countries have tightened controls through country-of-origin rules, and the loopholes are now of diminishing importance. However, trade controls can be evaded illegally through entrepôt trade: the rampant smuggling and barter trade between Singapore and Indonesia is an obvious example. Traders in Hong Kong revealed, in interviews with the author, that Indonesian tariffs have abetted Hong Kong re-exports to Indonesia, partly because Hong Kong traders have the connections to evade Indonesian tariffs using bribery. Indonesian tariffs appear to be particularly important in Hong Kong's re-exports of Chinese goods to Indonesia because Chinese state export corporations have little incentive to understate the value of exports to evade tariffs.

Foreign exchange control makes it difficult to trade and raises both the fixed and variable costs of a transaction. In itself, foreign exchange control does not generate asymmetries in transaction costs. However, given the cultural, geographical and political proximity of Hong Kong, it is not surprising that Hong Kong traders find it easier to get around foreign exchange controls by using the thriving black market in Hong Kong and Southern China.

Foreign exchange control encourages counter trade, as in the case of the Indonesia–Singapore barter trade. Counter trade increases the cost of transactions and the demand for intermediation. Foreign firms left with Chinese merchandise in counter-trade deals with China often enlist the service of trading firms to sell such merchandise. Hong Kong companies have arranged counter-trade agreements between China and other countries.

Internal distortions

Internal distortions are particularly important in trade with China because of the many rigidities that hamper trade in China's command economy. The internal distortions that are particularly relevant to Hong Kong's entrepôt trade include: (i) bureaucratic favouritism; and (ii) a seller's market syndrome. Some of these distortions generate asymmetric costs in transactions favouring Hong Kong and enhance the entrepôt position of Hong Kong.

(i) Bureaucratic favouritism

Bureaucratic favouritism for Hong Kong operates through export quotas, nepotism and corruption. In the past, central planners set export quotas for different commodities and different markets, and the treatment of Hong Kong was usually generous. Hong Kong traders often have surplus Chinese merchandise that is in great demand in China and on the world market. The Chinese have officially explained this favouritism as their support for 'Hong Kong compatriots'. However, other factors may also play a part, including the Chinese predilection for durable trade relationships, and the political influence of Chinese corporations in Hong Kong. Pro-Chinese Hong Kong merchants have long promoted Chinese exports, even in the days of the Korean War when the Chinese connection was a risk instead of a premium. These firms have economic and political influence.

In recent years, when decentralization has been the order of the day, some of the power of foreign trade has passed from central to provincial and lower echelon officials. Unlike the central planners who prefer political loyalty and a durable trade relationship, many lower officials prefer quick money and are willing to participate in nepotism and bribery. In Hong Kong, the influence of the old-time pro-China merchants has waned, and there is a rise in the influence of a new group of small traders prepared to bribe and speculate. Decentralization under irrational prices provides many opportunities for corruption and profiteering, and also makes it more difficult for central authorities to supervise and prevent nepotism and corruption.

Nepotism and bribery generate asymmetric transaction costs: the costs of insiders are lower than those of outsiders. Insiders include the many former cadres who have emigrated to Hong Kong and have good connections in China. They also include the many branch officers and trade representatives of Chinese enterprises in Hong Kong, as well as the sophisticated Hong Kong traders who know about the intricacies of China trade and are prepared to present gifts of television sets or automobiles to appropriate officials. Not surprisingly, many Chinese products have circumvented the control of the Chinese quota system and have been exported to Hong Kong illegally.

(ii) Seller's market syndrome

It is well documented that sellers' markets tend to prevail in command economies. In a seller's market, firms have very little incentive to market and promote their product. There is a lack of marketing services and firms are ill-equipped to compete in the international market. The seller's market syndrome increases both the fixed and variable costs of transactions, largely in a symmetrical way. However, given bureaucratic favouritism and the proximity of Hong Kong, Hong Kong traders have found it easier to deal with the syndrome than other traders, thus increasing the demand for Hong Kong middlemen.

The seller's market syndrome is manifested in many ways, including lack of attractive packaging, unwillingness to sort and pack consumer items to suit consumer demand, unwillingness to take small orders, erratic delivery schedules and poor quality control. The lack of marketing services is manifested in international trade as a lack of supporting services.

Packaging is not a particularly capital- or skill-intensive activity, and the considerable activity in re-packaging Chinese goods in Hong Kong for re-export reveals the seller's market mentality of Chinese firms. A good example of re-exports arising out of sorting is the labour-intensive sorting of Christmas decorations into variety packages. In terms of labour costs, such operations are more economically undertaken in China. Chinese firms may lack the knowledge of international markets to sort and package correctly, but Hong Kong firms can provide such information and allow the sorting to be done more economically in China. This is happening on an increasing scale with rising Hong Kong investment in China. China has recently imported modern packaging machinery to remedy its past negligence. In the long run, packaging and sorting will not contribute to Hong Kong re-exports.

Chinese firms are unwilling to take small orders; this enhances entrepôt trade in Hong Kong. Hong Kong traders take small orders from overseas buyers and aggregate them into bulk orders for Chinese firms. There are some signs that Chinese firms are becoming more flexible, and this distortion may become less important in time.

Because of erratic delivery schedules, merchants in Hong Kong keep stocks of Chinese merchandise for overseas buyers. To keep stock, traders have to re-export instead of trans-ship because they have to take legal possession of the product for storage in Hong Kong.

Quality control sometimes also induces Hong Kong traders to re-export instead of trans-ship, because the Hong Kong trader can examine the quality of the goods in Hong Kong for re-export, whereas he has no power to inspect trans-shipment goods in Hong Kong. However, with the opening up of China, it is now easier for the Hong Kong trader to inspect the goods at the factory gate. For Hong Kong investors who invest money in export industries in China, quality control is less of a problem. Quality control is no longer an important incentive for re-export.

It is interesting to note that the problem of delivery schedules sometimes induces Hong Kong traders to trans-ship Chinese exports through Hong Kong instead of Japan. Exports from northern or central China to the United States should logically be trans-shipped via Japan instead of Hong Kong. Chinese shipping companies handle such trans-shipment, and the goods may sit on Japanese piers for a long time before being loaded into containers bound for the United States. Chinese shipping companies can only quote a lengthy period during which the goods will be loaded in Japan; they cannot specify an exact date (another sign of the seller's market syndrome). Thus Hong Kong traders cannot notify US importers of the exact arrival date of shipment. Trans-shipping the goods through Hong Kong has the advantage that Hong Kong traders can call Chinese shipping companies in Hong Kong on the date of loading, and thus notify US importers about the date of arrival. When delays occur, Hong Kong traders can convert the trans-shipment into re-export, that is, take legal possession of the goods in Hong Kong, and re-export the goods to the United States through other shipping companies.

The lack of export-supporting services also enhances the entrepôt position of Hong Kong. In the early 1970s, many foreign banks could not finance imports from China directly because they had no connection with the Bank of China, and the financial arrangements were handled through Hong Kong. Nowadays, most large foreign banks can finance imports from China directly, and the financing factor is no longer significant.

The significance of distortions

Internal and external distortions are important for entrepôt trade, but their importance should not be over-emphasized. Though some distortions favour intermediation and entrepôt trade, there are many distortions that are unfavourable to entrepôt trade. Import-substitution policies, for example, are unfavourable to the growth of trade and entrepôt trade. Many developing countries do not allow market forces to determine trading channels, but pursue nationalistic policies to cut out the foreign middleman. In the case of China, few firms have complete freedom in the choice of trading agencies and channels. Like monopoly power, distortion is inefficient and is unlikely to be a source of dynamism and growth for trade. The entrepôt trade of Hong Kong has grown tremendously in recent years, despite the general decline in the importance of external and internal distortions in China's trade. The widening international political recognition of China and the increase in direct trade links since the 1970s have caused a decline in external distortion. The gradual liberalization of China's domestic economy and external trade means fewer rigidities and controls and a decline in both internal and external distortions. The thriving entrepôt trade of Hong Kong in recent years confirms that economic efficiency is the fundamental factor in the determination of entrepôt trade.

Singapore and China trade

Though the focus of this book is on Hong Kong, Singapore's case will be briefly discussed because Singapore is a major entrepôt with a stake in China's trade. Singapore lost its trade with China to Hong Kong after the opening of Hong Kong in 1840. Since the introduction of China's open-door policy, Singapore has tried to play a more important role in China's trade, but to little avail.

Singapore refuses to release statistics on re-exports by country of origin, and it is thus difficult to gauge the magnitude of Singapore's re-exports of Chinese goods. However, as shown in Table 7.2, Singapore's imports from China are only a small share of Chinese exports. Before 1980, food and textiles accounted for approximately half of the imports from China, and the greater portion of Chinese imports was believed to be for local consumption, as Singapore has a large Chinese population (Ng 1971:175). Singapore's re-export of Chinese goods is judged not to be significant (Ng 1971:177). The jump in imports to Singapore from China in 1984–85 was due to a surge in oil imports; non-oil imports actually declined. There can be no suggestion that Singapore re-exports Chinese oil, because oil is mostly traded directly (due to its homogeneity) and also because oil exports are handled centrally by state trading corporations in China. It is logical to conclude that Chinese oil is imported into Singapore (an oil-refining centre) for refining instead of for re-export. Non-oil imports into Singapore may be re-exported, but such imports have declined relative to China's exports from 1970, and declined absolutely in 1988. Furthermore, Hong Kong's re-exports of Chinese goods to Singapore increased during the period 1970–89 relative to Singapore's imports of non-oil products from China, indicating that Singapore is more and more dependent on Hong Kong for imports of non-oil products from China. In fact, Singapore dealers of Chinese merchandise sent a delegation to Beijing in 1983 to complain that their positions were threatened by Hong Kong traders (Yuan 1985a:81).

Singapore's re-exports to China declined absolutely from 1980 to 1985, largely as a result of a decline in rubber exports (Table 7.3). Though Singapore's re-exports increased from 1986 onwards, their shares in China's imports were small and the shares declined from 1980 to 1986.

Singapore permitted a trade mission to go to Peking in October 1971, the first since 1956. Singapore concluded a trade pact with China in December 1979 (Lu 1983:347–8) in order to take advantage of China's open-door policy. However, in the realm of entrepôt trade, Singapore's efforts with China have been a failure.

China's dependence on the entrepôt of Hong Kong

Table 7.4 shows China's indirect trade through Hong Kong with all countries, all non-Communist countries and all non-Communist countries except Japan. Hong Kong's share of imported Chinese goods for re-export to other countries relative to China's total exports (excluding direct exports to Hong Kong) has increased rapidly since 1975, rising from 5 per cent in 1975 to 41 per cent in 1989. Because China's trade with Communist countries was handled directly, the ratio of indirect exports to total exports was higher for China's trade with non-Communist countries, rising from 6 per cent in 1975 to 45 per cent in 1989. Since Japan has a long history of trade with China, and is China's foremost trade partner, most of Japan's trade is handled directly. The ratio of indirect to direct exports was even higher for China's trade with non-Communist countries excluding Japan, and this ratio rose from 8 per cent in 1975 to 51 per cent in 1989. The increase in the ratios of indirect to total imports (excluding direct imports from Hong Kong) after 1975 was even more dramatic. For China's trade with all countries, with all non-Communist countries and with all non-Communist countries except Japan, the ratios

Table 7.2 *Singapore's imports from China*

Year	Direct imports			Indirect imports: Hong Kong's imports of Chinese goods re-exported to Singapore	
	Total (US$m)	Oil (US$m)	Non-oil (US$m)	Amount (US$m)	% of Singapore's 'non-oil imports'
1956	33.5	0	33.5	—	
	(2.0)ᵃ	(0.0)	(2.0)		
1960	45.7	0	45.7	—	
	(2.3)	(0.0)	(2.3)	—	
1965	73.3	0	73.3		
	(3.6)	(0.0)	(3.6)		
1970	126	0	126	17	13.5
	(5.8)	(0.0)	(5.8)		
1975	287	0	287	42	14.5
	(4.0)	(0.0)	(4.6)		
1977	275	0	275	50	18.3
	(3.4)	(0.0)	(3.8)		
1980	622	67	555	102	18.4
	(3.3)	(1.6)	(3.8)		
1981	772	115	656	124	19.0
	(3.6)	(2.6)	(3.9)		
1982	879	230	649	133	20.4
	(3.9)	(4.7)	(3.7)		
1983	827	187	639	138	21.6
	(3.7)	(4.3)	(3.6)		
1984	1,351	732	618	128	20.7
	(5.2)	(13.0)	(3.0)		
1985	2,260	1,755	505	133	26.4
	(8.3)	(26.1)	(2.4)		
1986	1,431	809	622	173	27.7
	(4.6)	(25.6)	(2.2)		
1987	1,416	655	761	224	29.4
	(3.6)	(16.4)	(2.1)		
1988	1,683	699	984	357	36.3
	(3.5)	(20.7)	(2.2)		
1989	1,698	599	1,099	429	43.6
	(3.2)	(16.7)	(2.2)		

ᵃ Figures in brackets represent percentage share of China's exports.
Sources: Singapore data: 1956–77, *Singapore External Trade Statistics*; 1980 and after, *Singapore Trade Statistics*.
Chinese data: 1956–81, United States Central Intelligence Agency, National Foreign Assessment Centre, *China: International Trade*, various issues; 1982 and after, *Chinese Customs Statistics*.
Hong Kong data: Census and Statistics Department, Hong Kong.

Table 7.3 *Singapore's re-exports to China* (US$m)

Year	Total	Rubber
1980	166.3	99.0
	(0.9)[a]	(27.8)
1981	120.7	42.6
	(0.7)	(21.5)
1982	182.7	48.6
	(0.9)	(27.0)
1983	149.5	78.5
	(0.7)	(29.0)
1984	145.8	64.2
	(0.5)	(20.6)
1985	146.4	35.5
	(0.4)	(17.1)
1986	177.3	39.8
	(0.4)	(14.9)
1987	232.2	58.7
	(0.5)	(15.0)
1988	507.2	151.1
	(0.9)	(25.6)
1989	409.2	147.2
	(0.7)	(30.6)

[a] Figures in brackets represent percentage share of China's imports.
Sources: Singapore data: *Singapore Trade Statistics*; Chinese data: 1956–81, United States Central Intelligence Agency, National Foreign Assessment Centre, *China: International Trade*, various issues; 1982 and after, *Chinese Customs Statistics*.

in 1977 were 0.58 per cent, 0.64 per cent and 0.87 per cent respectively, and the corresponding ratios in 1989 were 23 per cent, 25 per cent and 24 per cent. China's dependence on the entrepôt of Hong Kong is substantial and growing. In 1989, the ratio of indirect exports to total exports was roughly 40 per cent to over one-half, depending on the choice of country group, and the corresponding ratio of indirect imports to total imports was roughly one-quarter.

The sharp rise in China's indirect trade with Taiwan and South Korea in recent years is not the main reason for the thriving China trade handled through Hong Kong. Table 7.5 shows the share of Taiwan and South Korea in Hong Kong's entrepôt trade with China. (China's indirect trade with Israel and South Africa, two other countries with no official trade links with China, is negligible, and is excluded from the table.)

The share of Taiwan in Hong Kong's re-export of Chinese goods declined sharply in the period 1977–86 because Taiwan's purchases from China were confined to items unavailable elsewhere (e.g. Chinese herbal medicine). Though Taiwan liberalized its imports from

Table 7.4 *China's direct trade through Hong Kong* (US$m)

Year		With all countries[a]			With non-Communist countries[a] excepting Japan	
		Exports	Imports		Exports	Imports
1966		94	9		—	—
	(i)	(4.8)	(0.45)			
	(ii)	(6.8)	(0.56)			
1970		97	6		84	—
	(i)	(5.1)	(0.29)	(iii)	(7.8)	
	(ii)	(7.3)	(0.32)			
1975		300	28		277	—
	(i)	(4.9)	(0.41)	(iii)	(8.1)	
	(ii)	(6.2)	(0.44)			
1979		962	263		842	191
	(i)	(8.3)	(1.7)	(iii)	(11.9)	(2.3)
	(ii)	(9.6)	(2.2)			
1981		1,907	1,386		1,735	1,124
	(i)	(10.2)	(6.5)	(iii)	(13.4)	(10.7)
	(ii)	(11.0)	(6.9)			
1983		2,185	1,539		2,055	1,076
	(i)	(11.8)	(7.5)	(iii)	(16.0)	(10.1)
	(ii)	(12.5)	(8.2)			
1984		2,826	3,320		2,594	2,107
	(i)	(12.9)	(12.9)	(iii)	(17.8)	(15.0)
	(ii)	(14.0)	(13.5)			
1985		3,434	5,512		3,128	3,645
	(i)	(14.8)	(13.8)	(iii)	(20.8)	(19.1)
	(ii)	(16.5)	(14.9)			
1986		5,161	4,700		4,804	3,557
	(i)	(20.1)	(11.7)	(iii)	(27.1)	(14.7)
	(ii)	(22.8)	(13.0)			
1987		8,511	7,716		7,893	6,058
	(i)	(25.0)	(19.5)	(iii)	(32.3)	(23.4)
	(ii)	(27.7)	(21.4)			
1988		13,350	11,013		12,125	8,045
	(i)	(32.3)	(22.4)	(iii)	(42.2)	(25.9)
	(ii)	(35.1)	(24.4)			
1989		19,201	11,721		17,568	8,713
	(i)	(41.3)	(22.5)	(iii)	(51.3)	(23.5)
	(ii)	(45.0)	(24.6)			

[a] Excluding Hong Kong and China. China's indirect exports (imports) are taken to be Hong Kong's imports from China for re-export to other countries (Hong Kong's re-exports from other countries to China).
(i) Percentage share of China's exports (imports) to (from) all countries.
(ii) Percentage share of China's exports (imports) to (from) all non-Communist countries. (Note that China's indirect trade through Hong Kong is directed almost exclusively to non-Communist countries.)
(iii) Percentage share of China's exports (imports) to (from) all non-Communist countries excepting Japan.
China's exports and imports referred to in (i), (ii) and (iii) exclude China's direct trade with Hong Kong but include China's indirect trade with other countries through Hong Kong.
Sources: Indirect trade data: *Review of Overseas Trade*, various issues; Direct trade data: *Chinese Customs Statistics*.

Table 7.5 *Share of Taiwan and South Korea in Hong Kong's entrepôt trade with China*

	Share in Hong Kong's re-exports of Chinese goods			Share in Hong Kong's re-exports to China			Share in Hong Kong's entrepôt trade with China		
	Taiwan	S. Korea	Total	Taiwan	S. Korea	Total	Taiwan	S. Korea	Total
1977	5.7	0.7	6.4	—	—	—	5.4	0.6	6.0
1979	4.9	1.8	6.7	8.1	2.2	10.3	5.5	1.9	7.4
1981	3.3	3.2	6.5	27.1	10.1	37.2	12.5	5.9	18.4
1983	3.5	4.3	7.8	10.1	2.7	12.8	6.0	3.7	9.7
1984	3.6	5.1	8.7	11.9	4.5	16.4	7.7	4.8	12.5
1985	2.6	5.6	8.2	16.7	6.0	22.7	10.7	5.8	16.5
1986	2.2	5.7	7.9	15.5	5.3	20.7	8.1	5.5	13.6
1987	2.7	6.0	8.7	15.9	10.3	26.2	8.2	6.4	14.6
1988	2.8	5.0	7.8	18.4	10.1	28.5	9.4	7.1	16.5
1989	2.4	3.8	6.2	21.8	7.5	29.3	9.3	5.1	14.4

Source: Review of Overseas Trade, various issues.

China in 1987–88, the rise in the share of Taiwan in Hong Kong's re-export of Chinese goods was quite slow from 1986 to 1988. In 1989, Taiwan's share fell as a result of the Tiananmen incident and economic retrenchment in China. In addition to these factors, the opening of unofficial direct trade between China and South Korea led to a sharp fall in the South Korea share. The total share of Taiwan and South Korea fell to 6 per cent in 1989, a figure too low to account for the sharp rise in Hong Kong's re-exports of Chinese goods.

The share of Taiwan and South Korea in China's indirect imports was more substantial. The Taiwanese share soared in 1980 after China tried to attract Taiwan by abolishing all tariffs on Taiwanese products, on the grounds that Taiwan is part of China. (Tariffs are still levied on Hong Kong products although China also claims sovereignty over Hong Kong.) The sudden surge of orders overwhelmed production capacity in Taiwan. Defective and low quality products were exported to China to fill orders (Long 1982:32), with the result that Taiwan's exports to China decreased in 1983. However, the surge in China's imports in 1985 led to another sharp increase in imports from Taiwan. In 1986, however, Taiwan's share in Hong Kong re-exports to China declined as China tightened controls on imports of consumer goods, Taiwan's main export to China. Taiwan's liberalization of trade with China in 1988 led to another sharp rise in the Taiwanese share.

The share of Taiwan and South Korea in Hong Kong's re-exports to China have been substantial but volatile. From 1977 to 1988, 29 per cent of the increase in Hong Kong's re-exports to China was supplied by Taiwan and South Korea.

The market and commodity composition of China's indirect trade

Tables 7.6 and 7.7 show Chinese exports to and imports from China's major trading partners. Communist countries are excluded because their trade is handled directly. Given that fixed costs in transactions are the basic reason for intermediation, countries with a long history of trading with China might find it worthwhile to pay the fixed cost of establishing trade links, and be less dependent on Hong Kong. In terms of Chinese exports, this is indeed the case. Japan and Europe have long histories of trade with China; their ratios of indirect to direct imports from China are much lower than those of the new traders (the United States, Canada, Indonesia and Saudi Arabia). Singapore has a long history of trade with China, but restricted the travel of its citizens to China for political reasons and only concluded a trade pact with China in December 1979. Singapore is thus treated like a new entrant and its dependence on Hong Kong for Chinese exports is high. Australia also has a long history of trade with China. Its dependence on Hong Kong for Chinese imports was low in 1970, on a level comparable with Japan. However, Australia's dependence on Hong Kong has grown rapidly, and by 1985, its level of dependence was comparable to that of the new entrants. This appears to indicate Australia's failure to develop carefully its historical trading relationship with China.

In the case of Chinese imports, Singapore and Indonesia confirm the expectation of greater dependency of new entrants on Hong Kong, but the dependence of the United States on Hong Kong for exports to China is low. This is because agricultural products constitute a substantial portion of United States exports to China, and trade in agricultural products is usually handled directly due to its homogeneity. In addition, there is also a long history of direct state involvement in agricultural trade.

A decrease in dependency on Hong Kong over time might be expected with political recognition of China and the conclusion of trade pacts. The decentralization of China's trading system in 1979, however, increased dependency on Hong Kong, and this pattern fits the theory. The dependence of Canada and the United States on Hong Kong for Chinese exports decreased in the early 1970s as each established political and commercial links with China. Indonesia established direct commercial relations with China in the late 1970s and its dependence on Hong Kong for both Chinese exports and imports declined in the 1980s. South Korea established direct commercial links with China in 1986 and its dependence on Hong Kong for China's trade also declined.

The dependence of all countries, except Singapore and Indonesia, (in Table 7.6) on Hong Kong for China's exports increased in 1985. This confirms the importance of the impact of the 1984 trade decentralization. The case of Singapore is not really an exception, as it is caused by an increase of direct exports of Chinese oil. Singapore's dependence on Hong Kong in non-oil imports from China has actually increased since 1980, as noted previously (Table 7.2). The exception of Indonesia is probably due to its recent establishment of direct commercial links with China. Dependence of all countries, except Indonesia and South Korea (Table 7.6), on Hong Kong for China's exports increased significantly in 1988, again confirming the impact of the 1988 trade decentralization.

All countries listed in Table 7.7, except Indonesia and South Korea, have become more dependent on Hong Kong for their exports to China since 1979. In fact, re-exports to China were insignificant before 1979. This again confirms the crucial impact of the 1979 decentralization of China's foreign trade system, and later the 1988 trade decentralization.

The commodity composition of China's indirect exports and imports through Hong Kong are shown in Tables 7.8 and 7.9 respectively. As the theory predicts, manufactures form the bulk of entrepôt trade. The share of manufactures in Hong Kong's imports from China for re-export has risen from 66 to 89 per cent in the period 1970–89, and the share of manufactures in Hong Kong's re-exports to China has risen from 76 to over 80 per cent in the 1980s. Hong Kong's imports from China for re-export were dominated by textiles (textile fabric, textile fibre and clothing) with a share of 46–47 per cent in the period 1984–86. Textiles were also important in re-exports to China. The share of textile fabrics (65) in re-exports to China was 40 per cent in 1981, declining to 25 per cent in 1987. The Chinese priority given to imports of machinery has meant that machinery is dominant in re-exports to China (the share of machinery in 1985 was 44 per cent).

China's dependence on Hong Kong is significant and increasing in many important commodities. In 1987, the ratio of indirect to total exports (excluding China's direct exports to Hong Kong) was over 30 per cent for clothing, over 31 per cent for textile fabrics, over 49 per cent for machinery, and over 28 per cent for manufactures as a whole. The ratio of indirect to total imports (excluding direct imports from Hong Kong) was over 72 per cent for textile fabrics, and 32 per cent for electrical machinery.

For China's exports, Hong Kong's share is high in commodities with a high growth potential, namely manufactures, especially textiles. Hong Kong's share is low in oil, which has a low growth potential due to supply bottlenecks and increasing domestic demand. The share of Hong Kong in Chinese exports is thus likely to continue to increase.

For China's imports, Hong Kong's share is high in electrical machinery, which is granted top priority on the import list. The share of Hong Kong in China's imports is thus likely to remain substantial.

There are at least two reasons for the dominance of textiles in China's trade via Hong Kong. Hong Kong is a big exporter of textiles and is experienced in both marketing and locating supplies of textiles. Hong Kong manufacturers have invested in textile industries in China, Macau and Southeast Asia. They import Chinese yarn and fabric in bulk, distributing these to their subsidiaries in Southeast Asia, or import yarn and fabric from non-Chinese sources, and distribute these to subsidiaries in China. As can be seen from Table 2.8, Hong Kong re-export of Chinese goods to China increased rapidly from 1982 to 1989 and over 70 per cent of these were textile

Table 7.6 *China's exports, direct and indirect (via Hong Kong), by destination (US$m)*

		1970	1975	1979	1983	1984	1985	1986	1987	1988	1989
Japan	(i)	224	1403	2,764	4,544	5,326	6,079	4,729	6,401	7,922	8,362
	(ii)	15	23	120	129	232	315	357	618	1,224	1,633
	(iii)	(5.5)	(1.6)	(4.2)	(2.8)	(4.2)	(4.9)	(7.0)	(8.8)	(13.4)	(16.3)
USA	(i)	—	129	595	1,732	2,397	2,340	2,617	3,037	3,380	4,391
	(ii)	0.28	24	125	640	955	1,228	2,033	3,024	4,708	7,192
	(iii)	(100)	(15.7)	(17.4)	(27.0)	(28.5)	(34.4)	(43.7)	(49.9)	(58.2)	(62.1)
Singapore	(i)	101	238	296	570	1,294	2,061	1,206	1,326	1,485	1,693
	(ii)	17	42	85	138	128	133	173	224	304	364
	(iii)	(14.4)	(15.0)	(22.3)	(19.5)	(9.0)	(6.1)	(12.5)	(14.5)	(17.0)	(17.7)
West Germany	(i)	69	220	459	864	800	745	1,010	1,225	1,485	1,609
	(ii)	—	6	32	46	76	121	209	478	811	1,273
	(iii)	—	(2.7)	(6.5)	(5.1)	(8.7)	(14.0)	(17.1)	(28.1)	(35.3)	(44.2)
UK	(i)	104	242	479	605	345	358	1,424	532	659	635
	(ii)	—	—	14	37	52	73	133	315	554	853
	(iii)	—	—	(2.8)	(5.8)	(13.1)	(16.9)	(8.5)	(37.2)	(45.7)	(57.3)
Canada	(i)	20	82	145	209	264	233	302	409	389	412
	(ii)	3	6	15	54	73	94	130	230	356	542
	(iii)	(13.0)	(6.8)	(9.4)	(20.5)	(21.7)	(28.7)	(30.1)	(36.0)	(47.8)	(57.0)
Australia	(i)	32	70	156	182	228	184	208	298	362	423
	(ii)	2	9	25	55	85	79	119	207	332	487
	(iii)	(5.9)	(11.4)	(13.8)	(23.2)	(27.2)	(30.0)	(36.4)	(41.0)	(47.8)	(53.5)

(i)   China's direct exports.
(ii) China's indirect exports via Hong Kong (taken to be Hong Kong imports from China for re-exports).
(iii) Percentage share of indirect exports in total (direct and indirect) exports.

Table 7.6 *continued*

		1970	1975	1979	1983	1984	1985	1986	1987	1988	1989
Indonesia	(i)	14	—	0.02	49	72	124	140	188	236	223
	(ii)	—	48	116	190	166	140	196	200	234	264
	(iii)	(100)	(100)	(100)	(79.5)	(69.7)	(53.0)	(58.3)	(51.5)	(49.8)	(54.2)
Saudi Arabia	(i)	1.1	3.9	68	150	138	133	133	247	230	249
	(ii)	—	—	—	94	82	93	110	165	192	232
	(iii)				(38.5)	(37.3)	(41.2)	(45.3)	(40.0)	(45.5)	(48.2)
South Korea	(i)	—	—	—	—	—	—	238	217	406	806
	(ii)	—	—	18	98	157	212	320	553	714	772
	(iii)			(100)	(100)	(100)	(100)	(57.3)	(71.8)	(63.8)	(51.1)
Taiwan[a]	(i)	—	—	—	—	—	—	—	—	—	—
	(ii)	—	—	—	115	230	99	122	240	407	497
	(iii)				(100)	(100)	(100)	(100)	(100)	(100)	(100)
All countries[b]	(i)	1,790	5,881	10,620	16,338	19,008	19,782	20,480	24,661	28,134	27,272
	(ii)	97	300	962	2,185	2,826	3,434	5,161	8,511	13,350	19,201
	(iii)	(5.1)	(4.9)	(8.3)	(11.8)	(12.9)	(14.8)	(20.1)	(25.7)	(32.2)	(41.3)

[a] China has unofficial direct trade with Taiwan. However, the value of this trade is difficult to estimate.
[b] Excluding Hong Kong and China.

(i) China's direct exports.
(ii) China's indirect exports via Hong Kong (taken to be Hong Kong imports from China for re-exports).
(iii) Percentage share of indirect exports in total (direct and indirect) exports.

Sources: Indirect trade data: Census and Statistics Department, Hong Kong; Direct trade data: 1970–79, *Almanac of China's Foreign Economic Relations and Trade*, 1984; 1981 and after, *Chinese Customs Statistics*.

Table 7.7 China's imports, direct and indirect (via Hong Kong), by country of origin (US$m)

		1979	1981	1983	1984	1985	1986	1987	1988	1989
Japan	(i)	3,944	6,292	5,530	8,578	14,395	12,424	10,100	11,057	10,535
	(ii)	72	262	463	1,213	1,867	1,143	1,658	2,968	3,008
	(iii)	(1.8)	(4.0)	(7.7)	(12.4)	(11.5)	(8.4)	(14.1)	(21.2)	(22.2)
USA	(i)	1,857	4,757	2,770	4,052	4,792	4,648	4,818	6,631	7,863
	(ii)	26	101	201	375	575	567	792	1,228	1,316
	(iii)	(1.4)	(2.1)	(6.8)	(8.5)	(10.7)	(10.9)	(14.1)	(15.6)	(14.3)
West Germany	(i)	1,739	1,366	1,216	1,312	2,346	3,606	3,148	3,434	3,379
	(ii)	8.4	21	44	75	137	133	173	288	330
	(iii)	(0.5)	(1.5)	(3.5)	(5.4)	(5.5)	(3.6)	(5.2)	(7.7)	(8.9)
UK	(i)	501	238	563	520	713	1,013	901	898	1,084
	(ii)	9.2	19	26	51	120	118	156	207	249
	(iii)	(1.8)	(7.4)	(4.4)	(8.8)	(14.4)	(10.4)	(14.8)	(18.7)	(18.7)
France	(i)	406	404	640	371	683	736	900	987	1,420
	(ii)	—	13	25	53	73	58	71	125	118
	(iii)	—	(3.0)	(3.7)	(12.5)	(9.6)	(7.3)	(7.3)	(11.2)	(7.7)
Italy	(i)	309	351	305	465	859	1,137	1,237	1,549	1,835
	(ii)	—	10	14	39	98	81	96	155	197
	(iii)	—	(2.8)	(4.5)	(7.7)	(10.3)	(6.7)	(7.2)	(9.1)	(9.7)

(i) China's direct imports.
(ii) China's indirect imports via Hong Kong (taken to be Hong Kong re-exports to China).
(iii) Percentage share of indirect imports in total (direct and indirect) imports.

Table 7.7 continued

		1979	1981	1983	1984	1985	1986	1987	1988	1989
Singapore	(i)	105	116	114	160	229	556	616	1,018	1,499
	(ii)	1.8	25	35	49	55	78	107	223	493
	(iii)	(1.7)	(18.0)	(23.3)	(23.5)	(19.4)	(12.4)	(14.8)	(18.0)	(24.7)
Indonesia	(i)	—	64	150	232	311	321	589	682	582
	(ii)	21	33	33	49	58	56	117	208	159
	(iii)	(100)	(34.1)	(19.1)	(17.5)	(15.7)	(14.9)	(16.6)	(23.4)	(21.5)
Taiwan[a]	(i)	—	—	—	—	—	—	—	—	—
	(ii)	—	52	135	270	988	811	1,227	2,240	2,897
	(iii)	0	(100)	(100)	(100)	(100)	(100)	(100)	(100)	(100)
South Korea[a]	(i)	—	—	—	—	—	391	333	471	437
	(ii)	5.8	144	45	160	355	276	538	1,224	1,000
	(iii)	(100)	(100)	(100)	(100)	(100)	(41.4)	(61.9)	(72.2)	(69.6)
All countries[b]	(i)	15,382	20,054	18,859	22,377	34,395	35,354	31,926	38,221	40,325
	(ii)	263	1,386	1,539	3,320	5,512	4,700	7,716	11,013	11,721
	(iii)	(1.7)	(6.5)	(7.5)	(12.9)	(13.8)	(11.7)	(19.5)	(22.4)	(22.5)

[a] China has unofficial direct trade with South Korea. However, the value of this trade is difficult to estimate.
[b] Excluding Hong Kong and China.

(i) China's direct imports.
(ii) China's indirect imports via Hong Kong (taken to be Hong Kong re-exports to China).
(iii) Percentage share of indirect imports in total (direct and indirect) imports.

Sources: Indirect trade data: Census and Statistics Department, Hong Kong; Direct trade data: 1970–79 *Almanac of China's Foreign Economic Relations and Trade*, 1984; 1981 and after, *Chinese Customs Statistics*.

Table 7.8 Hong Kong imports from China for re-export by SITC commodity (US$m)

| Year | Food | Beverages & tobacco | Crude materials (2,3) | | Oils & fats | Chemicals | Manufactures (6,7,8,9) | | | | Total |
| | | | Textile fibre | Sub-total | | | Textile fabric | Machinery | Clothing | Sub-total | |
	(0)	(1)	(26)		(4)	(5)	(65)	(7)	(84)		(0–9)
1970	20.4	0.05	0.58	9.4	0.48	3.5	38.5	3.7	5.8	66.3	96.9
(i)	(4.5)	(0.34)	(0.56)	(2.2)	(2.8)	(3.2)	(10.9)	(5.3)	(6.7)	(8.5)	(5.4)
(ii)	(20.4)	(0.05)	(0.58)	(9.2)	(0.5)	(3.5)	(38.6)	(3.7)	(5.8)	(66.4)	(100)
1975	48.6	0.70	1.4	40.8	1.3	17.1	83.3	17.0	22.1	191.3	300.1
(i)	(3.9)	(1.08)	(0.68)	(2.4)	(3.3)	(5.6)	(9.0)	(6.8)	(6.5)	(7.7)	(5.0)
(ii)	(16.3)	(0.23)	(0.45)	(13.6)	(0.4)	(5.7)	(27.9)	(5.7)	(7.3)	(63.8)	(100)
1979	122.4	2.0	11.9	112.2	2.6	68.9	283.1	38.3	123.3	648.6	962.2
(i)	(6.3)	(2.5)	(2.6)	(3.0)	(3.8)	(10.0)	(14.7)	(8.9)	(12.9)	(12.6)	(10.7)
(ii)	(12.7)	(0.20)	(1.2)	(11.7)	(0.27)	(7.1)	(29.4)	(4.0)	(12.8)	(67.1)	(100)
1981	210.8	3.1	53.6	277.8	2.3	143.7	414.8	116.5	279.7	1,282.7	1,950.8
(i)	(9.0)	(4.1)	(10.9)	(4.9)	(2.5)	(11.6)	(17.0)	(17.3)	(16.3)	(16.1)	(10.8)
(ii)	(10.8)	(0.16)	(2.8)	(14.2)	(0.12)	(7.4)	(21.3)	(6.0)	(14.3)	(65.8)	(100)
1983	266.1	7.7	68.0	241.4	5.7	146.2	436.1	110.3	478.6	1,622.7	2,300.1
(i)	(11.7)	(8.3)	(10.8)	(3.8)	(6.4)	(12.5)	(18.1)	(15.9)	(20.4)	(16.6)	(11.4)
(ii)	(11.6)	(0.33)	(3.0)	(10.5)	(0.25)	(6.4)	(19.0)	(4.4)	(20.8)	(70.5)	(100)
1984	264.1	6.0	166.6	336.6	5.8	170.9	629.0	139.4	618.8	2,265.3	3,055.8
(i)	(10.4)	(8.1)	(17.9)	(4.3)	(6.1)	(13.3)	(21.9)	(15.9)	(23.3)	(19.5)	(12.9)
(ii)	(8.7)	(0.19)	(5.4)	(11.0)	(0.19)	(5.6)	(20.6)	(4.6)	(20.3)	(74.1)	(100)

(i) Percentage share in Chinese exports to the world excepting direct exports to Hong Kong.
(ii) Distribution of Hong Kong's imports from China for re-exports (per cent).

Table 7.8 continued

| Year | | Food (0) | Beverages & tobacco (1) | Crude materials (2,3) | | Oils & fats (4) | Chemicals (5) | Manufactures (6,7,8,9) | | | | Total |
				Textile fibre (26)	Sub-total			Textile fabric (65)	Machinery (7)	Clothing (84)	Sub-total	(0–9)
1985		321.3	7.3	191.3	393.6	4.0	212.5	754.8	132.6	782.0	2,829.7	3,778.3
	(i)	(10.2)	(10.4)	(15.6)	(4.0)	(4.4)	(14.7)	(25.2)	(25.0)	(27.8)	(23.2)	(14.0)
	(ii)	(8.5)	(0.19)	(5.1)	(10.4)	(0.11)	(5.6)	(20.0)	(3.5)	(20.7)	(74.9)	(100)
1986		460.4	6.8	161.5	401.2	4.6	278.0	1,071.9	283.9	1,388.1	4,470.2	5,520.2
	(i)	(11.0)	(8.7)	(133.0)	(5.8)	(4.3)	(15.7)	(27.9)	(43.7)	(30.5)	(25.9)	(18.1)
	(ii)	(8.2)	(0.12)	(2.9)	(7.1)	(0.08)	(4.9)	(19.1)	(5.0)	(24.7)	(79.5)	(100)
1987		525.0	12.9	280.3	653.3	6.2	420.8	1,647.2	895.1	1,896.4	7,566.7	9,185.7
	(i)	(11.1)	(11.0)	(17.2)	(10.5)	(6.2)	(18.2)	(31.4)	(49.5)	(30.3)	(28.5)	(21.9)
	(ii)	(5.7)	(0.14)	(3.0)	(2.1)	(0.07)	(4.6)	(17.9)	(9.7)	(20.6)	(82.4)	(100)
1988		798.2	14.3	356.5	853.7	8.1	540.4	2,057.4	2,112.9	2,585.3	12,118.2	14,333.0
	(i)	—	—	—	—	—	—	—	—	—	—	—
	(ii)	(5.6)	(0.09)	(2.5)	(6.0)	(0.06)	(3.8)	(14.4)	(14.7)	(18.0)	(84.5)	(100)
1989		763.4	18.0	366.6	919.6	7.2	645.2	2,594.9	3,642.4	3,911.1	18,163.2	20,516.7
	(i)	—	—	—	—	—	—	—	—	—	—	—
	(ii)	(3.7)	(0.09)	(1.8)	(4.5)	(0.04)	(3.1)	(12.6)	(17.8)	(19.1)	(88.5)	(100)

(i) Percentage share in Chinese exports to the world excepting direct exports to Hong Kong.
(ii) Distribution of Hong Kong's imports from China for re-exports (per cent).

Sources: Hong Kong's imports from China for re-exports: Census and Statistics Department, Hong Kong; Chinese exports: United States Central Intelligence Agency, National Foreign Assessment Centre, *China: International Trade*, various issues.

Table 7.9 *Hong Kong re-exports to China by SITC commodity* (US$m)

Year	Food & crude materials (0–4)	Chemicals (5)	Manufactures (6,7,8,9)			Total (0–9)
			Textile fabric (65)	Electrical machinery (72)	Sub-total (6–9)	
1979	43	19	44	31.4	199	262
(i)	(1.1)	(1.3)	(17.2)	(6.0)	(2.3)	(1.8)
(ii)	(16)	(7.4)	(17)	(12)	(76)	(100)
1981	140	67	564	26.3	1,186	1,431
(i)	(2.1)	(3.3)	(38.2)	(20.9)	(13.2)	(8.2)
(ii)	(9.8)	(4.7)	(40)	(18.5)	(83)	(100)
1983	226	112	432	287	1,316	1,664
(i)	(4.6)	(5.1)	(55.4)	(27.9)	(12.8)	(9.5)
(ii)	(14)	(6.7)	(26)	(17.1)	(79)	(100)
1984	313	210	834	901	3,045	3,590
(i)	(5.3)	(6.2)	(65.3)	(45.4)	(21.2)	(15.2)
(ii)	(8.7)	(5.8)	(23)	(24.8)	(85)	(100)
1985	393	372	1,236	1,511	5,106	5,907
(i)	(8.0)	(10.3)	(63.0)	(33.3)	(17.8)	(15.8)
(ii)	(6.7)	(6.3)	(21)	(25.9)	(86)	(100)

(i) Percentage share in Chinese imports from all countries except direct imports from Hong Kong.
(ii) Percentage distribution of Hong Kong re-exports to China.

Table 7.9 *continued*

Year	Food & crude materials (0–4)	Chemicals (5)	Manufactures (6,7,8,9)			Total (0–9)
			Textile fabric (65)	Electrical machinery (72)	Sub-total (6–9)	
1986	531.2	446	1,443	874	4,224.4	5,241
(i)	(10.2)	(13.1)	(68.9)	(23.5)	(15.9)	(14.9)
(ii)	(10.1)	(8.5)	(27.5)	(16.7)	(81.4)	(100)
1987	705.6	804	1,902.6	1,346.9	6,202.7	7,716
(i)	(10.6)	(16.8)	(72.5)	(31.8)	(24.2)	(20.8)
(ii)	(9.1)	(10.4)	(24.7)	(17.45)	(80.4)	(100)
1988	1,116	1,764	2,361	724	9,286	12,166
(i)	—	—	—	—	—	—
(ii)	(9.2)	(14.5)	(19.4)	(6.0)	(76.3)	(100)
1989	1,489	1,592	3,018	780	10,187	13,268
(i)	—	—	—	—	—	—
(ii)	(11.2)	(12.0)	(22.7)	(5.9)	(76.8)	(100)

(i) Percentage share in Chinese imports from all countries except direct imports from Hong Kong.
(ii) Percentage distribution of Hong Kong re-exports to China.

Sources: Hong Kong data: *Hong Kong Trade Statistics,* various issues; Chinese data: United States Central Intelligence Agency, National Foreign Assessment Centre, *China: International Trade,* various issues.

yarn and fabrics, representing mostly processed re-exports. Chinese grey cloth can be imported into Hong Kong for pre-shrinking, then re-exported to China for dyeing and finishing, then re-imported into Hong Kong for re-export to other countries.

Hong Kong as a centre of trans-shipment

The value of goods trans-shipped through Hong Kong is not available; they do not pass through customs. Their weight, however, is known. Table 7.10 shows the rapid growth by weight in the trans-shipment of goods to and from China through Hong Kong. Trans-shipment of goods from China increased 2.5 times between 1983 and 1988, and the trans-shipment of goods to China increased 15-fold in the same period. Trans-shipment to China fell in 1989 as a result of the Tiananmen incident and the retrenchment of the Chinese economy. The weight of the trans-shipment of goods from (to) China through Hong Kong was only 2 (2) per cent of China's ocean-going sea cargo in 1989. However, the share by weight may bear little relation to the share by value. For instance, the total exports and imports of Hong Kong were about equal in value in 1986 (approximately US$35 billion), but imports weighed more than four times as much as exports because Hong Kong exports mostly light consumer goods.

Fortunately, the commodity compositions (by weight) of trans-shipment of goods to and from China are known. Trans-shipment of goods from China consists mainly of textiles, canned goods, miscellaneous manufactures of metal and non-metallic minerals, and miscellaneous crude animal and vegetable materials. These goods are not particularly bulky. In 1988, trans-shipment of goods from China represented over 21 per cent of imports from China by weight. As Hong Kong's imports from China in 1988 represented 41 per cent of Chinese exports by value (Table 2.3), the trans-shipment of goods from China through Hong Kong appears to constitute a substantial portion (around 9 per cent) of China's exports by value. This estimate appears to understate the share of trans-shipment from China by value, as the trans-shipment of goods from China appears to be less bulky than imports from China (which consist mainly of coal and petroleum).

Trans-shipment of goods to China consists of more bulky items, including chemicals, fertilizers, plastic materials and iron and steel. Hong Kong's direct shipment of goods to China (i.e. exports to China) also consists of bulky items such as petroleum, cement and chemicals. Thus, the share by weight of the trans-shipment of goods to China in exports to China should be a good indicator of its share

Table 7.10 *China's trans-shipment of goods through Hong Kong* (tonnes)

Year		Goods from China	Goods to China
1983		783,815	102,332
	(i)	(1.6)	(0.2)
	(ii)	(14.9)	(9.9)
1984		882,566	299,627
	(i)	(1.6)	(0.5)
	(ii)	(16.0)	(17.0)
1985		1,045,811	1,043,167
	(i)	(1.6)	(1.6)
	(ii)	(19.5)	(41.0)
1986		1,537,658	829,127
	(i)	(2.1)	(1.1)
	(ii)	(20.3)	(26.6)
1987		1,809,558	1,270,262
	(i)	(2.3)	(1.6)
	(ii)	(19.5)	(36.0)
1988		1,945,789	1,547,812
	(i)	(2.3)	(1.8)
	(ii)	(20.8)	(30.8)
1989		2,122,967	1,356,192
	(i)	(2.4)	(1.5)
	(ii)	(20.9)	(21.6)

(i) Percentage share in China's ocean-going sea cargo.
(ii) Percentage share in Hong Kong's imports (exports)[a] from (to) China.
[a] The weight of imports (exports) from (to) China is taken to be the weight of direct shipment from (to) China plus the weight of imports (exports) transported to Hong Kong by rail and by road because China is the only country that can transport goods to Hong Kong by land. The weight of imports (exports) carried by air is relatively small and is ignored because the data are not broken down by country.
Sources: Hong Kong data: *Hong Kong Shipping Statistics* and *Hong Kong Monthly Digest of Statistics*, various issues. Chinese data: *Chinese Statistical Yearbook*, various issues.

by value. In 1988, the share by weight was 31 per cent. As Hong Kong's exports to China in 1988 represented 31 per cent of China's imports (Table 2.4), Hong Kong's trans-shipment of goods to China appears to constitute a substantial portion (about 10 per cent) of China's imports by value.

Tables 7.11 and 7.12 show the distribution of Hong Kong's trans-shipment of goods from and to China by destination and origin respectively. Transportation costs being the main determinant of trans-shipment, distant countries would be expected to rely more on trans-shipment from Hong Kong. This is indeed the case. EC countries such as West Germany, the Netherlands, the United Kingdom and France figure importantly in trans-shipment of goods from

Table 7.11 Trans-shipment from China via Hong Kong by destination (tonnes)

Destination		1983	1984	1985	1986	1987	1988	1989
USA		123,100	183,065	197,029	229,087	271,277	331,018	460,639
	(i)	(15.7)	(20.7)	(18.8)	(14.9)	(15.0)	(17.0)	(21.7)
	(ii)	(30.7)	(35.8)	(35.4)	(39.3)	(36.1)	(35.7)	(37.4)
West Germany		89,952	101,162	97,097	172,468	194,338	200,886	242,959
	(i)	(11.5)	(11.5)	(9.3)	(11.2)	(10.7)	(10.3)	(11.4)
	(ii)	(2.2)	(2.8)	(3.5)	(4.0)	(5.7)	(6.1)	(6.6)
Netherlands		52,180	64,601	78,318	127,265	177,790	181,418	227,483
	(i)	(6.6)	(7.3)	(7.5)	(8.4)	(9.8)	(9.3)	(10.7)
	(ii)	—a	—	—			—	—
Australia		35,889	37,612	46,760	55,641	77,027	75,234	81,323
	(i)	(4.6)	(4.3)	(4.5)	(3.6)	(4.3)	(3.9)	(3.8)
	(ii)	(2.6)	(3.2)	(2.3)	(2.3)	(2.5)	(2.5)	(2.5)
United Kingdom		34,385	34,199	41,939	86,323	100,781	80,195	102,525
	(i)	(4.4)	(3.9)	(4.0)	(5.6)	(5.6)	(4.1)	(4.8)
	(ii)	(1.8)	(1.9)	(2.1)	(2.6)	(3.8)	(4.2)	(4.4)

a 'not available' because the amount is small.

(i) Percentage distribution of trans-shipment from China.
(ii) Percentage distribution of re-exports originating from China (excluding re-exports from China to Taiwan and South Korea).

Table 7.11 *continued*

Destination		1983	1984	1985	1986	1987	1988	1989
Singapore		30,628	23,017	27,016	53,339	64,102	105,342	128,418
	(i)	(3.9)	(2.6)	(2.6)	(3.5)	(3.5)	(5.4)	(6.0)
	(ii)	(6.6)	(4.8)	(3.8)	(3.3)	(2.7)	(2.3)	(1.9)
France		29,208	27,634	29,442	46,195	63,007	65,364	86,197
	(i)	(3.7)	(3.1)	(2.8)	(3.0)	(3.5)	(3.4)	(4.1)
	(ii)	—	—	—	—	—	—	—
Japan		26,267	—	—	29,260	44,109	78,321	96,648
	(i)	(3.4)	—	—	(1.9)	(2.4)	(4.1)	(4.6)
	(ii)	(6.2)	(8.7)	(9.1)	(6.9)	(7.4)	(9.3)	(8.5)
Sub-total		441,503	471,290	517,561	799,578	992,431	1,118,778	1,426,192
	(i)	(56.3)	(53.4)	(49.5)	(52.0)	(54.8)	(57.5)	(67.2)
	(ii)	(50.1)	(57.2)	(56.2)	(58.4)	(58.0)	(60.1)	(61.3)
Total		783,815	882,566	1,045,811	1,537,658	1,809,558	1,945,789	2,122,967
	(i)	(100)	(100)	(100)	(100)	(100)	(100)	(100)
	(ii)	(100)	(100)	(100)	(100)	(100)	(100)	(100)

(i) Percentage distribution of trans-shipment from China.
(ii) Percentage distribution of re-exports originating from China (excluding re-exports from China to Taiwan and South Korea).
Sources: *Hong Kong Shipping Statistics* and *Review of Overseas Trade*.

Table 7.12 Trans-shipments to China via Hong Kong by origin (tonnes)

		1984	1985	1986	1987	1988	1989
USA		108,061	583,789	319,796	472,120	423,025	455,251
	(i)	(36.1)	(55.99)	(38.3)	(37.2)	(27.3)	(33.6)
	(ii)	(11.8)	(12.6)	(13.6)	(12.2)	(14.1)	(14.0)
Canada		—a	21,374	56,322	94,399	103,340	46,786
	(i)	—	(2.0)	(6.8)	(7.4)	(6.7)	(3.4)
	(ii)	—	—	—	—	—	—
Netherlands		—	—	—	27,753	87,012	75,612
	(i)	—	—	—	(2.2)	(5.6)	(5.6)
	(ii)	—	—	—	—	—	—
Belgium and Luxembourg		14,783	41,521	52,406	74,808	70,543	52,030
	(i)	(4.9)	(4.0)	(6.3)	(5.9)	(4.6)	(3.8)
	(ii)	—	—		—	—	—
Italy		35,398	—	—	—	—	58,150
	(i)	(11.8)	—	—	—	—	(4.3)
	(ii)	(1.2)	—	—	—	—	(2.1)
Australia		25,701	80,669	—	—	—	32,329
	(i)	(8.6)	(7.7)	—	—	—	(2.4)
	(ii)	—	—	—	—	—	—

a 'not available' because the amount is small.

(i) Percentage distribution of trans-shipment to China.
(ii) Percentage distribution of re-exports to China (excluding re-exports from Taiwan and South Korea to China).

Table 7.12 *continued*

		1984	1985	1986	1987	1988	1989
Japan		—	—	—	—	—	11,249
	(i)	—	—	—	—	—	(0.8)
	(ii)	(38.3)	(40.9)	(27.5)	(25.6)	(34.1)	(32.1)
W. Germany		—	—	36,446	61,682	91,581	74,542
	(i)	—	—	(4.4)	(4.9)	(5.9)	(5.5)
	(ii)	—	—	(3.2)	(2.7)	(3.3)	(3.5)
Sub-total	(i)	(61.4)	(69.6)	(55.8)	(57.5)	(50.1)	(51.4)
	(ii)	(51.3)	(53.5)	(44.3)	(40.6)	(51.5)	(51.7)
Total		299,627	1,043,167	829,127	1,270,262	1,547,812	1,356,192
	(i)	(100)	(100)	(100)	(100)	(100)	(100)
	(ii)	(100)	(100)	(100)	(100)	(100)	(100)

(i) Percentage distribution of trans-shipment to China.
(ii) Percentage distribution of re-exports to China (excluding re-exports from Taiwan and South Korea to China).

Sources: Hong Kong Shipping Statistics and *Review of Overseas Trade.*

China; the Netherlands, West Germany, Italy, Belgium and Luxemburg figure importantly in trans-shipment of goods to China. Direct shipping is more convenient for countries to the north, such as Japan, whereas Hong Kong lies in the shipping lanes of countries such as Australia and Singapore, and the EC countries. Indeed, the Australian share of trans-shipment in both directions and the Singapore share of trans-shipment of goods from China were much greater than that of Japan, although Japan has much more valuable trade with China.

The distribution of Hong Kong's re-exports of Chinese goods, both exports and imports, by destination, is shown in Tables 7.11 and 7.12 for comparison with the distribution of trans-shipment. The re-exports of Chinese goods to Taiwan and South Korea are excluded from the re-exports total in computing their distribution because Hong Kong can re-export but cannot trans-ship Chinese goods to Taiwan and South Korea. The comparison shows that the determinants of trans-shipment are quite different from those of re-exports. The shares of the EC countries in trans-shipment of goods from and to China are much higher than their corresponding shares in re-exports. On the other hand, Japan's share in re-exports of goods from and to China is much higher than its shares in the trans-shipment of goods from and to China.

Transportation costs are not determined solely by distance. It would seem easier, because of the shorter distances, to ship goods directly between Shanghai and the United States or to trans-ship through Japan, rather than to trans-ship through Hong Kong. However, the schedule of ships between Hong Kong and the United States is more frequent than that between Shanghai and the United States, and the freight rates are sometimes lower because of greater competition. The huge share of the United States market in trans-shipment is difficult to understand in terms of geography alone. Shipping services, freight rates and internal distortions are among a variety of factors which have created this phenomenon.

Prospects for trans-shipment

Geographically, southern China is the natural hinterland of Hong Kong. Shanghai and Zhanjiagang (a port near Nanjing) are the ports which link central China with the outside world, while Tianjin, Qingdao and Dalien are the ports performing the same service for northern China. However, Table 7.13 shows that, of the goods trans-shipped from and to China via Hong Kong in 1989, 70 per cent were accounted for by ports in northern and central China. Moreover these percentages increased from 1983 to 1986.

The high level of trans-shipment through Hong Kong may reflect the lack of container facilities in Chinese ports, the infrequency of direct voyages to countries of destination, and internal distortions (particularly unreliable shipping schedules). In the long run, China is likely to solve most of the above problems, and the share of Chinese exports trans-shipped through Hong Kong can be expected to decline. For the present, however, as Table 7.14 indicates, the bottleneck in harbour facilities in China worsened in the period 1984–86: the average docking time of external trade vessels increased from 8.7 to 11.1 days. In Hong Kong, the average is only 2.5 days and only 13 hours for container vessels. Unfortunately, data on the average docking time in Chinese ports after 1985 are unavailable because they are no longer published in the *Chinese Statistical Yearbook*.

Table 7.15 compares the volume of cargo carried by sea and air in Hong Kong and China. As expected, Hong Kong has a huge lead in the capacity to transport air cargo. In 1987 Hong Kong transported 610,565 tonnes of air cargo, twice that of China. Also, only one-fifth of China's air cargo is international cargo, whereas all of Hong Kong's cargo is international. For cargo carried by ocean-going vessels, the Hong Kong figure in 1989 was 65 million tonnes, or 72 per cent of China's ocean cargo. Although the volume of China's cargo carried by ocean-going vessels exceeded that of Hong Kong, from 1979 to 1987, Hong Kong's cargo volume grew faster than that of China, despite the considerable efforts made by the latter in expansion of port facilities. China is particularly weak in container facilities. In 1982, only six ports in China had container facilities; they handled 250,000 containers, about 8 per cent of Hong Kong's figure for the same year. China expanded its container capability to handle 500,000 containers in 1985, but that was still only 23 per cent of Hong Kong's capacity. The Hong Kong Government is further expanding the container terminals in anticipation of more Chinese merchandise being shipped through the colony. The Chinese authorities have tacitly indicated that the expansion of container facilities in Hong Kong is important for Chinese interests.

Harbours, container terminals, airports, ships and aircraft are capital-intensive and expensive. Hong Kong boasts the world's largest shipping company and one of the world's best container terminals. Hong Kong became the world's busiest container port in 1987, surpassing New York and Rotterdam in 1986 and 1987 respectively. All indications are that China will still be heavily dependent on Hong Kong for trans-shipment, at least in the medium term.

Table 7.13 *Share of ports in Northern and Central China in China's trans-shipment via Hong Kong* (per cent)

Ports	1983	1984	1985	1986	1987	1988	1989
From Shanghai	29.6	28.8	30.5	29.2	27.3	29.5	29.5
To "	—	28.5	22.8	35.0	26.4	34.0	28.5
From Tianjin	13.0	15.4	18.0	19.4	19.5	20.8	19.7
To "	—	13.8	21.7	19.2	18.6	18.8	15.3
From Qingdao	9.3	9.6	11.3	12.3	11.6	12.1	13.2
To "	—	24.4	13.0	6.7	7.3	5.6	7.4
From Dalian	12.1	11.3	8.0	7.8	8.8	7.8	7.4
To "	—	12.5	13.0	9.6	6.4	7.5	8.5
From Zhangjiagang	—	—	—	—	—	—	—
To "	—	—	7.1	12.0	8.4	8.4	10.0
From Sub-total	64.0	65.1	67.7	68.7	67.2	70.2	69.8
To "	—	79.2	77.6	82.5	67.1	74.2	69.6

Source: Hong Kong Shipping Statistics, various issues.

Table 7.14 *Average docking time in Chinese ports* (days)

Year	Internal trade vessels	External trade vessels	All vessels
1984	1.6	8.7	3.3
1985	1.7	11.1	4.4

Source: *Chinese Statistical Yearbook*, 1986.

Table 7.15 *Cargo volumes carried by sea and air, Hong Kong*

Year	By ocean-going vessels ('000 tonnes)	By air (tonnes)
1979	27,879 (65.6)[a]	257,408 (322)
1980	30,692 (71.5)	257,866 (290)
1981	31,969 (70.6)	290,305 (309)
1982	32,964 (71.6)	305,757 (298)
1983	37,932 (79.7)	368,166 (317)
1984	35,293[b] (63.6)	417,146 (278)
1985	39,689 (60.0)	429,983 (221)
1986	47,469 (65.7)	536,760 (240)
1987	53,557 (67.1)	610,565 (204)
1988	61,321 (71.9)	694,064 (212)
1989	64,655 (71.6)	730,020 (236)

[a] Bracketed figures denote comparative percentages for cargo carried by ocean-going vessels or by air in China.
[b] The definition of Hong Kong cargo carried by ocean-going vessels changed from 1984.
Source: *Hong Kong Monthly Digest of Statistics*, various issues.

Triangular trade

Not much data exist on the role of Hong Kong trading firms performing a purely brokerage role in China's direct trade. This trade is called 'triangular trade' because the Hong Kong firm acts as a

middleman between offshore production bases and overseas customers. Based on the data from its 1988 survey, the Hong Kong
Trade Development Council estimated that the value of triangular
trade conducted by Hong Kong in 1988 was HK$140 billion, or
US$18 billion (Hong Kong Trade Development Council 1988). If it is
assumed that the shares of trade involving China in Hong Kong's
triangular trade and Hong Kong's re-exports are identical (82 per
cent in 1988), the estimate for the triangular trade conducted by
Hong Kong involving China (either as producer or as customer)
would be US$14.8 billion in 1988, or 7 per cent of China's trade in
1988.

Table 7.16 shows the value of loans extended by Hong Kong banks
to finance 'trade not touching Hong Kong'. Such trade is likely to
involve mostly triangular trade, because trade that does not touch
Hong Kong and does not involve Hong Kong firms as brokers is
unlikely to be financed by Hong Kong banks. Such loans grew very
rapidly from 1984 to 1988, indicating a rapid growth in triangular
trade. The shares of such loans in bank loans to finance Hong Kong's
trade jumped upwards during the second and third waves of the
decentralization of China's trade system in 1984 and 1988, and this
again confirms the important impact of decentralization on intermediation. Such loans fell in 1989 as a result of the Tiananmen
incident and the retrenchment of the Chinese economy.

Table 7.16 *Hong Kong bank loans used to finance 'trade not touching
Hong Kong'*

Year	US$m	Percentage of loans used to finance Hong Kong's trade
1980	383	11.0
1981	395	10.1
1982	377	8.7
1983	397	9.8
1984	570	13.7
1985	479	12.1
1986	589	12.9
1987	898	15.8
1988	1,581	21.6
1989	1,337	16.4

Source: Hong Kong Monthly Digest of Statistics, various issues.

The multi-faceted middleman functions of Hong Kong

China's reliance on Hong Kong for loan syndication and tourism (analysed in Chapter 2), and on its role in commodity trade presented here, indicates the importance of the multi-faceted middleman functions performed by Hong Kong. In 1988, China's indirect trade through Hong Kong (including both Hong Kong's imports from China for re-export and Hong Kong re-exports to China) accounted for 28 per cent of China's trade; China's trans-shipments via Hong Kong (both outgoing and incoming shipments) and the triangular trade conducted by Hong Kong involving China were estimated to be 10 per cent and 7 per cent of China's trade respectively. There is likely to be substantial overlapping between trans-shipment and triangular trade because Hong Kong is the central hub of transportation between China and the rest of the world, and a major portion of triangular trade may be trans-shipped through Hong Kong.

In loan syndication, tourism, entrepôt trade and triangular trade, economic decentralization has led to dramatic increases in the demand for intermediation. As China plans to further decentralize its economy, the prospects for Hong Kong as middleman are decidedly bright.

8

Summary and conclusions

More than a decade has elapsed since the beginning of Deng's open-door policy. By the standard of Stalinist economies, China has taken giant strides in institutional reforms in order to open its door: the power of foreign trade and investment has been significantly decentralized, the renminbi has been devalued substantially, a grey market for foreign exchange has been introduced, foreign joint ventures and fully owned foreign enterprises have been allowed, special economic zones have been established, and the formula of 'one country, two systems' has been promulgated for Hong Kong and Macau. The last two innovations are unheard-of in communist countries.

However, so far, the results of the open-door policy are mixed. Export expansion has been rapid but uneven, and the 1979–80, 1984–85 and 1988 reform drives have resulted in severe internal and external imbalances. On each of the three occasions, economic planners were forced to recentralize and adopt restrictive macro-policies. China succeeded in lessening its dependence on oil exports, but its dependence on textile exports is high and increasing. China relies increasingly on Hong Kong for marketing, re-exporting and trans-shipment. Service exports have boomed, especially tourism, but most foreign tourists are Hong Kong residents. Reform of the trading system has not met initial expectations, and the radical 1984 trade reforms have been only partly implemented. The existing system of trade controls is not effective and leads to many inefficiencies. Planners have tried to devalue the renminbi to a more realistic level, but the effort has stalled through fear of inflation. However, the grey market for foreign exchange is spreading and trading is becoming increasingly active.

The quantity and quality of direct foreign investment are both disappointing. Most foreign investment comes from Hong Kong, and China has had limited success in moving beyond its Hong Kong connection. China has also experienced difficulties in moving from low-technology, small-scale, import-substitution-oriented foreign investment in services to high-technology, export-oriented industrial investment. Moreover, pledged foreign investment has slumped since 1985 because of dissatisfaction with the Chinese investment environment. Compensation trade agreements have been used, principally by Hong Kong businessmen, as shelters for illicit trading activities. However, Chinese planners are making efforts to improve the investment environment; the share of foreign investment in manufacturing has risen, and pledged foreign investment has slowly recovered.

Although the results of the open-door policy are mixed, it must be stressed that the opening and reform of a command economy is a complex process; China has made good progress when compared with other Communist economies. Other Communist countries, which began their economic reforms much earlier than China, are now trying to learn from the Chinese experience. The open-door policy commands political support from both liberals and conservatives in China. In the long run, the success of the policy will depend on the success of the reform of China's economic system.

Summary of Hong Kong's roles

A summary of the economic relationship between China and Hong Kong using balance of payments accounts would be useful. However, Chinese data on balance of payments are brief and the Hong Kong government does not record capital movements. It is therefore necessary to rely on estimates to construct current and capital accounts.

In terms of the balance of payments, too much emphasis has been placed on China's foreign exchange earnings from Hong Kong. Many sources estimate that China earns 30–40 per cent of its foreign exchange through Hong Kong.[1] The estimates are biased upwards because Chinese exports re-exported through Hong Kong are regarded as China's foreign exchange earnings from Hong Kong. If re-exports of Chinese goods from Hong Kong are deducted, China's current account foreign exchange earnings from Hong Kong fall from 30–40 per cent of the total to 20 per cent (see the next section for estimates). Moreover, the amount of foreign exchange earnings overstates the direct economic benefits China obtains from the Hong Kong market. If there were no Hong Kong market, Chinese exports would be lower, but by an amount appreciably smaller than Chinese exports to Hong Kong. The goods sold to Hong Kong could be sold elsewhere or used

---

[1] For a detailed estimate, see Jao (1983).

for import replacement (market substitution), and the resources used in producing exports for Hong Kong could be used to produce other goods of economic value (commodity substitution). The possibility of substitution is increasing; from 1975 to 1987, the share of food in Hong Kong's retained imports of Chinese goods dropped from 57 to 15 per cent, whereas the share of manufactures rose from 26 to 72 per cent (Table 6.4).

Another common fallacy concerns the trade surplus China has with Hong Kong. The popular idea is mercantilistic; China's economic gain from Hong Kong is frequently measured by the size of the trade surplus (or current account surplus). This is clearly incorrect, as both economies benefit from the trade even if their trade is not balanced.

Current account transactions

Table 8.1 summarizes the deficits in the visible trade of Hong Kong with China. In 1951–52, Hong Kong had surpluses due to China's stockpiling for the Korean War. However, after the United Nations' and United States' embargoes, Hong Kong suffered deficits from 1952 to 1984. Recently the picture has changed: from 1977 to 1985, Hong Kong's domestic exports to China increased 279 times, and re-exports to China increased 155 times. Moreover, in 1985, Hong Kong's domestic exports and re-exports to China increased by 25 and 65 per cent respectively over the figures for 1984. On the other hand, China's direct exports to Hong Kong (Hong Kong's retained imports from China) dropped by 7 per cent, and Hong Kong had a small trade surplus in 1985. Owing to tightening controls on imports in China after April 1985, Hong Kong's re-exports to China dropped in 1986 and there was also an upsurge of imports from China for re-export. Hong Kong again ended with a deficit in 1986–88, though the size of these deficits was smaller than those in the period 1980–83.

The 1985 surplus is misleading in that Hong Kong's re-exports to China are regarded as Hong Kong exports. In fact, only the re-export margin should be regarded as exports of the entrepôt service of Hong Kong. Because of soaring Hong Kong re-exports to China, the 1985 trade balance is a more accurate indicator of trade between Hong Kong and China. In 1985, Hong Kong still had a large direct trade deficit with China, but the deficit peaked in 1981, and has been dwindling due to a rapid increase of Hong Kong domestic exports. The deficit dwindled to a very small amount (US$210 million) in 1988, and in 1989 Hong Kong ended up with a direct trade surplus of US$850 million. The increase in Hong Kong domestic exports to China is due partly to growing intra-industry trade as Hong Kong invests in China, and partly to China's imports of Hong Kong consumer goods.

Visible trade accounts for the bulk of China's foreign exchange earnings from Hong Kong, but invisible and non-traded income are also important. Table 8.2 summarizes China's current account earnings from Hong Kong. Jao (1983:58) estimated the non-trade items from 1977 to 1980, and this book extends the exercise up to 1989. The method of estimation is described here.

Private unrequited transfers (row 2)

Jao's 1977–80 estimates are scaled down because they appear to be biased upwards by one-third in comparison with the 1982–84 figures later released by China. Jao assumed that from 1979, 83 per cent of overseas remittances came from Hong Kong residents. This percentage is applied to official figures on private unrequited transfers to give the estimates from 1982 to 1988. The 1981 estimate is based on the assumption that the 1981 percentage share of remittances in Hong Kong's gross national product (GNP) was the same as that of 1980. This is not unreasonable, as Jao's estimates indicate that remittances as a percentage of GNP have been remarkably stable.

Tourism (row 3)

The figures are taken from Table 2.5 and the method of estimation is explained in Chapter 2.

Investment income (row 4)

Jao's estimates were used for the period 1977–80. Jao assumed that China's investment income from Hong Kong grew at the same rate as Hong Kong's GDP. Extending this assumption beyond 1984 does not give reasonable estimates as Hong Kong's GDP increases steadily, whereas China's official figures on total investment income, available from 1982 onwards, dropped rapidly in 1985 and 1986. This drop appears to reflect China's investment in failing enterprises and banks in Hong Kong in attempts to shore up the Hong Kong economy during 1983–85. In this period, the uncertainty over the political future of Hong Kong led to economic and monetary crisis. Applying Jao's assumption to the 1982–84 period, the share of China's investment income arising from Hong Kong is seen to be two-thirds. Such a ratio is reasonable as a predominant share of China's overseas investment in Hong Kong, though the exact share is not known (*Hong Kong Economic Journal* 28 Mar. 1989). The ratio was then applied to official figures of China's investment income since 1982 to give the estimates for 1982 to 1988. No estimate is available for 1981, and it must be assumed that the 1981 investment income was equal to the mean of the figures for 1980 and 1982.

Table 8.1 *Visible trade balance between Hong Kong and China* (US$m)

Year	Direct trade			Indirect trade			Total trade		
	Domestic exports	Retained imports from China	Trade balance	Re-exports to China	Imports from China re-exported	Trade balance	Exports to China	Imports from China	Trade balance
1950	—	—	—	—	—	—	221	137	+84
1955	—	—	—	—	—	—	32	157	−125
1959	2	—	—	18	—	—	20	181	−161
1960	2	—	—	19	—	—	21	207	−186
1965	3	—	—	10	—	—	13	406	−393
1966	3	394	−391	10	94	−84	12	487	−475
1970	5	373	−368	6	97	−91	11	470	−459
1975	6	1,083	−1,077	28	300	−272	33	1,383	−1,350
1977	7	1,286	−1,279	38	455	−417	44	1,741	−1,697
1979	121	2,076	−1,955	263	962	−699	383	3,038	−2,655
1980	323	2,977	−2,654	933	1,434	−501	1,255	4,411	−3,155
1981	523	3,325	−2,802	1,438	1,951	−513	1,961	5,276	−3,315
1982	627	3,367	−2,740	1,316	2,057	−741	1,943	5,424	−3,441
1983	856	3,588	−2,732	1,675	2,300	−625	2,531	5,888	−3,357
1984	1,443	4,075	−2,632	3,590	3,056	+534	5,033	7,131	−2,097
1985	1,950	3,790	−1,840	5,907	3,778	+2,129	7,857	7,568	+289
1986	2,310	4,842	−2,532	5,241	5,620	−379	7,550	10,462	−2,912
1987	3,574	5,591	−2,017	7,716	9,185	−1,469	11,290	14,776	−3,486
1988	4,874	5,084	−210	12,157	14,322	−2,165	17,030	19,406	−2,376
1989	5,548	4,698	850	13,268	20,517	−7,249	18,816	25,215	−6,399

Sources: Tables 2.3 and 2.4.

Table 8.2 *China's current account foreign exchange earnings from Hong Kong* (US$m)

	1977	1978	1979	1980	1981	1982	1983	1984	1985	1986	1987	1988	1989
1 Chinese exports	1,741	2,262	3,038	4,414	5,276	5,424	5,888	7,131	7,568	10,462	14,776	19,406	25,215
2 Private unrequited transfers	229	275	314	377	407	440	362	253	142	212	216	362	—
3 Tourism	117	195	337	457	534	573	649	792	875	979	1,199	1,461	1,358
4 Investment profit	368	461	610	825	720	614	906	1,250	911	512	651	979	—
5 Gross earnings (include re-exports)	2,455	3,193	4,299	6,073	6,937	7,051	7,805	9,426	9,496	12,165	16,842	22,208	—
	(26.4)	(28.3)	(27.2)	(28.3)	(28.3)	(27.8)	(30.7)	(32.5)	(31.9)	(39.3)	(41.7)	(46.8)	
6 Re-exports of Chinese goods	−455	−664	−962	−1,434	−1,951	−2,057	−2,300	−3,056	−3,778	−5,620	−9,185	−14,322	−20,517
7 Gross earnings (exclude re-exports)	2,000	2,529	3,337	4,639	4,986	4,994	5,005	6,370	5,718	6,545	7,657	7,886	—
	(21.5)[a]	(22.5)	(21.1)	(21.6)	(20.4)	(20.4)	(21.7)	(21.9)	(19.2)	(21.2)	(18.9)	(16.6)	
Hong Kong													
8 Domestic exports	−7	−17	−121	−323	−523	−627	−856	−1,443	−1,950	−2,310	−3,574	−4,874	5,548
9 Entrepôt service exports	−6	−7	−39	−140	−216	−197	−251	−539	−886	−786	−1,157	−1,824	−1,990
10 Partial current account balance	1,987	2,505	3,177	4,176	4,247	4,170	3,898	4,388	2,882	3,449	2,926	1,188	—
11 China's total current account earnings[b]	9,390	11,247	15,805	21,437	24,512	25,408	25,418	29,029	29,812	30,938	40,407	47,452	—

[a] Figures in brackets represent percentage share of China's total current account foreign earnings.
[b] Excluding official donations.
Source: See text.

China's current account earnings (row 11)
The 1977–79 figures are taken from Jao. The 1982–88 figures are obtained from balance of payments data released by China. The 1980–81 figures are based on the statement of the head of China's foreign exchange management bureau that China's foreign exchange earnings were around 1.25 times the value of visible exports (*Jingji Ribao* 10 Feb. 1984). Foreign investment and loans were about 8 per cent of visible exports in 1983, hence the 1980–81 estimates are obtained by scaling China's commodity exports by 1.17 (i.e. 125 per cent minus 8 per cent).

Some items such as transportation and the earnings of China's foreign contracted projects and labour service in Hong Kong are omitted due to lack of data. They are probably exceeded by Hong Kong's export of services to China. Hong Kong's earnings from Chinese tourists visiting Hong Kong are omitted as they are quite small. Moreover, a substantial portion of these trips is financed by the tourists' relatives in Hong Kong. Hong Kong's profits from investment in China are substantial, probably on a par with China's profits from investments in Hong Kong.

China's gross current account earnings (including re-exports) from Hong Kong (row 5) were about 30–40 per cent of its total current account earnings. After deducting Hong Kong's re-export of Chinese goods (row 6), the gross earnings from Hong Kong (row 7) emerge as about 20 per cent of total current account earnings.

To calculate the current account balance, Hong Kong's domestic exports to China and Hong Kong's export of services (largely entrepôt services) — that is the re-export margin of Hong Kong's re-exports to China, which was estimated to be 15 per cent — must be subtracted. The resulting partial current account balance is given in row 10.

Table 8.2 shows that the partial current account balance peaked in 1984 at around US$4.4 billion, and declined to US$1.2 billion in 1988, or 3 per cent of China's current account earnings. Hong Kong's investment profits in China and Hong Kong's export of shipping services to China are substantial. These items have not been deducted from the partial current account balance. After deducting these items, Hong Kong's share would be even less than 3 per cent.

Before 1979, China's gross foreign exchange earnings (excluding re-exports) were only slightly larger than the partial current account balance. The partial current account balance should have been close to the complete current account balance as Hong Kong's investment in China was minimal. Before China's adoption of the open-door policy in 1979, it was justifiable to use China's gross foreign earnings (excluding re-exports) as a substitute for the current account surplus.

Thus, China's current account surplus with Hong Kong before 1979 was quite substantial, representing approximately 20 per cent of China's total current account earnings.

Some countries dislike large bilateral deficits, but the Hong Kong economy is exceptional in this respect; it is founded on a liberal free-trade philosophy and is indifferent to bilateral deficits and surpluses. Hong Kong allows China to run large surpluses, and Hong Kong benefits tremendously from the competitive prices of Chinese food and manufactures. China's large surplus with Hong Kong enhances its ability to import capital goods from developed countries because China's trade with the developed countries is usually in deficit. Thus, China's current surplus with Hong Kong does have some economic significance, despite the popular mercantilistic fallacy.

However, it should be noted that since China's adoption of the open-door policy in 1979, its imports of goods made in Hong Kong, of entrepôt services and other services, have grown rapidly. Moreover, Hong Kong's investment profits in China have also soared. China's gross foreign exchange earnings from Hong Kong have diverged increasingly from its current account surplus with Hong Kong, and Hong Kong's importance as a source of current account surplus for China has decreased substantially.

The role of Hong Kong in China's commodity trade has shifted from that of a consumer of Chinese goods to that of a middleman and a supplier of goods to China. The quantity of Chinese exports consumed in Hong Kong is still large, but the market is close to saturation. Unless China can improve the quality of its exports or diversify its exports rapidly into electronic and consumer durables, the Chinese share of the Hong Kong market will stagnate or even decline.

Chinese exports retained in Hong Kong have seen a shift from foodstuffs to semi-manufactures for Hong Kong's export industries (particularly clothing). The role of Hong Kong has shifted from that of a consumer of Chinese exports to that of a processor of Chinese goods for export to the world market. Such processing includes: pure re-exports, where the process is the intangible one of marketing; processed re-exports; and processing of Chinese semi-manufactures into Hong Kong domestic exports. In 1989, the last item constituted at least 3 per cent of China's exports to the world, and the total of the three items was 42 per cent of China's exports. Moreover, illicit exports of Chinese clothing using the Hong Kong quota should be regarded as Hong Kong re-exports. In 1988, these illicit exports were 0.33 per cent of China's exports.

The changing role of Hong Kong from consumer to processor implies that Chinese exports to Hong Kong tend to overstate the amount of foreign exchange earnings of China from Hong Kong. In any case, the mercantile emphasis on China's foreign exchange earnings from Hong Kong is both erroneous and outdated. Trade between Hong Kong and China is now more balanced, reflecting the growth of a complicated network of economic relationships. These relationships benefit both parties, though they are intangible and difficult to quantify.

Capital account transactions

China's capital account transactions with Hong Kong are described in Chapter 5. Hong Kong is the source of approximately two-thirds of direct foreign investment in China. Since 1984, Hong Kong has become an important source of loans, and Hong Kong's commercial loans (both direct and syndicated) to China in 1987 represented 64 per cent of total commercial loans to China, or over 36 per cent of total foreign loans to China. The share of Hong Kong in China's total utilization of foreign capital in 1989 was around 42 per cent.

Before the adoption of the open-door policy in 1979, capital account transactions between Hong Kong and China tended to be one-sided: China invested in Hong Kong on a considerable scale in the absence of Hong Kong investment in China. Since 1979, Hong Kong investment in China has grown rapidly, and is now probably as large as Chinese investment in Hong Kong. Furthermore, since 1979, banks in China and Hong Kong have actively lent to each other (Table 5.1). Since 1985, China has tended to be a net borrower from Hong Kong.

The benefits and costs to China of the Hong Kong connection

The benefits of Hong Kong to China as trading partner, middleman, financier, and facilitator have been discussed in detail. In addition, Hong Kong aids China's thriving black market and illicit trade. The sharp drop in Hong Kong's retained imports from China in 1985 was largely attributable to illicit trade.

Hong Kong is an efficient and flexible instrument for the promotion of trade and investment, but China has not yet mastered its use. Given the efficiency and versatility of Hong Kong as a promoter of China's trade and investment, irrational policies in China will be manifested quickly in the Hong Kong market, and Chinese planners can avail themselves of this rapid feedback to assess their policies in trade and investment.

It has been repeatedly stressed that in the long run, the viability of China's open-door policy depends on the success of economic reforms. Hong Kong plays a crucial role in China's reform drive, especially in the reform of China's external sector. The dynamism of the Hong Kong market directly activates market forces in China, and the best example is the growth of the black market in foreign exchange in China. The presence of the black market forces planners to devalue the renminbi and also to create a thriving grey market for foreign exchange. The presence of Hong Kong also exerts pressure on China to decentralize its trade, as many localities and enterprises are able to trade with the outside world covertly through their Hong Kong connections.

Foreign travellers have noted that Guangdong is the Chinese province most coloured by market forces, forces which are attributable to its proximity to Hong Kong. Hong Kong will undoubtedly also play a crucial role in the colossal experiment to marketize the Hainan SEZ.

The impact of the Tiananmen incident

As is mentioned in Chapter 1, China was quick to reassure Hong Kong investors and to re-emphasize the important role of Hong Kong in China's open-door policy after the Tiananmen incident. The Tiananmen incident is likely to have severe adverse impacts on foreign investment, loans and tourism for some time. Political uncertainty is obviously detrimental to foreign investment and commercial loans, and OECD countries have suspended official loans following the Tiananmen incident. Tourism also slumped due to the military control of Beijing and sporadic acts of terrorist activity. The slump in tourism, foreign loans and investment will mean a cutback in commodity imports because of China's difficulties in financing its trade deficit. However, exports have to be maintained to finance essential imports. Thus, China's exports are likely to grow faster than its imports.

The Tiananmen incident has triggered a confidence crisis in Hong Kong, and the slump in China's imports, foreign loans and investment will imply a significant fall in China-related business. However, in relative terms, China is likely to be even more dependent on Hong Kong as a result of its economic isolation. During the Korean War, China was isolated by the United States ban on imports from China and the United Nations embargo on export of strategic commodities to China. Strategic materials were smuggled into China from Hong Kong and Hong Kong acted as China's link to the capitalist world for a long time.

In 1988, Hong Kong's share in China's exports was 41 per cent whereas its share in China's imports was 31 per cent. As China's exports are likely to grow faster than its imports, Hong Kong's share in China's commodity trade is likely to rise further. As for loans, Hong Kong does not extend official loans to China but its share in commercial loans is high. With the suspension of official loans, China will be forced to rely more on commercial loans and hence Hong Kong's share in total foreign loans is likely to rise. In the case of foreign investment, Hong Kong's investment in China tends to relate to strictly commercial operations whereas part of the investment of other countries is supported by official loans. The adverse impact of the suspension of official loans for foreign investment in China will be much greater for other countries than for Hong Kong. Moreover, Hong Kong's share in foreign investment is particularly high in Guangdong. As Guangdong has remained relatively stable in the recent political turmoil, Guangdong's share in national total foreign investment is likely to rise, and this tendency will lead to a higher share by Hong Kong in total foreign investment in China. The same regional factors operate for tourism. There will be a shift of foreign tourists from the North to the South as the South is more stable, and this will lead to a rise in Hong Kong's share in tourism.

As for shipping and trans-shipment, the plans of Japan and other countries to build ports in Shenzhen and other coastal cities will be held up by the Tiananmen incident, and China will be even more dependent on Hong Kong for shipping and trans-shipment. One important impact of the Tiananmen incident has been the increasing regionalization of the Chinese economy. The prestige and authority of the Central Government and the Party have suffered severely, while the role of the army has been enhanced. The Chinese army is divided into seven military regions, and there have been obvious signs of conflict between some of these military regions over the Tiananmen incident. There are many signs that Beijing has made concessions to regional authorities to gain their support for the political hard line. For instance, among the three new faces in the new standing committee of the Politburo elected in June 1989 by the Fourth Plenum, two were powerful local party chiefs: Jiang Zemin, the new General Secretary (formerly the Shanghai party chief), and Li Ruihuan (formerly Tianjin's party chief). It is also interesting to note that while thousands of arrests have been made in Beijing, the Guangdong authorities did not arrest any local pro-democracy supporters in June and July of 1989, and the Shanghai authorities have only made a very limited number of arrests. Southern China, especially Guangdong, stands to benefit from the further regionalization of the Chinese economy, and the important role of Hong Kong in the regional development of the coastal provinces is likely to be further enhanced.

Though the Tiananmen incident has had very negative impacts on the Hong Kong economy, the quick action taken by Chinese officials to re-emphasize the strategic role of Hong Kong in China's open-door policy again underlines the fact that Hong Kong is the key to China's door to the outside world.

As is mentioned in Chapter 1, the tension between communist orthodoxy and economic modernization has not been resolved. The tension may erupt again and Hong Kong may suffer more shocks. However, barring major wars and disasters, economic rationality is likely to triumph over ideology in the long run.

In the long run, the biggest role Hong Kong can play in the Chinese economy is that of a successful market model. China can choose to utilize, learn from, adapt, or even destroy the Hong Kong model, but cannot ignore it.

Appendix

Appendix *Estimates of retained imports from China by commodity* (HK$m)

SITC		1971	1975	1979	1983	1984
Estimates of Hsueh and Woo (1981)						
Food	(i)	1,320	2,410	2,828	4,902	4,609
(0)	(ii)	1,266	2,900	3,698	6,623	6,960
	(iii)	(104)	(83)	(76)	(74)	(66)
Fuels	(i)	2.3	201	877	1,495	1,224
(3)	(ii)	4.0	274	1,372	2,645	2,327
	(iii)	(58)	(73)	(64)	(57)	(53)
Other goods	(i)	1,249	2,451	5,762	16,744	21,813
	(ii)	1,301	1,888	4,397	13,873	18,359
	(iii)	(96)	(130)	(131)	(121)	(119)
Estimates of Hsu (1983)						
Foodstuffs	(i)	1,687	2,660	3,108	4,920	4,695
(0,1)	(ii)	1,694	2,984	3,779	7,018	7,393
	(iii)	(99.6)	(89)	(82)	(70)	(64)
Raw materials	(i)	215	888	2,400	5,522	6,662
(2,3,4)	(ii)	168	710	1,816	3,503	3,509
	(iii)	(128)	(125)	(132)	(158)	(190)
Chemicals	(i)	104	273	755	1,901	2,120
(5)	(ii)	55	173	350	651	550
	(iii)	(189)	(158)	(216)	(292)	(385)
Manufactures	(i)	554	1,220	3,167	10,693	13,926
(6,7,8)	(ii)	634	1,244	3,607	12,065	16,015
	(iii)	(87)	(98)	(88)	(89)	(87)

(i) Estimates. The 1983–84 estimates are not in the original papers, but they are estimated according to the same methodologies.
(ii) Correct data.
(iii) Ratio of estimates to correct data (per cent).
Note: Retained imports are defined as the difference between total imports and re-exports. For consistency with the estimates of Hsueh and Hsu, no adjustments are made for the trade margin of re-exports.

References

Almanac of China's Foreign Economic Relations and Trade, various issues.

Almanac of China's Foreign Relations and Trade, various issues.

Annual Report, Department of Trade, Singapore, various issues.

Asian Banking, various issues.

Asian Finance, various issues.

Bhagwati, J. N. and Srinivasan, T. N., 1983. *Lectures on International Trade*, MIT Press, Cambridge, USA.

Buchanan, I., 1972. *Singapore in Southeast Asia: An Economic and Political Appraisal*, Bell, London.

Chan, T. M. H., 1986. Reform in China's foreign trade system. Paper presented to the Conference on China's Systems Reforms sponsored by the Centre of Asian Studies, University of Hong Kong in Hong Kong, 17–20 March (mimeo.).

China: International Trade, various issues.

Chinese Customs Statistics, General Customs Department, various issues.

Chinese Statistical Yearbook, State Statistical Bureau, various issues.

Chung, S. Y., 1969. 'The role of manufacturing industry in the economy of Hong Kong', in J. W. England (ed.), *The Hong Kong Economic Scene*, University of Hong Kong, Hong Kong.

Du, W., 1985. 'The foreign exchange rate and tariffs', *International Trade Journal*, April:64–5 (in Chinese).

Findlay, C. and Xin, L., 1985. Management not motivation; questions and answers about China's open door policy (mimeo.). Paper presented at meetings in Adelaide and Melbourne on August 18 and 19, 1985 on the research project China's entry into world markets, sponsored by the National Centre for Development Studies, Australian National University.

He, X., 1988. 'Will a debt crisis explode in China?', *Hong Kong Economic Journal Monthly*, September:99–102 (in Chinese).

178   References

Hicks, J., 1969. *A Theory of Economic History*, Oxford University Press, London.

Ho, S. P. S. and Huenemann, R. W., 1984. *China's Open Door Policy: The Quest for Foreign Technology and Capital*, University of British Columbia Press, Vancouver.

Hong Kong Monthly Digest of Statistics, Census and Statistics Department, Hong Kong, various issues.

Hong Kong Shipping Statistics, Census and Statistics Department, Hong Kong, various issues.

Hong Kong Trade Statistics, Census and Statistics Department, Hong Kong, various issues.

Hong Kong Trade Development Council, 1986. China's demand for Hong Kong-made machinery, September (mimeo.).

———, 1988. Survey on Hong Kong re-exports: summary report, November (mimeo.).

Hsia, R., 1984. *The Entrepot Trade of Hong Kong with Special Reference to Taiwan and the Chinese Mainland*, Chung-Hua Institute for Economic Research, Taipei.

Hsu, J. C., 1983. 'Hong Kong in China's foreign trade: changing role', in A. J. Youngson (ed.), *China and Hong Kong, the Economic Nexus*, Oxford University Press, Hong Kong.

Hsueh, Tien-Tung and Woo, Tun-Oy, 1981. Trade between Hong Kong and China: Issues and prospects, Contemporary Chinese Studies Programme, Working paper no. c.c. 12, Centre of Asian Studies, University of Hong Kong.

International Financial Statistics, International Monetary Fund, Washington, various issues.

Jao, Y. C., 1983. 'Hong Kong's role in financing China's modernization' in A. J. Youngson (ed.), *China and Hong Kong, the Economic Nexus*, Oxford University Press, Hong Kong.

———, 1988. 'The China factor and Hong Kong's evolution as an international financial centre' in Y. C. Jao and C. Lai (eds), *The Economic Relationship between China and Hong Kong during the Transitional Period*, Joint Publishing Co. Ltd, Hong Kong:31–48 (in Chinese).

Krueger, A. O., 1978. *Liberalization Attempts and Consequences*, National Bureau of Economic Research, New York.

Kueh, Y. Y., 1986. Economic decentralization and foreign trade expansion in China. Paper presented to the Conference on China's Systems Reforms sponsored by the Centre of Asian Studies, University of Hong Kong in Hong Kong, 17–20 March 1986 (mimeo.).

——— and Howe, C., 1984. 'China's international trade: Policy and organizational change and their place in the economic readjustment', *The China Quarterly*, December:813–48.

Li, W., 1987. On structural reform of China's foreign trade and functions of foreign trade bodies. Speech at the Seminar on China's Foreign Trade sponsored by the Hong Kong Trade Development Council in Hong Kong, 29 May (mimeo.).

Lin, J. Y., 1989. 'Choice under a difficult situation', *Newsletter of the Development Institute*, Research Centre of Rural Development, 15 February, 108 (in Chinese).

Long, F. Z., 1982. 'The rise and decline of China–Taiwan trade', *Economic Digest*, 2(36):32–3 (in Chinese).

Lu, L. T., 1983. 'Singapore and East Asia' in P. S. T. Chen (ed.), *Singapore Development, Policies and Trends*, Oxford University Press, Singapore.

Lucas, R. E., 1985. The mechanics of economic development, Marshall Lecture, Cambridge University, Cambridge (mimeo.).

Ma, S. Y., 1985. 'The means and adverse consequences of over-invoicing imports', *Hong Kong Economic Journal Monthly*, 10(9):104–7.

McClellan, J., 1971. 'Entrepôt trade' in Y. P. Seng and L. C. Yah (eds), *The Singapore Economy*, Eastern Universities Syndicate, Singapore.

Ng, H. W., 1971. 'External trade: trend, composition and direction' in P. Seng and L. C. Yah (eds), *The Singapore Economy*, Eastern Universities Syndicate, Singapore.

Qi, X., 1985a. 'From an import spree to a sudden damp-down', *The Nineties* June:47–52 (in Chinese).

———, 1985b. 'Fire and smoke all over the Shenzhen issue', *The Nineties*, August:52–8 (in Chinese).

———, 1986. 'China cheapens the price while foreign investors hesitate and wait', *The Nineties*, December:32–5 (in Chinese).

Review of Overseas Trade, Census and Statistics Department, Hong Kong, various issues.

Sha, M., 1988. 'The second Hainan fever', *The Nineties*, January:61–3 (in Chinese).

Singapore External Trade Statistics, Department of Statistics, Singapore, various issues.

Singapore Ministry of Finance, 1961. *Development Plan 1961–1964*, Ministry of Finance, Singapore.

Singapore Trade Statistics, Department of Statistics, Singapore, various issues.

Stuart, C., 1979. 'Search and spatial organisation of trading' in M. Lippman and T. McCall (eds), *Studies in Economics of Search*, North Holland, Amsterdam.

Sung, Y-W., 1984. Structural change of the Hong Kong economy: some preliminary results. Discussion paper no. 36, Department of Economics, University of Hong Kong (mimeo.).

———, 1985. The role of Hong Kong and Macau in China's export drive. Working Paper no. 85/11, National Centre for Development Studies, Australian National University, Canberra.

———, 1988. The impact of the devaluation of the renminbi on China's trade. Paper presented to the Allied Social Science Association Annual Meeting in New York, 28–30 December (mimeo.).

——— and Chan, T. M. H., 1987. 'China's economic reform I: the debates in China', *Asian Pacific Economic Literature*, 2(1) May:1–25.

Tian, L. et al., 1986. 'The change in the instruments of macro-control on

China's foreign trade', *Caimao Jinji* (The Economics of Finance and Trade), February:36–40 (in Chinese).

Tom, C. F., 1957. *Entrepôt Trade and the Monetary Standards of Hong Kong, 1842–1942*, University of Chicago Press, Chicago.

Townsend, R. M., 1978. 'Intermediation with costly bilateral exchange', *Review of Economic Studies*, 45:417–25.

Wang, Shenzhong, 1986. 'Changes in the exchange rate and economic development in the external sector', *Jingji Yanjiu*, April, pp. 44–51 (in Chinese).

World Bank, 1985a. *China: Long-Term Issues and Options*, Report no. 5206-CHA, Washington.

——, 1985b. Alternative international economic strategies and their relevance for China (mimeo.), background paper to World Bank, 1985a.

——, 1988. *China: External Trade and Capital*, Washington D.C.

Wu, N., 1987. 'A discussion on the decontrol of the foreign exchange market in China', *China's Foreign Trade*, May:9–10 (in Chinese).

Xie, M., 1987. 'A brief analysis of the investment environment in China', *Wen Hui Pao*, 7 May (in Chinese).

Xuc, M., 1986. 'A discussion of the reform of the foreign trade management system', *Quoji Maoyi* (International Trade), March:4–8 (in Chinese).

Yamamura, K., 1976. 'General trading companies in Japan: their origins and growth' in Hugh Patrick (ed.), *Japanese Industrialisation and Its Social Consequences*, University of California Press, Berkeley.

Yearbook of International Trade Statistics, United Nations Statistical Office, various issues.

Yearbook of Statistics, Department of Statistics, Singapore, various issues.

Yuan, L., 1985a. 'The abrupt change in trade among China, Hong Kong, and Singapore — the difficulties of Singapore's dealers of Chinese merchandise', *The Nineties* 182:81–3 (in Chinese).

——, 1985b. 'The distinction between insiders and outsiders in import of technology', *The Nineties*:56–60 (in Chinese).

Zhao, W. and Liu, J., 1986. 'Formulation of export-promotion policies to increase the vitality of producer enterprises', *Jingying yu Guanli* (Enterprise and Management), February:36–8 (in Chinese).

Zheng, T., 1984. 'Problems of reform in foreign trade', *Jinji Yanjiu* (Economic Research), November:27–33 (in Chinese).

Index